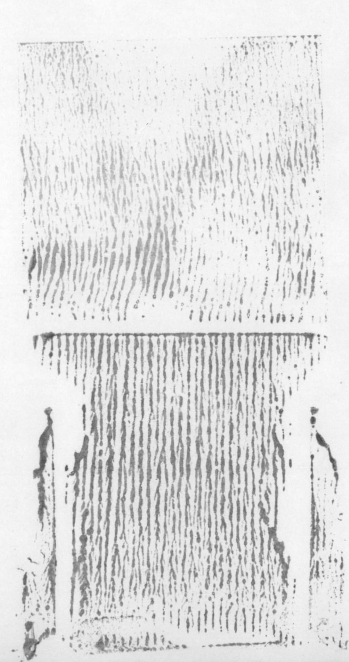

A MURDER

A MURDER

From the Chalk Outline to the Execution Chamber

Greg Fallis

M. Evans and Company, Inc.
New York

M. Evans and Company, Inc.
216 East 49th Street
New York, NY 10017

Library of Congress Cataloging-in-Publication Data

Fallis, Greg.
    Murder : from the chalk outline to the execution chamber / Greg Fallis
      p. cm.
    ISBN 0-87131-888-1
    1. Murder—United States—Popular works. 2. Trials (Murder)—United States—Popular works. 3. Criminal procedure—United States—popular works. 4. Criminal investigation—United States—popular works. I. Title.
KF9306. F35 1999
345.73'023523—dc21   99-046772

Book design and typesetting by Rik Lain Schell

Printed in the United States of America

9   8   7   6   5   4   3   2   1

CONTENTS

Part Four: The Trial

Part Five: The Sentence

ACKNOWLEDGMENTS

Writing a book is an odd process. A significant portion of the process takes place inside the writer's head. This means the writer is often distracted. In addition, writing a book about murder means one frequently has unpleasant and distasteful ideas and details scurrying about in one's mind. Not surprisingly, these two qualities can make the writer somewhat less congenial as a companion. A lucky writer—and I count myself as one—has friends and family capable of great tolerance.

I'd like to give special thanks to the following people for their friendship, support, and patience: Jeanne Flavin, Steve Wall, Joanna Panosky, Mary Ann Schwartz, and Linda Ireland. I'd also like to thank my brothers Roger Lee and Jesse Eugene, my sister Lisa, and their families.

INTRODUCTION

Murder. It's an ugly word that describes an ugly act. The deliberate taking of a life is generally considered to be the most serious crime a person can commit. We are repelled by murder . . . yet murder fascinates us. We have a perverse attraction to it.

Murder is the nucleus of much of our entertainment industry. Films, television programs, novels, theatrical plays, computer games, even board games revolve around murder. In recent years the advent of "reality-based" television programming has made the border between crime and entertainment even less distinct. That border became almost dreamlike during the murder trial of O. J. Simpson. It's no coincidence that the Simpson trial, with all its attendant fuss and tumult, was covered by serious news and information channels like CNN and Court TV as well as by E!, the entertainment channel.

Murder so permeates our society that we often forget the gravity of the crime. It's my hope that while reading this book you will periodically remind yourself of the enormity of the act. Remind yourself that murder not only deprives the victim of everything he or she *is* but of everything he or she might possibly *be*. To kill another person is an act of tremendous presumption. A murderer deprives his victim of the chance to ever again see the face of a loved one, to smell lilacs or taste a strawberry, to hear music or take a hot bath on a cold day.

And remind yourself that murder not only affects the victim, but the victim's family and friends. It's difficult enough to lose a loved one through illness or accidental death. It's almost incomprehensible to consider that somebody you care for could be *intentionally* taken from you forever.

And as you remind yourself of those things, consider this fact: approximately twenty thousand murders take place every year in the United States.

This book examines murder as a process—a series of actions, events, and operations conducing toward an end. Murder cases generally follow a linear course in which each step *tends* to lead to the next, like the ticking of dominos. The crime leads to a police investigation, which leads toward an arrest, which triggers a defense investigation, which precedes the pretrial hearings and jury selection that are a prelude to the trial itself, which is followed by sentencing, imprisonment, and execution.

Obviously, not every murder case includes each step. The process is generally linear, but it's not inevitable. The process can be derailed at any point. The manner in which each step proceeds affects and influences the succeeding steps.

Successful murders, in fact, only include the first step—the crime. The body of the victim may never be discovered, or perhaps the death isn't recognized as murder. Some cases end when the police investigation fails to uncover a suspect, or detectives are unable to obtain enough evidence to charge somebody. Still others end in dismissal of the charge before or during the trial. A very few cases end in acquittal of the accused. Of those cases that result in a conviction (or a guilty plea), most result in imprisonment. A small number of convicted murderers are executed.

Most studies of murder focus on only one or two aspects of the crime. They examine the crime itself, or the investigation of the crime, or the trial of the person accused of the crime. While such studies are valuable, they fail to reveal the full complexity of the process. To focus on a single aspect of the process is like reading only the very first scene of Act III in *Romeo and Juliet*, the scene in which Tybalt kills Mercutio and is killed in turn by Romeo. It's revealing, yes . . . but incomplete.

In this book we follow the process of a murder from its beginning to its end. Although no two murder cases are exactly alike, every murder process has elements in common. We examine a murder case (fictionalized, but based on a real crime) and the actions and events that result. We use each aspect of this particular murder case as a foundation for looking at murder in general.

The book is divided into five parts, each covering a major aspect of the murder process. Part One examines the crime itself. After describing the murder on which the rest of the book will be based, we look at murder as a crime of infinite variety. We explain the distinction between homicide and murder, we discuss alternative ways of understanding murder, and we look at various types of murder (*e.g.*, mass murder, drug-related murder, serial murder, etc.).

Part Two focuses on the police investigation. We follow the murder case from the discovery of the body, through the crime scene investigation, the interviews and interrogation, and the forensic examination of the evidence, all the way to the arrest of a suspect. We look at how murder cases are solved—the various ways physical and verbal evidence are collected. We also discuss the requirements the police must meet in order to make a legal arrest.

Part Three concentrates on the defense team and the defense investigation. The defense team is radically different from the prosecution team; their purpose is different, their rationale is different, and their approach to investigation is different. Because the focus of the defense is very often the defendant, this section examines the demographics of murderers: who kills who, and why? We also scrutinize the mindset and ethics of criminal defense lawyers and answer the question most commonly asked of them: "How can you defend these people?"

In Part Four we examine the trial itself. The course of the trial is often determined before the trial actually begins. The pretrial motions—the attempts by the prosecution and defense to exclude, limit, or control the evidence—and the selection of the jury are often as critical as the actual presentation of the evidence. In this section we examine the rules of evidence and the courtroom strategies employed by the lawyers involved. We also discuss jury deliberations—the wild card of the trial process. Finally, we look at a legal procedure unique to first degree murder trials: the penalty phase—the stage in which the decision is made whether the defendant will live or die.

The final section of the book, Part Five, examines what takes place after a guilty verdict. Although a death sentence may be delayed for many years before it's implemented, the sentence has an immediate effect on the offender. Here we compare the prison experience of an inmate serving life with that of a death row inmate. We also examine the most overlooked group of people in the entire murder process—the execution team, the people who actually strap the convict to the execution device and kill him. Finally, we walk through the execution itself, the actual techniques used to put a convict to death.

Throughout the book I use the pronoun "he" to refer to murderers. This, of course, is sexist. Sadly, it's also accurate. Men, after all, are the problem. Certainly women commit murders, but at drastically lower rates. For every murder a woman is involved in, nine murders are committed by men. Note I said murders women are "involved in." Many of the women convicted of murder are, in fact, accomplices to men who instigate or actually carry out the crime.

This book doesn't take any moral or political stance on controversial issues such as capital punishment or legal practices that may convict the innocent or allow the guilty to walk free. I simply report what takes place. This book deals with the justice system as it is, not as it should be.

The murder process is not a pretty one, but it's one that deserves close examination. It forces us to address some of the fundamental questions that define our society. Why do some people kill others? What are the limits of the State's power to catch and convict suspected criminals? How do we protect suspects who are, in fact, innocent? How do we balance the need to protect society with the need to protect individual civil rights? How should society treat those members who violate its most basic right—the right to live?

When we look at the act of murder and the ways we respond to it, we learn about ourselves.

PART ONE

The Crime of Murder

A MOST ORDINARY MURDER

He hadn't meant to kill her. Not really. It just sort of turned out that way.

They'd met as planned early that morning at a diner near his apartment. Over breakfast they'd discussed the photo shoot—the financial arrangements as well as what he expected from her during the shoot. He'd had her sign a model's release form for the photos and another stating she was of legal age. He'd also explained again that he was shooting the film on spec, that neither of them would see a dime from the photographs unless a magazine bought them. He would donate his time, his expertise, and his film; she would donate her time and her body. Together they might be able to make a few bucks.

Not that money was his main interest in shooting the photos.

He hadn't expected much to come from the shoot. After all, the woman wasn't really model material. It wasn't that she was homely; a lot of models had faces that weren't traditionally pretty. It was just that she had dozens of small flaws and imperfections. Her teeth were uneven, her skin was spotty, she was perhaps fifteen or twenty pounds too heavy, her nose was a bit too wide. Worst of all, she had a tattoo on her shoulder. It was a quality tattoo—not one of those cheesy reform school jobs. But it wasn't a very feminine tattoo, he thought. Some sort of snake. He thought it made her look cheap.

Still, some of that could be dealt with in the darkroom. He thought he might be able to sell a few nude shots to one of the lower-rung biker magazines. She had something of that "biker chick" look—a little cheap, a little sleazy, a little hard. That was why he'd picked her.

After breakfast they drove his small camper to Marshtown Park just south of town. The park was empty, as he'd known it would be. It was rarely used during the week. In fact, it was rarely used on weekends before noon. It was a perfect spot for an outdoor location and he'd used it several times before.

The light had been excellent. They'd spent nearly ninety minutes shooting photographs. He went through three rolls of film. Everything had gone surprisingly well, considering the woman wasn't a professional model. She listened and paid attention, she followed directions, she was enthusiastic and didn't complain. He'd known pros who weren't that good. It was a shame her body had so many flaws.

Three times during the shoot she'd used the camper to change clothes. He'd converted the little recreational vehicle into a traveling photography studio. It was perfect for location shoots: There was plenty of room for his equipment, it had a kitchen, and the tiny bathroom doubled as a dressing room. And it had a bed.

The shoot ended around noon. While she changed clothes in the bathroom he'd made sandwiches and mixed a couple of drinks. Seabreezes. Vodka, orange juice, cranberry juice.

In hers he'd dropped a tablet of Rohypnol.

Rohypnol. On the street, folks called called the drug "roofies" or "rope." The media called it the "date rape drug." For once the media got it right. He could pick up roofies for three bucks a tab. A remarkable price for a wonder drug. It dissolved easily in alcohol; it was colorless, odorless, and tasteless; it acted as a sedative; and—best of all—it caused short-term amnesia.

He'd been using roofies on models for nearly a year now. One drink, one roofie . . . and half an hour later they were out cold. Then he could do whatever he wanted with them. It had always worked perfectly before. He'd always been careful to clean them up when he was done. They'd wake up six hours or so later, confused and embarrassed, uncertain about what had happened. But none had ever complained. Some had even apologized for passing out on him. It was the stress, he always told them. It was a sign of artistic temperament. They liked that.

It wasn't as if he *had* to use roofies to get laid, he told himself. He'd done well enough before he discovered them. A lot of amateur models would do almost anything if they thought it might help get their photos published. The truth was he rather enjoyed the effect roofies had on women. He liked the feeling it gave him. The feeling of power. Control.

But this time something had gone wrong. Maybe he'd been sold a bad batch. Not that it mattered. All that mattered was this time the woman didn't stay drugged. She'd started to wake up while he was . . . in her. And she'd begun to struggle. She hadn't been alert enough to put up much of a struggle, but still he'd panicked.

They'd been on the narrow bunk of the motor home and he'd acted on instinct. He'd grabbed her by the throat. Not to kill her . . . just to keep her from shouting. But she kept struggling and kept moving her body and he'd become even more aroused. And, when he was finished . . . well, there she was. Dead.

Still, he hadn't meant for her to die. He hadn't even meant to hurt her. Not really. It was all just an accident.

Would that matter to the police? he asked himself. No, the police would look in the back of his camper and all they'd see was a dead, drugged woman with his semen leaking out of her. His life was about to be ruined . . . and for what? For a cheap biker slut he'd first met in a bar? For a woman who almost certainly would have slept with him—or anybody else—to get her photograph in even a cut-rate skin mag? For somebody no one would ever miss?

No, it wasn't fair. There had to be some way out of it.

MURDER—A CRIME OF INFINITE VARIETY

The terms *murder* and *homicide* are often used interchangeably. However, they actually have slightly different meanings. Homicide refers to the act of one person killing another; murder refers to an *unlawful* homicide.

There are a number of situations in which people *lawfully* kill others. Soldiers in combat, law enforcement officers in the prevention of a violent crime, executioners of a criminal convicted of a capital crime—these are acts of homicide, but not acts of murder. The result, of course, is the same—a person killed lawfully is just as dead as one killed unlawfully. However, a lawful killing is a regulated killing. Soldiers in combat, for example, must follow specified rules of engagement and the Geneva conventions. Law enforcement officers must abide by departmental policies and state laws regarding the use of lethal force. Execution teams follow a strict protocol. None of these people have a "license to kill."

The focus of this book is *murder*—the unlawful killing of another person. There are two primary ways to approach the concept of murder: from a legal perspective and from a criminological perspective. The legal perspective is the approach taken by those who make, enforce, and interpret the law. The criminological perspective is the bailiwick of scholars and students of behavioral and social trends.

Consider two different murders: A postal worker goes to work one morning and shoots three of his co-workers to death. A drug dealer shoots another drug dealer at an inner city street corner over a turf dispute. The legal approaches to these two very different crimes will differ radically from the criminological approaches.

The legal approach focuses on the act itself. Why did the postal worker shoot his co-workers? Was he targeting specific people, or shooting at random? Was he rational at the time of the crime or was he suffering from a psychiatric disorder? Was he under the influence of a mind-altering substance? The criminological approach, on the other hand, concentrates on the trend toward acts of violence among postal workers. Is there something about the social environment of post offices that contributes to acts of violence? What are the similarities and differences between the acts of post office violence? Are workers in certain employment positions—mail sorter, route carrier, drivers—more likely to engage in violence? Are there any similarities in the victims?

In the drug dealer murder the legal approach focuses on the ability to prove the case against the shooter. Are there witnesses? If so, can they identify the shooter? Are they willing to testify? Do the recovered bullets match the weapon found on the suspect? The criminologist, on the other hand, examines the crime with an eye toward learning about the culture of drug dealing. How is turf determined? What are other ways of settling turf disputes? Are there differences and similarities between a turf murder in Detroit and one in Boston or Des Moines?

Both legal and criminological perspectives are important; each offers a unique and valuable understanding of murder.

Legal Perspectives of Murder

This is the purview of lawyers, legislators, and police officers. The law is concerned with responsibility for actions. The questions asked by lawyers, legislators, and police officers deal with individual culpability. Who is responsible for a particular act? How do we hold people accountable for their behavior? How do we balance the search for justice with the rights due to people accused of crimes?

The first and most critical function of the legal perspective is to carefully define the behavior under question. You can't hold a person responsible for committing a crime unless you have clearly spelled out the elements of that crime—even a crime as obvious as murder.

One reason it's so critical to clearly define murder is because not all murders are alike. While all murders are bad, some are worse than others. What makes one murder worse than another? The legal perspective has one answer—the intent of the offender.

Intent matters. We know this intuitively. Even a dog, it has been said, knows the difference between being tripped over and being kicked. The greater the intent, the more serious the crime; the more serious the crime, the more severe the punishment.

In the following legal definitions of murder you'll notice a gradation of intent. The level of the offender's intent, in fact, is the primary distinction between the different categories of murder.

Categories of Murder

Legally, murder is divided into several categories or degrees. The designations of these categories vary in different jurisdictions; however, we can generally classify murder in the following categories.

Murder in the First Degree

This is the willful, deliberate, and premeditated killing of another person. This means the murderer *wants* to kill the victim (willful), *intends* to kill the victim (deliberate), and *plans* the crime before carrying it out (premeditated). All three elements are critical, but the primary consideration of first degree murder is premeditation. The length of time the offender plans the crime needn't be very long; the time it takes to walk from the living room into the bedroom to fetch a shotgun is time enough to be considered premeditation. All that is required is a sufficient length of time to demonstrate that an intent and a plan to kill had been established in the offender's mind. This state of mind is referred to as "malice aforethought."

An example of a first degree murder would be a husband who decides to kill his wife for her insurance money.

Murder in the Second Degree

In most jurisdictions this is the willful killing of another *without* the element of premeditation. The offender has the intent to kill the victim, but there is no malice aforethought. Generally, second degree murder is a crime of passion. These crimes are often committed in a fit of rage or fear. They tend to be reactive crimes; something happens that sparks the event. The offender acts on the spur of the moment, without really considering the consequences of the act.

An example of a second degree murder would be a woman who kills her boyfriend when she finds him molesting her daughter. She may intend to kill the boyfriend, but she didn't plan the crime in advance.

Manslaughter

Manslaughter is generally considered a crime of reckless indifference to human life. The offender doesn't intend to kill the victim, but nonetheless deliberately acts in a way he knows to be dangerous and possibly life-threatening.

An example of manslaughter would be two young men on a highway overpass, dropping balloons filled with paint onto cars as they pass beneath them. If a balloon causes a startled driver to crash into the bridge abutment and die, the two would be guilty of manslaughter. They may not have intended to kill the driver, but they knowingly acted in a manner that showed a reckless indifference to the fates of their victims.

Negligent Homicide

This is a crime in which the victim dies as a result of gross negligence. The offender has no intent to kill the victim, nor does the offender behave recklessly. The death of the victim is due to carelessness or neglect.

An adult who leaves a very young child alone for a weekend would be guilty of negligent homicide if that child accidentally starts a fire and dies of smoke inhalation. The adult didn't intend any harm to come to the child and yet the child is dead. It's the egregious carelessness of the act that makes it criminal.

FELONY MURDER

Most jurisdictions have a legal category known as "felony murder." This refers to a situation in which a person dies during the commission of a felony. *Anybody* involved in the commission of the felony is responsible for the death of the victim. It doesn't matter if the offender didn't play a direct role in the death. It doesn't even matter if the offender was aware of the death of the victim—the offender is nonetheless held responsible.

For example, Smith and Jones decide to rob a liquor store. Smith waits outside in the getaway vehicle while Jones enters the store. Jones robs the clerk at gunpoint. As he is leaving the store Jones shoots and kills the clerk. It's irrelevant that Smith waited outside. It's irrelevant that Smith may not have carried a weapon, or that he was entirely ignorant that Jones shot the clerk. Under the felony murder rule Smith is equally responsible for the clerk's death.

In fact, if the clerk had pulled a gun and killed Jones, Smith could be charged with felony murder in the death of his partner (although the clerk, acting in self-defense, probably would not be charged). Any death resulting from the commission of a felony can invoke the felony murder rule.

Not every felony counts, though. Some courts have ruled that the underlying crime "must be inherently or potentially dangerous to human life." If a death should occur during the commission of a forgery, for example, it's unlikely the felony murder rule would apply.

Non-criminal Homicide

As noted earlier there is a distinction between homicide and murder, the distinction being that murder is an unlawful homicide. We mentioned some of the more obvious forms of lawful homicide—soldiers in combat, police officers in the line of duty, execution teams. These, as we noted, are regulated killings by people authorized to commit them. However, there are also situations in which an ordinary citizen might commit a homicide that is considered either excusable or justified.

Excusable Homicide

An excusable homicide is, essentially, an accident in which one person kills another. There is no intent to kill, no reckless disregard for the safety of another, no negligence. For example, a subway motorman who runs over and kills a person who had fallen or jumped in front of his moving train has committed an excusable homicide. The motorman did, in fact, kill the victim; nevertheless, the killing may be excused because it was unintentional and unavoidable.

Justifiable Homicide

There are certain circumstances under which the intentional killing of another person by an ordinary citizen is considered justifiable. These circumstances vary from state to state, but generally include the defense of oneself or the defense of another from imminent danger of death or great bodily harm. In other words, a homicide is considered justified when the killer believes he is protecting himself or another from immediately being killed or badly injured.

Notice that the *belief* of imminent death or great bodily harm is enough to justify the killing. Several legal rulings have held that the danger need not be real so long as the person *reasonably believes* the danger exists and is imminent. For example, a clerk in a liquor store might reasonably believe he or she is in danger if a person enters the store with a pistol drawn. The pistol may be unloaded . . . or even a realistically crafted squirt gun. All that matters is that any reasonable person under the same circumstances would also perceive the situation as imminently dangerous.

Some states have a wider scope of situations in which a homicide committed by a common citizen may be considered justifiable, including:

- the defense of property (generally where the loss of the property would constitute a felony);

- the defense of an unauthorized attempt to enter a dwelling place
- situations in which a citizen has been commanded or authorized to act by a legitimate law enforcement officer; such as in the course of the retaking of a felon who has escaped, the suppression of a riot, or the lawful preservation of the peace

It should be noted that many states have passed laws specifically excluding the defense of unborn fetuses from the domain of justifiable homicide.

Criminological Perspectives of Murder

Where the legal perspective is primarily concerned with individual responsibility and intent, criminologists are concerned with the social circumstances and patterns of murder. Lawyers, legislators, and police officers want to know who is responsible for a particular act, the degree to which they are responsible, and the rules under which they are required to prove responsibility. Criminologists want to understand why murders happen and what that says about society and culture.

For that reason criminologists aren't interested in individual crimes so much as how those individual crimes can be categorized into meaningful groups. Rather than ask who killed the bank guard during the robbery of the Bailey Street Bank, criminologists will ask what the Bailey Street Bank robbery has in common with other bank robberies or what the person who committed that particular robbery has in common with other bank robbers.

These radically different questions lead criminologists to categorize murder differently than legalists. The following categories are examples of some of the ways criminologists look at murder.

Drug-related Murder

We often hear reports of "drug-related" murders on the evening news. The phrase seems to elicit a rather hazy image of young, urban men (usually

African-American) killing each other. That image is based in part on fact, in part on fiction, and in part on racism. Drug-related murders aren't as simple as news reports would lead us to believe. They are, in fact, very complex social crimes and include a variety of subcategories.

Turf Murders

Many drug-related murders are territorial in nature. Drug dealers, like all business operators, tend to stake out a territory, or turf. The territory might be based on geography or on product. A drug dealer may assert control over a specific physical area (a neighborhood, a street corner, a building) or over a specific drug category (such as heroin, cocaine, or crack) within an area. An attempt by another drug dealer to intrude on that territory leads to conflict, which might result in murder. It's nothing personal; just business. Legitimate corporations engage in similar, though usually less lethal, competition.

Business Practice Murders

Like all business operators drug dealers sometimes suffer as a result of deceitful business practices. They may be sold merchandise that isn't of the quality they'd been led to expect. They may not receive full payment for their merchandise (or not receive payment at all). They may enter into an agreement to launder money, only to discover that the launderer is now demanding a higher exchange rate. As with legitimate business operators, a drug dealer's reputation for consistently delivering a quality product is important. Drug dealers are as careful to preserve their reputations as IBM, General Mills, or Maytag.

Unlike legitimate business operators, however, drug dealers can't bring their business disputes to court. They must resolve these disputes themselves, and they often resolve them through violence. In fact, among drug dealers a reputation for lethality in resolving disputes is good for business. It reduces the odds others will engage in the same practice.

Robbery Murders

In an odd way drug dealers are attractive targets for very aggressive armed robbers. Drug dealers often carry large sums of cash, they are often holding significant quantities of drugs (which can either be used or resold), and they are unlikely to report a crime to the police.

However, it takes an extremely aggressive armed robber to consider robbing a drug dealer. In addition to carrying drugs and cash, dealers also often carry very powerful firearms. An encounter between an aggressive armed robber and a well-armed drug dealer frequently results in one or more dead bodies.

A less common form of drug-related robbery murder involves an attempt by a drug user to obtain money to buy drugs.

Intimidation Murders

Since their work is illegal, drug dealers frequently find themselves in conflict with the criminal justice system. One way some drug dealers attempt to avoid imprisonment is by intimidating or silencing potential witnesses against them. Dead men, as they say, tell no tales.

Drug-related murders are often difficult for the police to solve. The people involved—the killer(s) and victim(s)—rarely have any meaningful social connections to each other. They may barely know each other, and that means there are few obvious suspects. The people most likely to have seen the crime take place are rarely eager to help the police, and that means there are few willing witnesses. The venues in which drug-related murders take place—street corners and drug houses—frequently have a great deal of transient traffic, and that means the physical evidence is often confusing. As will be discussed later, it's no coincidence that the increase of drug-related murder corresponds with the decrease of murder clearance rates.

Mass Murder

Many people confuse mass murder, spree murders, and serial murder. All involve multiple killings but they are nonetheless very distinct modes of murder. The distinction depends largely on the length of time between the killings and, to a lesser extent, the area in which the killings take place. The killings in a mass murder are temporally proximate, meaning the victims are all killed within a short period of time—a few seconds to a few hours. They usually take place within the same general area. Spree killings take place over a slightly longer time frame and involve greater distances, sometimes several different states. The killings in a serial murder, by contrast, take place over a longer period of time—days, months, even years may pass between killings. Like spree killings, serial murders are not confined to one locale. Spree killings and serial murder will be discussed in more detail later.

Mass murder entered and became firmly lodged in the contemporary American consciousness in 1966. On the morning of August 1, a heavily armed twenty-five-year-old man named Charles Whitman made his way to the top of the bell tower on the campus of the University of Texas at Austin. After barricading the door he opened fire on the people below. Whitman killed twelve people that morning (he'd killed his mother and wife the night before) and wounded more than thirty others before being shot and killed himself by a police officer.

Whitman wasn't the first mass murderer in the United States. There are reports of mass murders as early as 1866 (a farmhand named Anton Probst murdered a family of eight with an axe) and it's certain other mass murders took place before then. Nor was Whitman the first to use semi-automatic firearms to systematically kill bystanders (in 1949 a twenty-eight-year-old pharmacy student named Howard Unruh took a walk through East Camden, New Jersey, shooting people he encountered; he killed thirteen people—including two children—in twelve minutes). Whitman, however, was the first mass murderer of the modern era, the disaffected sniper.

Data suggests that some type of mass murder takes place in the United States at least once a month, possibly as often as once a week. Murders with multiple victims are also slowly rising. In 1976 less than 3 percent of all murders had multiple victims; by 1997 that proportion had risen to 4 percent.

We can divide mass murders into two broad categories: public mass killings and private, domestic mass killings. In general, only public mass killings receive national news coverage; private, domestic mass killings are often perceived as community events and usually receive only local news coverage.

Public Mass Killings

These are the crimes that generally come to mind when we hear the term "mass murder." As the name suggests, public mass killings almost always take place in a very public arena—restaurants, shopping malls, post offices, schoolyards, office buildings, etc. Most of the offenders who commit public mass killings are white males. Although most mass murderers are between the ages of twenty and thirty-five, some have been as young as eleven and as old as sixty-four.

There doesn't appear to be any consensus in regard to the motives of mass murderers. In general they appear to be acting out of frustration and rage, but the spark that ignites a mass killing varies widely from case to case. Quite often the mass murderer attempts to resolve his frustration in other ways—by writing letters to officials or the editorial pages in newspapers. The mass murderer is frequently known by the people in his community as a crank or frightening eccentric.

In some instances, the mass killer will target a specific individual—an ex-wife, a former girlfriend, a representative of an institution. However, others in the vicinity of the targeted victim are also killed. For example, the most deadly non-political mass murder* in recent history took place in the Bronx, New York, in 1990. Julio Gonzalez, angry with a former girlfriend, set fire to the social club in which she worked. Eighty-seven people died in the resulting blaze.

---

*Political mass murders, such as the killing of 168 men, women, and children by Timothy McVeigh in the 1995 bombing of the federal office building in Oklahoma City, are qualitatively different from other acts of mass murder. The result, however, is the same.

In other cases the victims are simply selected at random. In July of 1981, for example, an unemployed security guard named James Huberty entered a McDonald's restaurant in San Ysidro, California, and opened fire on the staff and customers. He killed twenty-one and wounded more than twenty others.

Some public mass killings seem to be spontaneous outbursts sparked by an incident that seems trivial. For example, in August of 1982, a fifty-one-year-old Miami man named Carl Brown became unhappy with the repair work done on his lawn mower. He rode his bicycle to the repair shop, where he shot and killed eight men and women. Other mass killings appear to be well thought out and meticulously planned. When Charles Whitman climbed to the observation platform of the clock tower at U.T. Austin, he went prepared for a long siege. He brought along a footlocker containing food, toilet paper, extra weapons, and spare ammunition.

Mass murderers tend not to be concerned about being arrested for their crimes. These crimes are usually meant to be final acts. A large number of mass murderers are killed by the police or commit suicide at the end of their rampage. A smaller number surrender peacefully to law enforcement officers when they have finished their killing. It appears the more planning a mass murderer puts into his crime the less likely he is to survive the event.

As shown in the examples mentioned, the two weapons of choice for most modern mass murderers are semiautomatic weapons and fire. The large magazines available for semiautomatic pistols and rifles allow the offender to fire a great many high-powered bullets without having to pause to reload. This makes them ideal tools of mass murder. Fire is even more lethal. Arson is a comparatively inexpensive crime and requires less skill than shooting.

Private, Domestic Mass Killings

Although these crimes receive less attention, they are the most common type of mass killing. These are mass murders in which one family member kills some or all of the other family members.

We have much less data on these offenders than on the more tradition-al mass murderers. Researchers have only recently begun to regard domestic mass killings as a form of mass murder.

These crimes are almost always committed by a man—the father, step-father, husband, live-in boyfriend, or a former husband or live-in boyfriend. The killings are usually preceded by a turbulent relationship marked by violence and jealousy.

By and large, domestic mass killings result in a lower body count. One reason this is so is because there are simply fewer targets in a home than in a public arena. The killing stops when the rage recedes or the killer runs out of family members. These crimes often end with the offender committing or attempting suicide.

Private, domestic mass killings take place with alarming regularity. Even as this chapter was being written, Shon Miller of Gonzales, Louisiana, burst into the New St. John Fellowship Baptist Church during an evening Bible class and murdered his estranged wife and son. Shortly before arriving at the church, Miller had fatally shot his mother-in-law. Miller was later shot and killed by police.

In the two years before the rampage Miller had burned the family's trailer, slashed the tires on his wife's vehicle, and had been arrested and jailed for physically assaulting her. He had also been jailed for violating a restraining order prohibiting him from having contact with her.

Juvenile Mass Murder

In the recent past we have seen an alarming spate of multiple murders committed by juveniles. Juvenile mass murder appears to be the domain of small town or suburban white boys. Many of these crimes have taken place in a venue normally considered safe—the school.*

In October of 1997 a teenager in Pearl, Mississippi, killed two girls (one of whom was his former girlfriend) and wounded seven other students at his high school. The night before, he had stabbed his mother to death. Two months later a high school student in Paducah, Kentucky, opened fire

---

*As the writing of this book was nearing completion, the author was distracted by the most lethal episode of juvenile mass killing to date. In Littleton, Colorado, two students initiated a well-planned assault on their high school. Twelve students and a teacher were murdered; twenty-three others were wounded. The perpetrators also killed themselves.

4444444

444

44444444

444

on a group of fellow students gathered to say a prayer in the hallway before class. He killed three and wounded five others. The three dead students were all girls. Three months later, in March of 1998, the small Arkansas town of Jonesboro was horrified when two young boys ambushed their classmates. After triggering a fire alarm the two boys proceeded to shoot the teachers and students as they filed out of school. When they had finished, four students and one teacher were dead. Ten others were wounded. Two months later a recently suspended high school student in Springfield, Oregon, opened fire in the school cafeteria. He killed two and wounded eight before being subdued by fellow students.

What do these juvenile mass murderers have in common? Alienation from their classmates, resentment at real and perceived personal slights, a keen interest in violent media (movies and computer games), and access to firearms. Combined with a teenager's sense of drama and lack of skill in resolving conflict, it's a deadly combination. It's also no coincidence that so many of the killers are boys and so many victims are girls. There is a gender component to these killings that is usually ignored.

Spree Murder

A spree killer is a person who kills several people in two or more distinct locations. Spree killers are killers on a roll—they commit one murder, often on impulse, and then seemingly shuck off any inhibitions they might have had about committing more. They begin a killing and crime spree that may last days, weeks, or months, during which they may travel great distances, killing as they go. Spree killers are living from one intense experience to the next with little time to cool off between crimes; they usually have only vague thoughts about the future. Mass murderers often expect to die and serial killers usually expect to avoid getting caught, but spree killers seem to give little or no thought as to what might happen to them in the future. Unlike mass murderers or serial killers, spree killers don't appear to feel any compulsion to kill. Rather, the killing is an adjunct to some other need—money, sex, food, a car. Before the spree began, the spree killer might have robbed or raped to get want he wanted, but once the spree begins, another dead body doesn't seem to matter much.

The classic spree killers were Charles Starkweather and Caril Ann

Fugate. For eight weeks in the winter of 1957–58 the teenage pair (he was nineteen, she was fourteen) went on a two-state killing spree that left eleven people (including Fugate's mother, stepfather, and her two-and-a-half-year-old baby sister) dead. Starkweather and Fugate were the first spree killers to achieve a twisted sort of national celebrity. There was something disturbing and yet compelling about their story—star-crossed teenage lovers who turned their anger outward. Their story has provided the framework for half a dozen movies.

Alton Coleman and Debra Brown were a less traditional, but more lethal, team of spree killers. Coleman and Brown are both African Americans—rare among spree killers. In an eight-week period in the summer of 1984, the pair traveled through the Midwest, killing, raping, and robbing. They left behind at least eight bodies in five different states, as well as a large number of surviving victims who'd been abducted, raped, assaulted, and robbed. Both Coleman and Brown are currently in prison on death row.

Serial Murder

As noted earlier, the trait that distinguishes serial killers from mass murderers is a temporal one. Mass murderers kill their victims within a short period of time; serial murderers kill their victims over a longer period of time.

Serial killers have always been the object of a singular fascination. They represent our worst nightmares. They have become part of folklore and popular entertainment. There are more movies and books about Jack the Ripper than about Queen Victoria, during whose reign he committed his crimes. Serial killers are a popular theme for weekly television programs. American teens are more able to identify recent serial killers than Supreme Court justices.

The fascination, of course, is a product of the nature of serial killers. They are not like "ordinary" murderers. Most murders are committed for reasons the average person can comprehend—greed, revenge, fear, power, rage, jealousy. When the underlying emotion is assuaged, the killing stops.

Serial killers are an entirely different breed. They act out of motives that are far more convoluted and enigmatic, motives we can't always under-

SERIAL MURDER TYPOLOGY

In their 1996 book on the subject, Holmes and Holmes identify four main categories of serial killers.

- **Visionary.** These offenders are most commonly suffering from some form of psychosis. They are acting in response to "visions" or hallucinatory commands and suggestions, most often from some source of supreme good or evil.

- **Mission-oriented.** As the name indicates, mission-oriented serial killers are motivated by a great purpose or calling. They see their killing as a means to rid society of a certain group of people—racial minorities, for example, or people they perceive to be sexually deviant. These killers are operating out of a warped sense of duty. Many are proud of their work.

- **Hedonistic.** These offenders kill their victims for the pleasure in it, or for the personal gratification that occurs as result from the killing. Many hedonistic serial killers find sexual release in the murder or in certain sexualized acts that precede or follow the murder. These offenders frequently suffer from one or more sexual paraphilia, a reliance on some unusual stimulus or fantasy to achieve orgasm. Paraphilia can range from fetishes (such as an extreme attraction to certain types of underwear or bodily function) to necrophilia (sexual acts with the dead). These sexual serial killings are generally the ones that receive the most public notoriety. Other hedonistic serial killers see their killing as a means to a comfortable end. This would include people who kill for money. They may not take pleasure from the killing itself but from the amenities and comforts they can purchase with the money.

• **Power/Control-oriented.** These serial murderers also get pleasure from their crimes, but the source of the pleasure is in their ability to control, intimidate, terrify, and/or exert power over their victim. The offender is gratified by the sight of a cowering, groveling, whimpering victim, therefore they often prolong the killing for as long as possible.

Obviously, these categories are not fixed or mutually exclusive. Many serial killers fall into more than one category. Take, for example, the case of Calvin Jackson. In 1973 and 1974 Jackson raped, killed, and robbed nine women at or near the New York City residential hotel where he worked as a porter. Jackson fits the description of at least two of the categories described above.

stand even if the offender explains them. And serial killers often continue to kill until they are captured or killed themselves.

The vast majority of serial murderers are men. They are generally white, between twenty-five and thirty-four years of age, and clever (though not necessarily educated). Regardless of their race, serial killers tend to target members of their own race; white serial killers tend to kill whites, African-American serial killers tend to kill blacks. Many serial killers, curiously enough, have expressed a desire to work in some law enforcement capacity.

Based on evidence found at crime scenes and interviews of convicted serial killers, FBI profilers have categorized these offenders as being either *disorganized asocial* or *organized nonsocial*. Disorganized serial killers are considered asocial because they tend to be outcasts; they are shunned by others because they are perceived to be different, strange, or weird. They often have limited intelligence and poor personal hygiene. Many consider themselves to be "night people." Since they tend to be uncomfortable when outside their normal routine, they generally commit their murders near where they live or work. By contrast organized killers are called nonsocial because they elect to be socially isolated (rather than isolated because they are socially incompetent). Although they are often glib and charming they may feel nobody is quite good enough for them. They tend to be of at least adequate intelligence and are often quite clever. More self-assured than the disorganized asocial offender, these killers are willing to travel far to find their victims.

Women Serial Murderers

Aileen Wuornos, a drifter and prostitute who killed seven men in a ten-month period, is often proclaimed as the first woman serial killer. She wasn't; she was simply one of very few women whose killing fit the traditional public image forged by male serial killers. Women serial murderers are different. They tend to commit their crimes for different reasons than male serial killers. They generally choose their victims differently and kill by different methods than men. Women are stealth serial killers, flying below the radar of public awareness.

For the most part, women serial killers are caregivers; their victims tend to be the people under their care. They may be nurses who kill their patients or baby-sitters who kill their wards. Some women serial killers fit the "black widow" mold, women who serially marry and murder.

Many of these offenders kill for money (such as insurance settlements), others kill for emotional reasons (to relieve the suffering of the victim or the victim's family), and some for a combination of reasons. Women rarely seem to kill for the sexual or power thrill so common among male serial killers.

A classic woman serial killer was Nannie Doss. Between 1925 and 1954 Doss killed four of her five husbands (her first husband divorced her because of her continuous infidelity). When caught Ms. Doss claimed she killed for romance, that she was simply in search of the perfect mate. This assertion is undermined by the fact that she also killed her two children, her mother, her two sisters, one grandchild, and a nephew. Her weapon of choice: rat poison and arsenic mixed with stewed prunes.

Women have also occasionally teamed up with male serial killers. About a third of all known team serial killers include women. The vast majority of those women are followers in rather than initiators of the killing.

Consider Carol Bundy (no relation to serial killer Ted Bundy). She was a lonely, shy, myopic nurse recovering from a broken relationship when she became infatuated with Douglas Clark, a charming boiler room worker. He moved in with her but continued to have sex with other women. He brought teenage girls home with him. After his first killings—two teenage runaways—he showed the bodies to Bundy. She began to assist him in his deviant sexual acts and killings, even to the point of putting lipstick and makeup on the severed head of one of his victims (which he used sexually). Although she participated in the murders, Bundy claimed they were initiated by Clark. At one point, however, Bundy let some information about the killings slip when talking to her former boyfriend. Concerned he would report the information to the police, she lured him to a remote area where she had sex with him, stabbed him to death, and removed his head. Eventually Bundy talked to the police herself and became a witness against Clark.

How many serial killers are out there? Obviously, we have no way of knowing for certain. Experts in the field estimate that at any given time there are between thirty-five and a hundred serial murderers active in the United States. These offenders are responsible for somewhere between ninety and a thousand murders annually. This is an alarming number, but it's a relatively small proportion of the total murders committed in a year.

Juvenile Murder

It's common for adults of every generation to think the current group of teenagers is drastically worse than earlier generations. However, juveniles have always been responsible for a significant proportion of crime, including murder. In *Romeo and Juliet,* Shakespeare describes what is essentially a rumble between a pair of juvenile gangs, in which two teenage boys are murdered.

This shouldn't be dismissed as mere fiction. Accounts written by seventeenth-century Parisians complain about students attacking and killing passersby, carrying off women, ravishing virgins, committing robberies, and breaking into houses. In the eighteenth century the solicitor general of England reported to the House of Commons that there was an epi-

TABLE 1

Homicide offending rates by age of offender, 1976–97
(number of homicides for every 100,000 people)

		Age of offender			
Year	Under 14	14-17	18-24	25-34	35-49	50+
1976	0.2	10.6	22.4	19.4	11.1	4.0
1977	0.2	10.0	22.1	18.7	11.4	4.0
1978	0.3	10.1	23.1	19.0	11.4	3.7
1979	0.2	11.7	26.2	20.3	11.6	4.1
1980	0.2	12.9	29.5	22.2	13.3	3.8
1981	0.2	11.2	25.7	20.3	12.8	3.8
1982	0.2	10.4	24.2	19.0	11.3	3.5
1983	0.2	9.4	22.1	17.5	10.2	3.0
1984	0.2	8.5	21.5	16.9	9.5	3.0
1985	0.2	9.8	21.4	16.0	9.4	3.0
1986	0.2	11.7	23.4	17.6	9.9	2.9
1987	0.2	12.3	24.1	16.2	9.2	2.9
1988	0.2	15.5	26.9	16.5	8.9	2.7
1989	0.3	18.1	30.2	16.4	8.4	2.5
1990	0.2	23.7	34.4	17.6	9.5	2.5
1991	0.3	26.6	40.8	18.6	8.2	2.3
1992	0.3	26.3	38.4	16.8	7.7	2.3
1993	0.3	30.2	41.3	15.9	7.4	2.4
1994	0.3	29.3	39.6	15.2	7.4	2.0
1995	0.3	23.6	36.7	14.4	6.7	2.0
1996	0.2	19.6	35.7	13.4	6.2	1.8
1997	0.2	16.5	33.2	12.4	5.5	1.7

Source: FBI, Supplementary Homicide Reports, 1976–97.

demic of violent crime by young men. In the nineteenth century we saw outlaws such as Billy the Kid, so named because he was really just a kid.

Kids have always killed. In the United States the level of juvenile murder remained fairly stable until 1985, when there was a marked increase in the juvenile murder rate. As seen in Table 1, before 1985 approximately 10 percent of all murders were committed by people under the age of eighteen. For the next ten years that proportion grew steadily, and by 1993 juveniles were responsible for about 30 percent of all murders. Since that time, the proportion of murders by kids has declined somewhat. The most recent data gathered by the FBI indicates that juveniles are responsible for around 17 percent of all murders.*

How do we account for this explosion in the juvenile murder rate? According to reports by the National Institute of Justice and the FBI it's attributable to gun violence. More and more young people are either carrying or have easy access to handguns. Almost 80 percent of the victims of juvenile murders are killed with a firearm. Incidents that would have resulted in bloody noses twenty years ago now result in bodies in the morgue. There has, however, been no meaningful shift in the proportion of non-gun homicides.

Not surprisingly, the availability of firearms in inner city neighborhoods corresponds with the rise of the illegal drug culture. Drugs and firearms are a natural and lethal combination. Poverty breeds drugs and drugs bring firearms. It isn't surprising, therefore, that juvenile murder rates among African-American males aged fourteen to seventeen have been about four to five times higher than among white males of the same age group.

Who do juveniles kill? For the most part, according to a 1997 study done by the National Center for Juvenile Justice, they kill their friends and acquaintances. Over half of the victims of juvenile murder are acquaintances and friends. The second most common group of victims are strangers. More than one third of the victims were entirely unknown to their killers. Family members account for only 10 percent of the victims of juvenile murderers.

---

*It should be noted that juveniles between fourteen and seventeen years of age were responsible for the explosion in the juvenile murder rate; children under fourteen consistently account for only about 0.2 percent of all murders.

Neonaticide

Neonaticide is generally defined as the murder of a newborn baby in the first twenty-four hours of life. In recent years we've become increasingly aware of this peculiar form of murder. It's not a new phenomenon; we're simply more aware of neonaticide because of the existence and nature of modern news media.

The research on neonaticide focuses almost exclusively on mothers. Certainly fathers also kill their children and stepchildren—and at a much higher rate—but, for the most part, murders of newborn infants are committed by women.

The women who kill their newborn children tend to be young and single. They usually describe feeling isolated, frightened, and terribly ashamed about being pregnant. They often manage to conceal their pregnancy from their families and friends. Some are even able to deceive themselves about their condition. Others hope the pregnancy will somehow magically disappear. Obviously, these women do not get proper prenatal care.

Given the course of the pregnancy, it's not surprising that these young women are rarely prepared for the onset of labor. They often give birth alone, in secret and without help. The birth commonly takes place in a less than ideal environment—a bedroom, a motel room, a public bathroom. These circumstances further decrease the likelihood of the delivery of a healthy, living baby. In addition, some of these women report experiencing a dissociative reaction during the birth, feeling as if they were outside themselves and watching the event from a distance. Some are unable to recall the actual birth at all.

All these factors—lack of pre-natal care, denial of the pregnancy, childbirth in isolation and under poor circumstances, altered mental state—result in an untenable situation. These young women suddenly find themselves in possession of a baby (very possibly a baby in physical distress or dying) and the associated mess that comes with childbirth . . . and they don't know what to do. Often they take a step that seems to them both logical and horrible: they throw the baby and the mess in the trash.

Melissa Drexler is a classic case. She had concealed her pregnancy from her family, her friends, and her boyfriend. Then in June of 1997, Drexler went into labor while attending her senior prom. She delivered a baby boy in the bathroom of the ballroom, wrapped the baby in garbage bags and put him in a trash bin. She then returned to the prom and attempted to act as if nothing had happened. A maintenance worker, responding to reports of blood in the bathroom, discovered the dead baby in the trash.

Although it's difficult to understand how a mother can dispose of her helpless, newborn baby, the fact is these women are not moral monsters. Many of them are, in fact, deeply religious. They are young women and girls in deep distress. Research has indicated that women who have committed neonaticide often prove to be devoted and caring mothers when they later give birth under less distressing circumstances.

Murder for Hire

Assassins have always existed. The term "assassin" comes from the Arabic word *hashishin*. This term refers to a member of a secretive sect of Shi'ite Muslims said to have carried out political murders during the Crusades in the eleventh century. Members of this sect were said to act under the direction of a leader referred to as "the Old Man of the Mountain." They were allegedly given the drug hashish as a reward for their dedication and as a hint of the joys and wonders of the Paradise that awaited them.

In modern times murder for hire is considerably less romantic. Only a very small number of criminals are professional assassins—people who earn a living solely through murder. Most murders for hire are done by ordinary criminals and street hoodlums who agree to kill a person for a sum of money.

Consider the case of Alvin Weiss, a New York landlord who owns nearly two dozen buildings in and around Manhattan. In 1997 New York City passed legislation allowing landlords owning rent-stabilized apartments to substantially increase the rents on vacant units. Weiss bailed a young man out of jail and paid him four to five thousand dollars to murder two of his rent-controlled tenants, allowing him to rent their apartments for significantly more money. The would-be assassin, however, reported the incident to the police and cooperated with them to record an incriminating conversation. Weiss, who was arrested in his two-million-dollar home, pled guilty to attempted murder, attempted arson, and conspiracy and was sentenced to seven to fourteen years in prison.

A second type of murder for hire involves murders that take place in the course of routine criminal enterprises. These killers aren't hired killers; they are employees of criminal organizations who occasionally commit murders as part of their work. This would include the "enforcers" of organized crime.

The case of John Cuff is an example. In the 1980s Cuff, a housing police officer in the Bronx, New York, was recruited by a drug gang known as the Preacher Crew. When not working as a police officer, Cuff acted as a bodyguard, driver, and enforcer for the Crew. Cuff admitted being involved in the murder and dismemberment of several individuals, including members of the Preacher Crew and rival drug gangs. Murder wasn't his main job; it was simply one of those distasteful and awkward tasks that arise occasionally.

Hate-motivated Murder

A hate crime is one in which the victim was selected based primarily on the offender's perception of the victim's race, ethnicity, religion, sexual orientation, gender, or other immutable group affiliation. It's important to note that the perception need not be accurate. For example, an offender who assaults a man believing him to be gay is committing a hate crime even if the victim is heterosexual.

Although there is no single explanation for hate crime there is one common, consistent theme. Hate crimes are generally fueled by fear and rage. When given free rein, fear and rage often result in massive overaggression. A victim in a common stabbing murder might have three or four puncture wounds, whereas the victim of a hate-motivated murder may have thirty to fifty stab wounds as well as postmortem mutilation. For example, it wasn't enough for Emmett Cressell and Louis Ceparano to simply murder Garnett Johnson, Jr., in July of 1997. Cressell and Ceparano, both white, soaked Johnson, an African-American man, with gasoline and burned him alive. Afterward they beheaded Johnson's corpse with an ax.

Similarly, this rage- and fear-fueled need to overkill may result in mass murder. Although rarely described as such, a significant number of mass murders are also hate crimes. It's not uncommon for the victims of a mass murder to be of the same race, ethnicity, or gender. For example, Colin Ferguson, an emotionally disturbed Jamaican immigrant, blamed all white people for his personal failures and setbacks. This belief came to a crisis stage during the Christmas season of 1993. Ferguson, riding on a Long Island commuter train, began to open fire on the passengers. He killed six and wounded many others. All were white.

Women are frequent targets of hate-induced mass murderers. In 1989 Marc Lepine killed fourteen women at the Ecole Polytechnique in Montreal. Lepine felt he'd been denied admission to the university so that lesser qualified women students could attend. He wandered through a university building separating male students from females, and shooting the latter. As he fired Lepine was heard to shout, "You're all a bunch of feminists! I hate feminists!"

In many cases the victims of hate-motivated murders aren't seen as individuals by their killers. Instead they are symbolic representatives of an entire group. Marc Lepine had no motive to kill any of the individual women he targeted, nor did Colin Ferguson have any personal animosity against the commuters he killed. Rather, their victims were killed as an expression of their fear of and rage against an entire group.

Domestic Murder

Domestic murders are those committed by current or former spouses, boyfriends, and girlfriends. Contrary to popular belief, most homicides are not the result of attacks by strangers. Instead most murders are committed by a person known to the victim—often by a person with whom the victim is intimate or related.

This fact translates into bad news for women. As shown in Table 2, only 430 men were killed by intimate members of their households in 1997. By contrast, that same year 1,174 women were killed by current or former husbands and boyfriends. Women are actually more at risk from the men in their lives than they are from strangers. More than twelve times as many women are murdered by men they know than are killed by male strangers.

Violence committed against a family member is generally seen as less deviant than violence committed against strangers. Consider, for example,

TABLE 2

Gender of victims of murder by intimates (spouses, ex-spouses, boyfriends, and girlfriends).

	Gender of Victim	
Year	Male	Female
1976	1357	1600
1977	1294	1437
1978	1202	1482
1979	1262	1506
1980	1221	1549
1981	1278	1572
1982	1141	1481
1983	1113	1462
1984	989	1442
1985	957	1546
1986	985	1586
1987	933	1494
1988	854	1582
1989	903	1415
1990	859	1501
1991	779	1518
1992	722	1455
1993	708	1581
1994	692	1405
1995	547	1321
1996	515	1324
1997	430	1174

Source: Bureau of Justice Statistics

TABLE 3

Homicide victimization—1970–97

Year	Homicide Rate	Total Homicides
1970	7.9	13,649
1971	8.6	16,183
1972	9.0	15,832
1973	9.4	17,123
1974	9.8	18,632
1975	9.6	18,642
1976	8.8	16,605
1977	8.8	18,033
1978	9.0	18,714
1979	9.7	20,591
1980	10.2	21,860
1981	9.8	20,053
1982	9.1	19,485
1983	8.3	18,673
1984	7.9	16,689
1985	7.9	17,545
1986	8.6	19,257
1987	8.3	17,859
1988	8.4	18,269
1989	8.7	18,954
1990	9.4	20,045
1991	9.8	21,505
1992	9.3	22,540
1993	9.5	23,271
1994	9.0	22,076
1995	8.2	20,043
1996	7.4	15,848
1997	6.8	15,289

Source: FBI, Uniform Crime Reports, 1970–97

a parent disciplining a child in a supermarket. Other shoppers may frown at an adult swatting a child on the rump, but bystanders are unlikely to interfere if that child is related to the adult. However, an adult committing the very same act against an unrelated child will likely prompt a very different response.

Similarly, law enforcement has historically been reluctant to interfere in what are termed "domestic disputes." Police departments are becoming more sensitive to spousal abuse. However, data reveal that most of the women murdered by their domestic partners have previously been assaulted by that partner. Similarly, a significant proportion of the women who kill their domestic partners are killing men who have abused them. Violence in the home generally leads to still more violence in the home.

Conclusion

In 1997 the murder rate* in the United States was at the lowest level in thirty years (see Table 3). There were only seven murders for every one hundred thousand people in the U.S. The murder rate for the period between 1972 and 1995 ranged from eight to ten victims per one hundred thousand people. The difference between seven murders and ten murders for every one hundred thousand people may not sound like a lot, but in raw numbers it accounts for around eight thousand dead bodies.

Why has the murder rate dropped? Obviously, there is no simple, single answer. The drop appears to be the result of a confluence of several factors, including:

• Changes in the drug culture
• Changes in demographics
• Changes in policing styles
• Improvements in trauma care

*Criminologists use crime rates rather than the actual number of crimes in order to control for variations in the size of the population. Comparing the number of crimes for every 100,000 people in the U.S. provides a more accurate look at crime trends. For example, in 1971 there were 16,183 murders, a murder rate of 8.6 for every 100,000 people. By 1995 the population of the U.S. had increased, so the murder rate was lower (8.2) even though the number of murders was higher (20,043).

In the 1980s, crack cocaine became a popular drug in impoverished inner city neighborhoods where people could not afford powder cocaine. The crack trade became a lucrative business, and many young men, most of whom were minorities, were recruited into the supply side of the market. Competition between drug dealers was fierce and cash was plentiful—a condition that led to an inner city arms race. Now consider that historically most murders are committed by young adults aged eighteen to twenty-four (see Table 2). Combine this notoriously reckless age group with drugs and high-powered weaponry and you have an epidemic of anonymous violence and murder.

The conditions that fueled the increase in murder rates have slowly changed. The generation that was eighteen to twenty-four in the 1980s and early 1990s has aged (or been imprisoned or killed itself off). The generation entering the eighteen-to-twenty-four age range has witnessed the deleterious effects of crack and violence on their parents and older siblings. This appears to have reduced demand for the drug. In addition, the violent drug wars had the effect of reducing the competition through attrition. The surviving drug dealers have developed a more stable marketplace.

At the same time policing styles have changed. More police officers are being assigned to violent neighborhoods. These officers are trained to be more aggressive in stopping and searching "suspicious" individuals, and they are arresting more young people for "quality of life" crimes.* This has two primary consequences. First, the searches result in the discovery of more illegal guns. Fewer guns on the street decreases the chances that a disagreement will end in death. Second, the people arrested for carrying illegal guns—also the people most likely to be involved in a crime of violence—are incarcerated. More aggressive and intrusive policing removes the more volatile members from the community—although this often comes at the expense of civil liberties.

Finally, one rarely mentioned reason for falling murder rates is the improvement in trauma care. The emergency room physicians and nurses who treat gunshot wounds, and the emergency medical technicians who respond to the scenes of shootings have become more proficient in

---

*These are the minor crimes that make good citizens reluctant to spend time on the street: loitering, public intoxication, violations of noise ordinances, etc.

dealing with gunshot trauma. At the same time, however, the firearms used in street shootings have become increasingly powerful and lethal. E.R. doctors are seeing gunshot patients with more severe trauma than in the recent past. The severe trauma caused by more powerful firearms means more patients are dying on the way to the emergency room. But those fortunate enough to arrive alive have a much better chance of remaining alive. Incidents that would have resulted in death and a murder charge a decade ago now result in charges of first degree assault and attempted murder.

PART TWO

The Police Investigation

THE SCALES OF JUSTICE

Murder is generally considered the most serious crime. It's not surprising that murder cases get more investigative attention than other crimes. That increased attention pays off; murder has the highest clearance rate of all serious crimes.*

However, it's a fact of detective life that investigative resources are limited. In any large city there are always more dead bodies than homicide detectives. There is a finite number of detectives and evidence technicians available in a police department, and they have to divide their time between several cases. On a more mundane note, there is only so much space available in a police department's evidence control room. Not every possible piece of evidence can be collected, tested, and stored. One of the tricks of a good detective is finding the right balance between being thorough and wasting resources.

This translates into a need for police departments to prioritize investigative resources. Some murder cases will necessarily get more attention than others. Put more bluntly, some murder cases will be seen as more important than others. This isn't a fact police departments like to admit. Certainly no victim's family wants to hear that the life of their child/par-

---

*A case is generally considered "cleared" when at least one person is arrested and charged with the crime. Cases may also be cleared when an identified offender is killed during apprehension or commits suicide.

51

ent/sibling/spouse was less important than the life of another and merits fewer investigative resources. As ugly as the fact is, it's a fact nonetheless; not all murder cases are created equal.

What determines the importance of a case? It's the intersection of the victim, the accused murderer, the circumstances of the crime, and the crime's news value. Important cases usually require a combination of two or more of these factors; only rarely is one factor enough to boost an otherwise obscure crime to importance.

The Victim

The victim, of course, is the pivot point of a murder case. Everything revolves around the victim. The victim's race, gender, social class, age, marital status, and fame (or notoriety) can all play a role in determining the importance of the case. Rarely, however, is any single factor predominant.

Here are some very general, if ugly, realities (and I must emphasize these are generalities). White victims will generally receive more investigative resources than minority victims. Young victims will generally receive more attention than old victims. Victims of a higher social class will generally receive more attention than those of the lower classes. Famous (or infamous) victims will clearly get more attention than obscure victims.

I doubt if these realities will surprise the reader. As a society we intuitively know these things to be true. However, most of us prefer to avoid thinking about the implications behind the truth.

Consider the murders of Marvin Watson and Amy Watkins. Each of these young people (Watson was twenty-two, Watkins twenty-six) moved to New York City from someplace else; Watson from Jamaica, Watkins from the Midwest. Both hoped to achieve something in New York; Watson learned to be an electrician, Watkins was a graduate student in social work. They each moved into apartments in Brooklyn within about a mile of each other. Although they moved in different social circles, both were well liked.

Both Watson and Watkins were stabbed to death. Although their murders were unrelated, they took place within ten weeks of each other. The murder of Amy Watkins received national publicity. Watson died in obscurity. The investigation of Watkins's murder involved a team of more than two dozen detectives. Watson's murder received no special attention. Watson was a working-class black man and an immigrant. Watkins was a middle-class white woman from America's heartland. Both victims were important to their families. One, however, received more investigative resources.

The Accused

Some murder cases are elevated to importance because of the person accused of the crime. The murders of Nicole Simpson and Ron Goldman, although brutal, were not radically out of the ordinary. In many ways that crime was no different from thousands of other murders that take place after years of spousal abuse (Goldman, it appears, was simply in the wrong place at the wrong time). Ex-husbands kill former wives and ex-boyfriends kill their former lovers with alarming regularity.

What made the Simpson case important to the police was that the prime suspect and eventual defendant was O. J. Simpson, a football star turned ad-man and actor. When a famous person is accused of a crime, especially a serious crime, the pressure on the prosecution to obtain a conviction is magnified. That pressure inevitably filters down to the investigators. More resources are applied to the case.

The fact that Simpson was wealthy also played a role in determining the amount of police resources devoted to the case. Wealthier defendants can afford more—and usually better—attorneys, and more investigators. It is, therefore, more difficult to successfully prosecute a person of wealth. The defense in the Simpson case is estimated to have cost approximately six million dollars. The prosecution cost taxpayers approximately nine million dollars (over two and a half million was spent on housing and feeding the sequestered jury).

It's not that the law doesn't apply to the wealthy; it's just that the wealthy can buy more "justice."

The Circumstances of the Crime

Some murder cases become important because of unusual circumstances. A quirky murder will likely get more investigative attention than an ordinary murder. For example, a victim killed by a bow and arrow is likely to attract more investigative resources than a simple shooting. Detectives, like everybody else, appreciate novelty in their work.

The number of the dead can also make a case important. A triple murder will attract more attention than a single murder, if only because three bodies at a crime scene will require more forensic technicians to process the area. Even a mass murder in which the offender takes his own life demands a great deal of investigative resources. There is no mystery about *who* committed the crime, but there is a mystery as to *why* it took place.

The number of victims can influence the intensity of the investigation even if the victims are not killed contemporaneously. Relatively few resources will be spent on the murder of one black, inner-city, homeless street prostitute.* However, the collective weight of half a dozen black, inner city, homeless street prostitutes turning up dead in similar ways over a period of a few months will raise the importance of the case and the amount of resources devoted to it.

Murders that affect the economic well-being of a community can also generate a great deal of investigative resources. For example, the murder of a tourist in a resort town will likely spark an intense investigation. Although there may not be anything unusual about the actual murder, the potential effect on the tourism industry might elevate the crime. Similarly, an ordinary murder in an upscale shopping district will engage more investigative attention. It may not be openly discussed, but part of the investigative mission will be to demonstrate that the killing was a fluke and the area is actually safe.

---

*Many serial killers recognize that some victims will receive less investigative attention and have used this fact to their advantage. Prostitutes rank very high on the list of serial killer targets. Even as this is being written a serial killer is preying on prostitutes in Englewood, an impoverished, drug-ridden section of Chicago's South Side. Six victims have been linked to this one killer. In the past eight years two other serial killers chose to hunt in this same neighborhood; one killed six women, the other fourteen.

The News Value of the Crime

Newsworthiness—the qualities of an event that reporters feel make it worth covering—is difficult to define. But there is little doubt the news value of a crime often determines the level of investigative effort it's given. The factors already mentioned (the victim, the accused murderer, and the circumstances of the crime) also play key roles in newsworthiness.

The murder of JonBenet Ramsey is a model case—the perfect intersection of victim, suspect, and circumstance. JonBenet was the six-year-old daughter of wealthy white parents. She was a pretty child, one who had been involved in the curious subculture of child beauty pageants. The prime suspects in the murder were members of her family (it's important to note nobody has been formally charged with her murder at the time this is written). The murder itself was peculiar. She was strangled in her home while her parents were allegedly asleep. There were hints of sexual abuse. Finally, JonBenet was murdered late on Christmas Day, a fact that makes the murder seem somehow more tragic. This was a crime saturated with news value.

At the time this is written, the investigation of JonBenet Ramsey's murder has cost the city of Boulder, Colorado, over one and a half million dollars. One cannot, of course, put a price on justice. Yet it must be noted that JonBenet Ramsey was only one of approximately 980 children under the age of eight who were murdered in 1996. One has to wonder how much money was spent investigating those other child murders. One has to wonder how many other criminal investigations in that jurisdiction received short shrift due to budgetary and personnel constraints.

Few, if any, homicide detectives would admit that the death of one person is more important than the death of another. I suspect the vast majority of homicide detectives give every case as much effort as they possibly can. However, detectives are realists. They know more pressure will be put on them to solve the murder of a prominent member of society than the murder of a homeless man. They know that a case that draws a lot of media attention will also draw scrutiny from their superiors on the force. They know that justice isn't an equal-opportunity result. A good homicide

55

detective puts as much effort into a case as is demanded . . . and then moves on to the next case. There is always a next case.

It may not be right, but it's the way of the world.

FINDING THE BODY

The county dispatcher logged in the call at 0912 hours on a Saturday morning. A report of skeletal remains found in Marshtown Park. The caller, who identified himself as Tony Wingate, said he was calling from a convenience store on Old Marshtown Road. The dispatcher told Wingate to wait there until a patrol car arrived.

Sheriff's deputy Richard Cook arrived at the convenience store at 0925. Cook, a three-year veteran of the Calhoun County Sheriff's Department, was glad to get the call. Skeletal remains were something new, something different. He generally divided his time between ticketing speeders on county roads, responding to traffic accidents, and taking reports of minor break-ins and thefts from the small towns and farms in southern Calhoun County. Most of the crime handled by the Sheriff's Department was spillover from Stormont, the county seat of nearly one hundred twenty thousand people.

Skeletal remains. Probably just a deer, Cook thought. Still, it would make a good story. As he pulled into the convenience store parking lot Cook was already thinking how he'd tell his buddies after his shift ended. "Just another day," he'd say. "Spent the morning sorting out some skeletal remains."

Only one vehicle was in the parking lot—a late-model pickup with a young man leaning against it. The man headed toward Cook's cruiser even before it stopped.

57

He introduced himself as Tony Wingate.

"You're the one who, uh, found something unusual in the park?" Cook asked.

"A skeleton," Wingate said. "Or part of one. My buddy actually found it. We drove down from Stormont to ride our bikes. Mountain bikes. The park has these great trails, you know. Anyway, Jeff—that's my buddy, Jeff Hadden—Jeff stepped into the woods to take a leak. Next thing I know he's shouting for me to come see. And there's this human skeleton."

"How do you know it's human?" Cook asked.

"Got a human skull," Wingate said.

"Where's your buddy now?"

"Back at the park," Wingate said. "He thought maybe somebody should stay there to . . . I don't know, guard the body I guess."

"Let's go take a look."

Cook followed Wingate the few miles back to Marshtown Park. Jeff Hadden was waiting for them, riding his bicycle in slow circles around the gravel parking area. Hadden took Cook to a point south and east of the parking lot, just a few yards off from the bike trail.

There, among the small bushes scattered between the ash and hickory trees, Cook saw the torso of a human skeleton. The skull wasn't attached and one of the arms was missing.

Animals been at it, Cook thought. There seemed to be some skin still attached near the ribs. Been dead a while, Cook thought.

Cook circled the skeleton, finding a few more scattered bones. He squatted by the skull, reached out and gingerly touched it. He heard Hadden clear his throat.

"You boys touch anything here?" Cook asked.

Hadden shook his head.

"Well, let's head back to the parking lot," Cook said. "I need to get some information from you."

Cook radioed his supervisor then began to interview Wingate and Hadden.

Within twenty minutes a half-dozen members of the Sheriff's department had arrived to examine the skeleton. Cook's supervisor, Sgt. Wilton, arrived to find them in a loose huddle around it.

"Break it up," Wilton ordered. "Treat this like a crime scene." He sent one deputy off to fetch crime scene tape, another to call for a team of evidence technicians, and another to make a rough sketch of the entire area. He told the rest to scatter and look for any evidence and the rest of the skeleton.

"I want you to check the area around the skeleton," he said, "then move down along the trail. Both sides. And the wooded area around the entire parking lot perimeter. We might as well be thorough."

He sent Parisi to check the parking lot perimeter. Parisi was new, just ending his six-month probationary period. New guys always got the dull and dirty jobs. It was almost a tradition.

Once the men were busy Sgt. Wilton had Wingate and Hadden go over their story again. They were young men, both in their mid-twenties, both employed by the same manufacturing company in Stormont. They went riding at least twice a month from early spring to late fall, exploring different parks and trails within a few hours' drive from Stormont. They weren't certain when they'd last ridden the trails in Marshtown Park; maybe three months ago, maybe only two.

"How long do you think that's been there?" Hadden asked.

Wilton shrugged. "Two, three months," he said. "Four, maybe. Hard to say."

"You think it's a murder?" Hadden asked.

"Too early to say," Wilton said. "Could be some hiker or bum stepped off the trail to take a dump and had a heart attack."

"Like Elvis," Hadden said, laughing.

One of the deputies came to report that some more bones and some old clothing had been found.

"Men's clothes?" Wilton asked.

The deputy shook his head.

"What the hell is wrong with Parisi?" Sgt. Wilton asked. He could see the new deputy at the northwest corner of the parking lot, bent over and vomiting. "You'd better go check on him."

The deputy walked off with a look of disgust on his face. Newbies were a pain in the ass.

A moment later, as Wilton was having Wingate and Hadden write out their own statements, the deputy called out. "Sarge, you'd better come take a look at this. We got us a fresh one."

Fresh was a relative term, Sgt. Wilton thought as he approached. He could smell the decomposing body before he could see it. The body was naked, sprawled out face down, crawling with maggots and beetles, but clearly that of a woman.

"We're gonna need more people here," Wilton said.

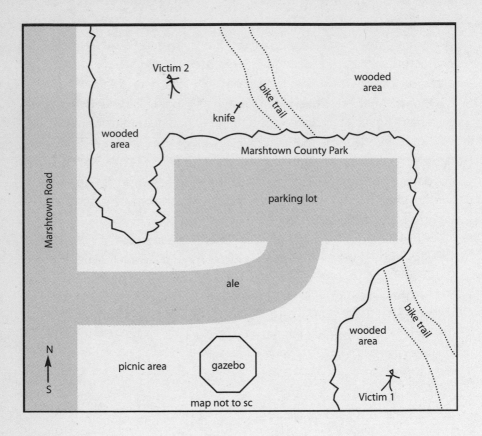

CRIME SCENE INVESTIGATION

The Latin root of the term "evidence" is *videre*, which means "to see." When we can see a thing clearly, we say it is evident. Evidence is what we call the information we gather in order to more clearly see the truth.

In legal matters evidence comes in a variety of forms, but most commonly it falls into the categories of verbal evidence and physical evidence. By verbal evidence we mean the statements people make about what took place. We'll discuss interviewing and interrogation, the methods by which verbal evidence is obtained, in a later chapter. In this chapter we'll focus on physical evidence.

In very simple terms, physical evidence refers to the tangible residue of crime—the concrete things left behind that suggest what took place and who might have been involved. Fingerprints, bloodstains, footprints, pry marks, tire tracks, bullet holes, shell casings, dead bodies—these are all examples of physical evidence. By carefully examining the patterns and inconsistencies in the physical evidence, detectives attempt to reconstruct as best they can what took place.

Physical evidence is usually considered more reliable and more meaningful than verbal evidence. One reason for this is that physical evidence exists in a moral vacuum. A bullet hole doesn't have an agenda, a fingerprint doesn't have a motive. These things are just *there*.

DUELING INTERPRETATIONS

One of the most well-known examples of differing interpretations of evidence involved the bloody glove reported to have been found on the property of O. J. Simpson after the brutal murder of his ex-wife and her friend. There can be no doubt that two dark brown, cashmere-lined gloves were seized as evidence. There can be no doubt that the gloves were saturated with blood. Given the nature of DNA testing, there is statistically no doubt that most of the blood on the gloves was that of the two victims. Nor is there much doubt that blood consistent with the DNA of Simpson was found near the cuff of the right hand glove.

However, during the trial there was much disagreement about virtually everything else pertaining to the gloves. The prosecution maintained the right hand glove had been found on O. J. Simpson's property; the defense maintained the glove had been planted on the property in order to frame Simpson for the crime. The prosecution stated the gloves belonged to Simpson; the defense claimed they did not.

The bloody gloves exist. But whether they were seen as evidence of Simpson's guilt or of his innocence depended entirely on who was doing the interpreting.

Moreover, physical evidence doesn't lie. It is, however, open to interpretation. Consider something as simple as a pry mark on a window sill. Different people may offer different explanations about how the pry mark got there. They may disagree about what tool or device was used to make the pry mark. They may even dispute that it's a pry mark at all. Nonetheless, the mark is there; it exists independent of any interpretation. A pry mark just *is*.

Generally, most physical evidence is found by the police at the scene of the crime and transported to the crime laboratory for analysis. The crime scene investigation is very often the most crucial step in any murder investigation. Evidence at a crime scene not only suggests what happened, but it may also indicate why it happened and who was responsible. In addition, evidence collected at a crime scene may eventually be introduced at a trial. It's essential, therefore, that the police take great care to ensure the evidence is valid, reliable, and untainted.

What the police do at the crime scene often determines the success or failure of the investigation as well as the success or failure of any resulting prosecution.

Crime Scene Protocol

Any technical task can be broken down into many individual steps. Raising a circus tent, for example, is an immensely complex chore involving a large number of workers and a great deal of material. However, it's made easier and is done more safely by following the same steps in the same order every single time.

Processing a crime scene, like raising a circus tent, also involves following a basic protocol to ensure it's done properly. There are four primary steps involved in the crime scene protocol:

1. Secure the crime scene.
2. Examine the scene.
3. Locate and interview witnesses to the crime.
4. Gather the physical evidence.

Step three will be discussed in a later chapter. The remainder of this chapter will examine the other three steps.

Although each of these is important, the first step, securing the crime scene, is paramount. This is written in stone: *Thou Shalt Secure and Protect the Crime Scene.* Once the scene is secure the other steps may be considered.

Securing the Crime Scene

An undisturbed crime scene can often offer detectives the best account of the crime. However, crime scenes are very delicate environments and are easily damaged. The simple act of entering a crime scene taints it. Every person who sets foot behind the yellow tape brings along dust, loose fibers, and hair that might be left at the scene. Each person who enters a crime scene increases the risk of contamination. This is especially true as forensic science becomes more sophisticated. In major crimes in some of the larger cities, forensic techs wear clean-suits like surgeons. However, the most common technique for maintaining the integrity of a crime scene is simply to keep anyone unnecessary out.

This isn't as easy to do as it sounds. Crime scenes are people magnets. At any given murder scene it's likely the following people have entered: the person(s) who discovered the crime, the first uniformed officer(s) to respond to the scene, emergency medical personnel, the watch commander summoned by the uniformed officers, the detectives summoned by the watch commander, the medical examiner staff, the forensic team, and possibly an attorney from the prosecutor's office. If the case is recognized as an important murder, it isn't uncommon for senior police personnel and local politicians to arrive at the scene, each wanting to view the scene. The danger of contamination is further compounded by the arrival of public spectators and the news media.

Various methods are used to maintain the integrity of the murder scene. They include:

- **Erecting barriers.** The simplest form of barrier is the yellow police tape we see so often on television. This is also the least effective method. People quickly become accustomed to ducking under the police tape. Double perimeters are more effective, but not foolproof.
- **Visitor logs.** Requiring every person who enters a crime scene to provide their name and purpose for entering the scene tends to discourage those police personnel who are basically just curious spectators.
- **Specimen release forms.** Some departments require individuals entering a crime scene to sign a consent form stating they'll provide fingerprints, hair samples, shoe prints, blood samples, and semen specimens for comparison purposes. This also discourages idle observers; nobody wants to submit blood and semen specimens.

The size of the crime scene and the number of access points directly relates to the difficulty of keeping it secure. A murder committed in a motel room is easier to secure than one committed in a tavern. A murder committed in a tavern is easier to secure than one committed in the lobby of a large hotel. A murder committed in a hotel is easier to secure than one committed in a public park.

Consider the problem that faced the police of Jasper, Texas, during the 1998 murder investigation of James Brooks. Brooks, an African-American man, was murdered by three white racists who chained him to the back of their pickup truck and dragged him to death. The crime scene covered an area of county road three or four miles long.

The case on which this book is based involved a body discovered in a wooded area inside a park. This poses a serious problem for the police. How big should the crime scene be? Five square yards around the body? Twenty square yards? A hundred?

The decision is generally based on instinct and available personnel, balanced against the perceived importance of the crime. There may simply not be enough officers and technicians to adequately search a hundred square yards (ten thousand square feet) of woods—unless, of course, the case is perceived as a high publicity case.

A crime scene can't be kept secure forever. Eventually the yellow crime scene tape will come down and the scene will open up. The more public the scene, the sooner the detective will lose control over it. A private apartment might be sealed for weeks, but a busy street will be opened as soon as possible. Once a crime scene is open the chances of obtaining reliable or useful evidence from it decreases radically.

The remaining steps in the crime scene protocol are more fluid. They rarely take place in strict order. In fact, they often take place concurrently. For example, one detective may be examining the scene while others locate and begin to talk to witnesses. Some detectives prefer to make an initial examination of the scene before talking to witnesses. They feel the information they obtain from the scene will help them determine when the witnesses are telling the truth. Other detectives prefer to talk briefly with witnesses before paying attention to the crime scene. They operate

65

on the premise that any information they have about the events that took place will help them evaluate the scene more clearly.

Examining the Scene

Because crime scenes are so fragile, police officers and detectives are repeatedly reminded of the cardinal rule of crime scene protocol: *don't touch anything*. This seems obvious. And yet every detective who has ever worked a murder scene can tell you horror stories about trained police officers—including high-ranking supervisors—who have picked up, handled, moved, stolen, or otherwise disturbed crucial evidence. In the famous Sam Sheppard murder case (the case on which the television program and movie *The Fugitive* were based), a police officer literally flushed potentially critical evidence down the toilet. The officer noticed a cigarette butt floating in the toilet—and flushed it without thinking. Later it was discovered that neither Sheppard nor his wife smoked. The cigarette butt may have been the clue that would have solved the crime.

To resist the tendency to touch things, police officers are often trained to keep their hands in their back pockets while moving through a crime scene. The back pockets are used because it's not the natural place to put one's hands. The odd feeling of walking around with your hands in your back pockets acts as a constant reminder to be careful.

Although crime scene protocols vary from department to department, they all include the following steps:

- examine the perimeter
- examine the body
- photograph the scene
- sketch the scene
- process the scene

A homicide detective generally begins the initial examination of the murder scene by scrutinizing the perimeter of the crime scene rather than the body itself. This is done for two reasons. First, because the body isn't going anywhere. It's going to stay exactly where it is until the detective allows the medical examiner's staff to take it away. So long as it's protected against contamination, the body can always wait. Second, the farther any evidence is from the body the more likely it is that somebody will disturb it and ruin it as evidence for trial. Even the most raw recruit will recognize a bloody knife lying beside the body as evidence. However, if that same recruit discovers a bloody knife down the hall, through the kitchen, and in the mud room he or she may pick it up to look at it. To be safe, then, most detectives begin their initial examination of the scene at the periphery of the crime scene and slowly work their way toward the body.

During this examination the detectives ask themselves two very basic questions: What is at the scene that shouldn't be? And what is not at the scene that should be? The first question pertains to any evidence

EVIDENCE COLLECTION PROTOCOLS

BLOOD STAINS

Blood in liquid pools should be picked up on a gauze pad or other clean sterile cotton cloth and allowed to air dry thoroughly at room temperature. If not completely dry, label and roll in paper or place in a brown paper bag or box and seal and label the container. Place only one item in each container. Do not use plastic containers. The sample should be transported to the crime lab as soon as possible. Delays beyond 48 hours may make the samples useless.

Dried blood stains on clothing should be wrapped in clean paper and placed in a brown paper bag or box, which is then sealed and labeled. Do not attempt to remove stains from the cloth. When dried blood is found on small solid objects the entire object should be transported to the lab, after labeling and packaging. When dried blood is found on large, immovable objects the stained area should be covered with clean paper, the edges sealed with tape to prevent loss or contamination. Before the scene is cleared the stain should be scraped onto a clean piece of paper, which should be folded and placed in an envelope. Do not scrape the dried blood directly into an evidence envelope. The scraping should be done using a freshly washed and dried knife or similar tool; the tool should be washed and dried before being used to scrape another stain.

the offender may have left behind, evidence that may lead the detective to the offender. The second question pertains to evidence the offender may have taken from the scene, evidence that will tie the offender to the crime and possibly supply a motive.

It's during this initial examination that many of the decisions regarding evidence are made. The detective decides what surfaces should be fingerprinted; what areas should be searched for fiber evidence or bullets; what items should be seized, bagged, and tagged. As noted, these decisions have to be weighed against the importance of the case and the resources at the detective's disposal. You can't collect and analyze everything.

After the perimeter has been examined the detective can focus on the body. The detective knows that the *real* examination of the body will be done later by a medical examiner under more clinical conditions, but an undisturbed body at a crime scene offers the good detective a great deal of information. Is there an obvious cause of death—gunshot wounds, stab wounds, asphyxiation? Are there any signs of foul play—defensive wounds, pockets rifled, the absence of a weapon that could make the wounds? Are there indications that the body was moved—a lack of blood, dragging marks, a trail of blood?

Once the initial examination is finished, photographs are taken. Photographs of everything. Detectives don't always know what information is going to be important in solving the crime and getting the perpetrator convicted. It's better to waste film on photographs that may not be needed than to need a photograph not taken. Film is cheap. Two types of photographs are taken—general location shots to establish what the scene looked like and close-up shots of evidence.

After the photographs are taken the scene is sketched. It may seem redundant for a detective to sketch a scene that has just been photographed, but it's a critical step. Although unlikely, it's possible that something may happen to the film during processing and all the photographs will be ruined. In addition, a sketch includes measurements. A sketch, for example, will indicate the bloody knife lying next to the body is exactly seventeen inches from the victim's left hand. Again, that sort of information may turn out to be unimportant—but there is no way for a detective at the crime scene to know. It's always better to have too much information than not enough.

TAINTED EVIDENCE

Sloppy evidence collection techniques and poor evidence management contributed to the acquittal in the O. J. Simpson murder case. A blanket taken from inside the home of victim Nicole Brown Simpson was used to cover her body. It was a considerate gesture by the police, but it may have contaminated trace evidence found on her body. The defense argued that hair and fibers on the blanket could have been transferred to the victim's body, and that Simpson could have left hair on the blanket during a visit to his ex-wife's home. The primary criminalist at the scene was forced during the trial to admit the use of the blanket was an error.

Later a blood sample taken from Simpson at the jail was carried by the lead police investigator to Simpson's home, where the criminalist was still collecting evidence. The vial of blood should have been taken directly to the Evidence Control Unit. The criminalist testified he could not recall a single instance in which a suspect's blood evidence was brought directly to him at a crime scene. By not following the standard protocol, the detective gave the defense lawyers the opportunity to suggest the blood had been taken to the Simpson home in order to frame him for the crime.

The sheer quantity of such evidentiary irregularities and prosecutorial errors led Vincent Bugliosi, the prosecutor who convicted Charles Manson, to label the Simpson case as "the most incompetent criminal prosecution that I have ever seen."

After the scene has been examined, after the photographs have been taken, after the sketching has been complete . . . only then is the evidence actually collected. The criminalists move in and begin to gather the physical material on which a murder conviction might be obtained.

Collecting Physical Evidence

The collection, analysis, and interpretation of physical evidence is known as criminalistics. This is an extremely diverse field and draws on a wide

EVIDENCE COLLECTION PROTOCOLS

SEMINAL STAINS

Seminal stains are often found on clothing, blankets, sheets, or towels. The stain should be allowed to air dry, then be wrapped in paper and packaged in paper bags. Plastic bags are not appropriate.

Victims should always be examined by a physician using a sexual assault evidence collection kit. All garments should be collected and packaged separately, and handled as little as possible.

variety of sciences and disciplines, including chemistry, anatomy, zoology, physics, archeology, and entomology.

Collecting physical evidence can be a routine process, or it can be a highly technical procedure involving special training and technology. Whether routine or complex, the sheer variety of techniques used to gather physical evidence makes it impossible to discuss in any detail in a book of this nature. Included in this chapter, however, are basic collection protocols for some of the more common types of physical evidence collected in murder cases.

Chain of Custody

It's critical for the prosecution to be able to demonstrate that the evidence collected at the scene of the crime is the same evidence introduced in the courtroom. It's equally important to show the evidence hasn't been tampered with. This is done by maintaining a strict chain of custody.

When physical evidence is collected, it's sealed in an appropriate container. Attached to that container is an evidence label, which includes a description of the evidence, the signature of the collector, the location from which it was collected, the time and date it was collected, and an investigation case number. Every time that evidence container switches hands, the person who accepted it must sign and date the evidence tag. In that way the prosecution can assure the court, the defense lawyer, and the jury that the evidence has not been tampered with. A piece of evidence for which the chain of custody has been broken may be found inadmissable in court.

EVIDENCE COLLECTION PROTOCOLS

HAIR

Human hair can reveal the possible race of the individual it came from and the part of the body from which it originated. It can be compared with other samples to determine if the samples had a common origin.

Hair should be recovered using tweezers, placed in paper bindles or coin envelopes that should then be folded and sealed in larger envelopes. The outer sealed envelope should be labeled.

Hair caught in dried blood or in metal or a crack of glass should not be removed unless the object is too large to be moved. If the object is small it should be marked, wrapped, and sealed in an envelope.

In cases involving sexual contact, the victim's pubic region should be combed prior to collecting standards. When obtaining hair samples from living persons (suspects, officers who may have contaminated the crime scene) for comparison, the recommended method is to have the subject bend over a large sheet of clean paper, then rub or massage his or her hands through the hair so that loose hair will fall out on the paper. In addition, hairs should be gathered by plucking (not cutting) them from representative areas all over the head. A total of fifty to a hundred hairs is desired.

DNA Evidence

The development of DNA testing technology may be the most important advance in investigative history. It has revolutionized criminal investigation. The use of DNA evidence allows police and prosecutors to establish the guilt of an accused offender with a much higher degree of certainty than had previously been possible. In addition, the development of DNA "fingerprint" archives offers investigators a new tool for identifying and apprehending criminals. At the same time, DNA evidence serves the search for truth by exonerating the innocent.

"DNA" is the acronym for deoxyribonucleic acid. The inherited characteristics of people come from the genes on their chromosomes.

EVIDENCE COLLECTION PROTOCOLS

FIBERS AND THREADS

Examination of fibers can be conducted to determine the type or color of fiber. Such examinations will sometimes indicate the type of garment or fabric from which they originated. Fibers and threads can also be compared with a suspect's clothing.

Threads and large fibers can be treated much like hair: picked up with tweezers, placed in a paper bindle, then in a coin envelope, which is sealed and marked. Loose threads and fibers should not be placed directly into an envelope.

Chromosomes consist of self-replicating molecules of DNA, and our genes consist of subsets of these very large molecules. The underlying concept of DNA analysis is that every person* (with the exception of identical twins) has a unique combination of genes encoded in their DNA. By comparing a known sample of DNA with a sample of DNA collected from a crime scene it's possible to determine the probability that both samples came from the same individual. The probability of one individual's DNA matching the DNA of another is generally measured in the hundreds of millions. One-hundred-percent certainty is not achieved because comparing all the billions of elements of DNA in each sample is not technically feasible at this time. Nor is it necessary—enough elements of the DNA are tested to establish statistical certainty. Still, explaining the scientific and statistical ramifications of DNA testing to a jury is sometimes a hurdle for prosecutors.

DNA can be obtained from a variety of biological sources—hair, blood, semen, saliva. Hair strands require a follicle (the root of the hair) in order to provide a DNA profile, and seminal fluid requires the presence of sperm. Saliva can be obtained from a suspect simply by wiping a swab on

---

*DNA analysis has also been used on dog blood. In 1996 a man and a woman were murdered along with their puppy. Seattle police found blood spatters on the jacket of one of the suspects. Lab analysis determined the blood to be that of the puppy, placing the suspect at the scene of the murder.

the inside of the mouth, which is less intrusive than collecting a blood sample. Each type of sample offers the same basic information with the same degree of precision.

The FBI has been conducting forensic DNA testing since 1989. They report that approximately 60 percent of all the DNA samples they receive have matched DNA of the primary suspect in the case. Interestingly, one quarter of the samples exonerate the primary suspect. The rest are inconclusive.

This illustrates the tremendous benefits of DNA testing: It not only inculpates the guilty, but exculpates the innocent. The fact that DNA analysis can be so effective in establishing innocence has sparked the creation of the Innocence Project. This organization, based at Cardozo School of Law and founded by attorneys Barry Scheck and Peter Neufeld, relies on volunteer law students and attorneys to review cases of people who claim to have been falsely convicted. They also make arrangements for DNA testing in cases that seem appropriate.

DNA testing has revealed a startling number of wrongfully convicted people serving long prison sentences. Consider the case of Ronald Cotton. The evidence in two separate 1984 rape cases suggested a single perpetrator had commited both crimes. In both cases the assailant broke into an apartment, cut the telephone lines, then sexually assaulted the woman who lived there. Afterward the rapist searched her belongings, taking money and other items. Following a month-long investigation Cotton was arrested and charged with both rapes. The evidence against him was circumstantial but compelling. A flashlight found in Cotton's home resembled one used by the assailant, and rubber from Cotton's tennis shoe matched rubber found at one of the crime scenes. Most damning, however, was the fact that one of the victims picked Cotton's picture out of a photographic lineup.

Cotton was convicted of each crime in two separate trials and received sentences of life imprisonment and fifty-four years. He appealed the convictions based on the fact that the second victim had picked a different man out of a lineup and the trial court had not allowed this evidence to be presented to the jury. The appellate court agreed with Cotton. The following year the court ordered that he receive a new trial on each of the two rape cases.

Before a retrial took place, however, a remarkable thing happened. A

EVIDENCE COLLECTION PROTOCOLS

INSECTS

Chemical changes occur in the body almost as soon as it dies, and insects—especially flies—take note of those changes. If the body is outdoors, the first flies arrive to lay their eggs within ten minutes of death.

Forensic entomologists can often determine the approximate time of death, how long human remains have been undetected, whether the body has been moved after death, perhaps even the location of the murder by examining the insects found on, and in, bodies.

Larvae and pupae of all sizes should be collected from different parts of the body and placed in a container of 70 to 80 percent isopropyl alcohol. Each container should hold only those larvae and pupae collected on a particular part of the body, and should be labeled accordingly—for example "groin area" or "eye socket." If a large number of insects are placed in a single container, the alcohol should be changed a few hours later. Insect bodies contain a large proportion of water, which will dilute the alcohol to a point at which it will be ineffective as an agent to prevent decay.

Living insects should be captured using a net and placed in containers. If they can't be caught, extra larvae and pupae should be collected and kept alive in order that they may be raised by the lab. Adult insects are easier to identify. Larvae and pupae to be raised to adulthood for identification should be placed in a container filled with a wet cotton ball to prevent drying out. The lid of the container should be replaced with a coffee filter, which allows the larvae to breathe. Again, each container should only contain insects from a particular part of the body.

man serving a prison sentence for crimes similar to the assaults for which Cotton had been convicted told another inmate he had committed the crimes Cotton had been charged with. The judge at Cotton's new trial, however, refused to allow this new information into evidence. Cotton was again convicted of both rapes and sentenced to life.

A second appeal was rejected in 1988, and Cotton's conviction was reaffirmed. In 1994, however, a third appeal was successful in getting the court to order DNA testing of both Cotton and the inmate who had confessed to the crimes. The testing was conducted in 1995. The results of the testing excluded Cotton as the rapist and matched the inmate who had admitted to the crimes eight years earlier. The district attorney dismissed the charges against Cotton, the governor of North Carolina pardoned him, and he was released from prison. To compensate him for the ten and a half years he spent in prison for crimes he didn't commit, the State of North Carolina offered him $5,000.*

---

*Most states have sovereign immunity laws that preclude citizens from suing them for wrongful imprisonment. Some states permit very limited awards to wrongfully imprisoned citizens. Only New York and West Virginia allow wrongfully imprisoned citizens who are later exonerated to seek substantial damages.

SORTING THROUGH THE MESS

Within two hours of the time Jeff Hadden stepped off the trail to relieve himself, nearly twenty uniformed officers and half a dozen detectives from three different agencies arrived at Marshtown Park. Interagency rivalries boiled up.

The park was only a mile south of the city limits of Stormont. Officers from Stormont P.D. arrived to offer help. They were more familiar with handling murder scenes than the Calhoun County Sheriff's Department. The sheriff's deputies resented the implication that they couldn't handle the scene. While they argued matters of jurisdiction the first of the uniformed officers from the State Police arrived, along with a team of forensic evidence technicians from the state crime lab.

The Stormont police and the sheriff's deputies disliked the State Police more than they did each other, but they couldn't dispute their right of jurisdiction. The state police immediately blocked off the entrance to Marshtown Park and denied entry to anybody who didn't have a valid reason to be there. Even those who had a legitimate reason to be at the crime scene were forced to park in a field across the road from the park. That included State Police Lt. Carla Witherspoon.

Witherspoon didn't bother looking at the bodies. Bodies weren't her business. There were more important things to do. She set up a command post in the old gazebo in the picnic area and went about creating order out of the crime scene chaos.

Lt. Witherspoon's first command was for everybody but the evidence technicians to stay away from the bodies. She then had the two men who found the first body, Hadden and Wingate, separated and placed in different police vehicles. She had one officer note the licence numbers of all the police vehicles in the park parking lot. Another was ordered to gather the names of the various officers on the scene and their time of arrival. A third, stationed at the entrance to the park, began a log of everybody to enter and leave the scene.

Among the first to sign the log were State Police Detectives James Dietz and Glenda Woodward. Dietz would be the primary investigator; Woodward, the secondary.

Dietz frowned at the park. He hated outdoor crime scenes. There wasn't enough control. And he hated bodies found in parks more than anything else. A body found in a park often meant the victim had been killed else-where and dumped in the park. That meant the best crime scene evidence was probably somewhere else. And what about fingerprints? There were no walls, no light switches, no flat surfaces in a park—nothing to print. You get a dead body in a house, you have a place to start—the connection between the body and the house. If the body belongs there, you can look at who else belongs in the house. If the body doesn't belong there, you can look at how it got there. But a body in a park lacks that personal ground-ing. A body in a park was a pain in the ass. Two bodies in the same park was twice the pain.

Dietz found Lt. Witherspoon in the gazebo. "What have we got?" he asked her.

"We have one body recently dead and decomposing and one partial skeleton," she said, then filled him in on what she'd done. "I'm not sure if we have two crime scenes or just one large one. Or no crime scene at all. I decided to set it up like one large one, just in case."

"Good work," Dietz said. "I'll go take a look at the bodies. Glenda, you talk to the guys who found the skeleton. Especially this Hadden guy."

"Why especially him?" Woodward asked.

"Seems unlikely we're gonna have two accidental death victims in one small area," Dietz said. "So we're probably talking murder here. This

Hadden found the skeleton and stayed behind while his buddy went to make the call. Maybe he put the body there and got tired of waiting for somebody to find it."

Woodward nodded. "We should get the troops to walk the perimeter of this park, in case there are any more bodies out there."

"Good idea," Dietz said. He nodded to Witherspoon. "You set that up. Spread them out . . . say, five feet apart. Give them some evidence flags. Have them walk slow and mark anything that might be evidence."

Lt. Witherspoon began to organize the uniformed officers. Woodward went to put Hadden and Wingate through their story once again. Dietz headed for the nearest cluster of evidence techs huddled around Jane Doe #2, the more recently dead victim.

One was shooting photographs, another was using tweezers to pull insect larvae from the body and put them in small alcohol-filled containers, a third was using a small net to catch the living flies and insects that hovered around the body, another was taking soil samples near the body.

The body was naked, Dietz noted, and sprawled awkwardly on the ground. That suggested the killer had no concern for his victim. Some killers did show concern, oddly enough. Some tried to protect the bodies of their victims, wrapping them in blankets or sleeping bags. Some arranged the clothing of their victims so that it was smooth and presentable, and laid them out neatly on the ground. This one . . . this one had simply been killed and tossed away.

Dietz noticed the tattoo on the dead woman's right shoulder. It looked like some sort of snake-woman, half reptile and half seductress. He reminded the photographer to get a close-up of the tattoo.

The photographer nodded and kept shooting photographs. He didn't need the reminder; he was a professional. But he knew detectives felt the need to point out the obvious. And rightly so. If the case fell apart, it was the detective's responsibility.

"Detective?" A uniformed officer approached Dietz. "The lieutenant says to tell you the press is here."

"Somebody needs to develop a spray for reporters," Dietz said. "They're more irritating than mosquitoes. Tell Lt. Witherspoon to keep them on the other side of the road. Tell her I'll be available to mouth the usual meaningless phrases in half an hour or so."

79

The officer trotted off, only to be replaced by another.

"Detective, we found us a knife." He pointed to a spot less than ten yards away.

"Did you touch it?" Dietz asked.

"No sir."

"Did you mark the location with a flag?"

The officer nodded.

"Did you do anything at all that might disturb the knife?" Dietz asked.

"Nothing," the officer said. "I saw it, I marked it, I told Sgt. Wilton and he told me to come tell you."

For the first time that afternoon Dietz smiled. He pinched the officer's cheek. "You are my special angel," he said, and laughed as the officer blushed.

INTERVIEWS AND INTERROGATIONS

All criminal investigations involve witnesses of some sort. These aren't necessarily people who observed the crime. A witness can be any person who has some information about one or more aspects of the crime. It might be a neighbor with some background knowledge of the people involved, or a laboratory technician who can identify the brand of lipstick found on a murder victim, or an insurance agent who can advise a detective on the contents of an insurance policy. A witness is anybody who is aware of something that *might* be relevant to the case.

In fact, that's the origin of the term "witness." In old English, *wit* referred to knowledge or awareness. Witness, then, is the quality of having *wit*, just as cleverness is the quality of being clever. A witness is a person who has *wit*, a person who has knowledge of something.

Getting witnesses to share their knowledge can be a lot more difficult than collecting and interpreting physical evidence. While collecting physical evidence requires technical skill, it's a skill anybody of intelligence can be trained to do. Collecting a dried bloodstain requires a different technique than collecting wet blood, but once a criminalist learns the different techniques, becoming proficient at them is only a matter of practice.

People, obviously, are more complex than things. People make mistakes, people get confused, people withhold information, people lie. A detective can learn different techniques for getting witnesses to give information, but at the heart of interrogation and interviewing is an intuitive understanding of human nature. And that's something that can't be taught.

Interviewing and interrogation are the two primary methods used by detectives to obtain verbal evidence. They are radically different techniques grounded on different psychological principles and using different skills. Generally speaking, witnesses and potential witnesses are interviewed; people who are suspected of committing a crime or of having guilty knowledge are interrogated. Police detectives use both methods during the course of their investigation. In contrast, defense investigators rely almost exclusively on interviewing.

Interviews

An interview is simply an attempt to gather information from a witness. Anybody having information pertinent to the crime is likely to be interviewed. It's generally an unstructured and informal process. The subject of an interview could be anybody from the victim (this, of course, isn't possible in a murder case), to bystanders who were in the vicinity of the crime, to experts who have specific knowledge that might pertain to the crime.

In an interview an investigator merely asks the subject what he or she knows about the crime. It sounds simple . . . and in most cases it is. The real test of interviewing skill comes when the subject doesn't want to provide the information, can't recall the information, or isn't aware he or she has the information. In such instances interviewing becomes a form of verbal seduction. The success of an interview depends on the ability of the interviewer to get the subject to recall the information and to want to provide the information. It's often a very subtle and manipulative process.

Criminal defense investigators tend to make better interviewers than police officers. This is because police officers are accustomed to relying on their authority to get information. They *expect* people to answer when they ask a question, which means they aren't always as thoughtful and tactful as they could be. Private investigators, on the other hand, have no inherent authority in the community. The good ones learn a variety of techniques to get the witness to *want* to give up the important information.

In criminal cases the most common types of interview subjects are eyewitnesses, indirect witnesses, and expert witnesses.

Eyewitnesses

An eyewitness is exactly what the term implies—a person who was present during the commission of the crime and who observed it with his or her own eyes. Investigators have a love/hate relationship with eyewitnesses. A reliable eyewitness is an invaluable source of information about what took place.

The problem with eyewitnesses, however, is that they are notoriously unreliable. In a 1967 Supreme Court ruling, Justice Brennan wrote: "The vagaries of eyewitness identification are well known; the annals of criminal law are rife with instances of mistaken identification."

Why are eyewitnesses to crimes so unreliable? There are several reasons, the most common being simply that no two people experience an event in the same way. We all know this is true; we experience it in our daily lives. Two people walking down the street will notice and remember very different things. Two people observing a crime in progress will also notice and remember different things. It doesn't mean one of them is necessarily wrong and the other necessarily right; it simply means they experienced and processed the event differently.

In addition, the circumstances in which violent crimes occur are usually stressful. Adrenaline distorts the ability of a witness to reliably observe what is taking place. This is especially true when shots are fired. The noise and confusion makes it extremely difficult for a witness to pay close attention to who is doing what to whom.

Finally, people tend to see and hear what they expect to see and hear. All of a person's life experience, all the likes and dislikes and prejudices, all the person's fears and beliefs will influence the way that person perceives an event. Consider an argument between a black teenager and a white police officer. If the argument were observed by the Reverend Al Sharpton, the New York African-American activist, and Jesse Helms, the conservative legislator from North Carolina, it is unlikely they would agree on what was taking place.

Eyewitnesses are very often absolutely certain of the truth of their version of the event. Research shows that repeating a story increases the teller's confidence in it. Each time a witness tells the story—to the police, to friends and family, to the press, to the defense investigator—the witness becomes that much more certain of it, even if the final story bears only a passing resemblance to the very first telling. Witnesses may unconsciously add, omit, or change small details to make the story "better," that is, to make it more interesting. This isn't done to deceive, merely to improve. It's also a common, though mistaken, belief that a story with great detail is more likely to be accurate. In fact, research shows the amount of detail bears no relationship to the accuracy of a story.

Studies have shown that more than half of the people known to have been wrongfully convicted of crimes were convicted based on the errors of eyewitnesses. Those, of course, are only the cases in which the mistakes came to light. It's safe to assume most eyewitness errors go uncorrected.

Such would have been the case for Charles Dabbs. Dabbs was arrested in 1982 on a charge of rape. The victim had been attacked from behind by a single assailant and forcibly dragged into an alley. There she was pushed

MISTAKEN IDENTITY

In a 1980 trial involving the assault of an elderly man, a defense lawyer pulled an unorthodox trick. During a recess the lawyer asked a man sitting in the hallway if he would sit beside him at the defense table in order to test the credibility of some of the witnesses. The young man, Jeffrey Streeter, agreed. After the break the defendant sat behind the lawyer and Streeter joined him at the table. Three eyewitnesses who testified on the stand confidently identified Streeter as the man who had assaulted the victim. They simply *expected* to see the defendant sitting next to the defense lawyer.

Unfortunately for Streeter, the lawyer had neglected to inform the judge of the stunt. Based on the witness identifications, Streeter was actually convicted of assaulting the elderly man. He was taken into custody and forced to spend a night in jail before the matter could be straightened out.

down some stairs, after which she lost consciousness. When she awoke, the victim observed two other men who had joined her original assailant. One of the newcomers held her legs and the other held her arms while the original assailant raped her.

The victim was able to identify only one of the assailants—the original one, the man who raped her. She could identify him because she knew him. He was, she said, Charles Dabbs, a distant cousin. Dabbs was convicted of first-degree rape in 1984 in part based on the solid eyewitness identification and in part on physical evidence—forensic analysis of a semen stain found on the victim's underwear indicated that the rapist was of the same blood type as Dabbs. He was sentenced to serve twelve and a half to twenty years in prison.

Seven years later, however, a sample of Dabbs's DNA was compared to the DNA of the semen stain taken from the victim's underwear. Although the blood groups were the same, the DNA from the semen stain didn't match the DNA of Dabbs. Dabbs's conviction was vacated. His own cousin had mistakenly identified him as her rapist.

Indirect Witnesses

An indirect witness is one who has indirect knowledge of some aspect of the crime. Most indirect witnesses will have observed events preceding or following the crime itself. For example, a witness might have seen the accused and the victim arguing about a woman an hour before a murder took place. Similarly, a sales clerk at a sporting goods store might be able to say he'd sold the accused a weapon of the type used in the crime. These witnesses have no direct knowledge of the murder, but do have circumstantial information that may have some bearing on the matter.

Other indirect witnesses may have some specialized skill or knowledge that is pertinent to the crime. If, for example, a dead body is found inside the burned shell of a car, an engineer for the manufacturer might be able to tell an investigator the temperature at which the plastic of the dashboard would melt. Such information could be important if the temperature needed to melt a dashboard was higher than would be expected from a fire of natural origin.

Expert Witnesses

Expert witnesses are those with significant expertise in a given field. They are consulted by investigators or brought into court to explain or amplify evidence that is beyond the scope of laymen. Such experts in murder cases might include forensic entomologists, psychiatrists, firearms experts, DNA analysts, forensic dentists, fiber analysts, and accountants, to name only a few.

The fact is, nobody knows everything. Consider a body found in a trunk of a car. Snagged in the sweater worn by the corpse is a small twig and leaf. Obviously, the twig and leaf are evidence; they may reveal something about where the crime took place. The trick is in identifying the twig and leaf. For that, an expert must be consulted.

Expert witnesses can be critical in a criminal trial. Dr. Henry Lee, the forensic specialist hired by the O. J. Simpson defense team, was a pivotal person for the defense. After the verdict, several jurors cited Dr. Lee as the most credible witness of the trial. His testimony that there was "something wrong" in the way the police handled the blood evidence collected at the crime scene was enough to create reasonable doubt as to Simpson's guilt in the minds of some jurors.

Interrogation

As stated earlier, interrogation is generally used on persons suspected of a crime or who have guilty knowledge of a crime.* It's a much more intense and focused technique than interviewing.

Interrogation relies on the power and authority behind the interrogator to compel the subject to cooperate. The police have a tremendous amount of civil power, ranging from the power to detain and arrest to the power to use deadly force. It's the subject's respect or fear of that power that underlies interrogation. The subject of interrogation is made to understand that he or she is, to some extent, under the control of the interrogator.

---

*Guilty knowledge refers to information pertaining to the commission of the crime: who committed it, how it was done, why it happened, or where it took place.

First and foremost, interrogation is about control. Control of the setting of the interrogation, control of information, control of access to the interrogation subject by other people, and control of the subject himself.

Control of the Setting

Interrogation rooms in police departments throughout the United States. tend to resemble each other. They are purposefully utilitarian; stark, bleak, bare, harshly lit rooms with purely functional furniture—a table and a few uncomfortable chairs. More and more interrogation rooms also include a two-way mirror, a tape recorder, or a video camera system. The ambience of most interrogation rooms is deliberately austere and unfriendly.

Controlling the setting allows the detective to set the mood, and many detectives feel the proper mood for an interrogation is isolation and helplessness. There is little in the room to link the subject with the outside world. The lighting and temperature are beyond the subject's control. There is nothing for the subject to look at; no photographs, no paintings, preferably no windows—nothing to distract the subject from the fact that he is alone in a hostile environment.

In recent years we have seen the beginning of a trend toward interrogation rooms that appear more businesslike and professional, and less spartan and intimidating. Although the subject is still isolated it's thought that a more office-like interrogation room will disconcert the suspect and break down interrogation defensiveness. It's like being brought to the principal's office.

Control of Information

In addition to isolating the subject physically, police detectives also control his access to information. This includes information about activity outside the interrogation room, the presence of others in the police station (other witnesses, other suspects, friends or family of the subject), and most importantly, the nature of the evidence in the case. Information is power; by controlling the information available to the subject the police reinforce his sense of powerlessness.

There are, of course, legal considerations involved. The police are

87

required to inform an interrogation subject if his attorney arrives and wishes to see him. For the most part, however, an interrogation subject receives only such information that the police think might induce him to talk.

The control of information extends to the control of *mis*information. The police are granted a great deal of latitude in regard to the truth when interrogating a subject. The police can, and frequently do, tell lies to get the subject to confess (or reveal the guilty knowledge they are suspected of having). A detective might inform the suspect that the crime took place in an area monitored by a video surveillance camera and suggest that if the suspect wants to cut the best deal he can he'll have to do it before the surveillance tape is processed.

The danger of lying to an interrogation subject isn't that the courts might disallow a confession obtained through deception; the danger is that the suspect might discover the lie. For example, a detective might tell a suspect that his fingerprint was found at the crime scene—but the suspect knows he wore plastic gloves when committing the crime. The detective's credibility, and therefore his power and the likelihood of obtaining a confession, is greatly diminished when caught in an obvious lie.

Control of Access to Other People

An isolated subject is a vulnerable subject. The more alone and forlorn the interrogation subject feels, the more likely he is to talk. One of the biggest impediments to a successful interrogation is other people—especially a lawyer.

The reasons for this are obvious. First, an interrogation subject gains emotional strength from knowing that friends or family are there to support him. Second, the subject may be unlikely to admit certain embarrassing acts in front of friends and family members. A child molester might be induced to confess to a police detective he doesn't know, but would be unlikely to admit it to his mother.

The most important reason for isolating a subject, however, is that an outsider is likely to advise the subject not to talk. Again, this is especially true of a lawyer. Lawyers know it's almost never in a suspect's best interest to talk to the police. At least not until some favorable arrangement has been made.

Detectives are under certain constitutional constraints when they interrogate a suspect. The law states, "A suspect may not be subjected to custodial interrogation unless he or she knowingly and intelligently has waived the right to remain silent, to the presence of an attorney, and to appointed counsel in the event the suspect is indigent." The police are obligated to stop questioning a suspect if he asks them to stop and requests a lawyer.

Good detectives, however, quickly learn techniques to prevent a suspect from asking for a lawyer. The most common technique is for detectives to claim that once a defense lawyer is involved the process becomes more official and the police won't be able to "help" the suspect. Detectives are so adept at these techniques that, according to research, nearly 85 percent of people suspected of a crime waive their right to counsel and answer the questions of the police.

Controlling access to other persons doesn't always mean isolation. On occasion the police will allow the suspect to see a family member or a minister. In such cases the family member or minister has previously indicated he or she will counsel the suspect to "do the right thing" and confess. It's also not uncommon to allow a suspect to obtain a quick glimpse of accomplices and witnesses to the crime without letting them exchange any words. This is done to suggest that others are cooperating with the police and that it would be wise for the subject of the interrogation to tell his version of the criminal events.

Control of the Subject

The subject himself is physically controlled during an interrogation. The detective controls the subject's body and his ability to meet his bodily needs.

The subject's movement is restricted. He may be physically restrained by handcuffs during the interrogation. He isn't allowed to leave the interrogation room without permission. The subject sits while the detectives stand and move around the interrogation room and tower menacingly over the subject.

The subject's speech is controlled. The interrogators might shout, whisper, bellow, and curse, but the subject is usually required to speak in a normal tone of voice. The interrogators may mock and insult the subject, but the subject is expected to remain respectful.

The subject's bodily needs and demands are controlled. Anything the subject wants—a cup of coffee, a cigarette, an aspirin, a sandwich—must come from the interrogator. Any of the subject's physical needs—to eat, sleep, or go to the bathroom—are granted or denied by the interrogator. The subject is dependent on the interrogator and under his control, a fact that is impressed on the subject both overtly and subtly.

Once control over the subject is established, it can be relaxed or strengthened at the discretion of the detective. Small considerations normally taken for granted, such as going to the toilet or smoking a cigarette, are presented to the subject as gifts and acts of kindness for which the subject should be, and often is, grateful. How can he express his gratitude? By telling the interrogator what he wants to hear.

Despite what we see in the entertainment media, the use of violence during an interrogation is extremely rare. Intimidation isn't uncommon, but modern detectives generally find violence both unnecessary and ineffective. Not only can the use of violence lead to a confession being excluded by the courts, it can also spark both civil and criminal proceedings against the interrogator. The day of the third degree is long gone.

The key to a successful interrogation is in convincing the suspect that it's in his best interest to confess—that by confessing he will feel better, that he will be doing the proper "manly" thing, that he will benefit from giving his version of the crime. In reality, of course, this is almost never true.

False and Coerced Confessions

The nature of interrogation is such that false and coerced confessions are inevitable.* It's an intimidating process, and some suspects will give a confession simply in order to end the interrogation. To be considered legal, a confession must be given voluntarily. This means the suspect:

> • Must be aware of whether he is in custody or is free to leave. It isn't uncommon for suspects to agree to admit almost anything under the mistaken belief they will be free to leave after confessing.

---

*It's also true that confessed criminals will often claim confessions were false or coerced, even when they were given voluntarily. Criminals are not known for their honesty.

90

THE THIRD DEGREE

During the Inquisition—tribunals of the Catholic Church devoted to discovering, suppressing, and punishing heresy and witchcraft—unspeakable forms of torture were used to obtain confessions. Confession was seen as good for the soul of the person confessing. Any device or technique that might produce a confession was considered justified for the good of the subject.

Notions of Christian benevolence evolved, however, and efforts were gradually introduced to reform the brutal techniques used by Inquisitors. In the eighteenth century the Empress Marie Therese of Austria instituted reforms that came to be known as the Three Degrees of the Question.

The First Degree of the Question allowed only the use of the thumbscrew—a device which basically crushed the subject's thumbs. If the subject refused to confess, the Inquisitor moved on to the Second Degree. This involved stripping the subject to the waist, securing his or her arms so that they were raised above the head, then using a flame on the tender areas of the torso, from the waist to the armpits. If the subject continued to resist confession, the Third Degree of the Question was implemented. This involved the strappado, a technique in which the subject's arms were tied behind the back and then attached to a winch on the ceiling. The subject was then hoisted off the ground by his or her arms.

A suspected witch or heretic who managed to endure the Three Degrees of the Question without confessing was judged to be innocent and was required to be released. While these practices seem horrifically brutal to us, it must be remembered they were considered a reform effort at the time. Like all reform efforts, they were criticized and resisted as coddling the offenders and unfairly tying the hands of the Inquisitors.

- Must have been given the Miranda warnings prior to the interrogation, *understood* these warnings, and voluntarily waived his rights. It's not enough merely to read a suspect his rights; the suspect has to actually understand them.
- Must not have been subjected to an overt or implied threat or a promise in exchange for the confession. This is the "Godfather Clause"—making the suspect an offer he can't refuse. Clearly, an agreement made under such conditions can't be considered voluntary.
- Must not have been subjected to extreme methods and/or styles of interrogation or been interrogated for an excessive length of time.

That's the theory. Reality, of course, is less clear. When these constitutional constraints are tested in court, the law generally supports the interrogators if it appears they were acting in good faith. The fact remains that some suspects give confessions to crimes they did not commit.

Young people are especially susceptible to giving false confessions. A 1998 Chicago murder case received international news attention after the two suspects confessed to the crime. The suspects were two boys, aged seven and eight—the youngest murder suspects in U.S. history. The two boys had confessed, after six hours of questioning, to killing an eleven-year-old girl for her new bicycle. They admitted stuffing her underwear in her mouth and playing sexually with her dead body. However, the two boys had done no such thing. In fact, the crime had been committed by a thirty-year-old man with a history of child molesting. The boys had confessed under police pressure. Unfortunately, it took two months before their innocence could be established.

Michael Pardue was less lucky. In the summer of 1973, Mobile, Alabama, police arrested sixteen-year-old Michael Pardue for a series of three shotgun murders. There was no physical evidence linking him with the crimes, but Pardue was interrogated for a period of nearly eighty hours. By the end of the interrogation he tape-recorded a confession, admitting he had committed the murders. In 1997, after Pardue had served twenty-four years in prison, the Alabama courts ruled his confession had been coerced. His murder convictions were overturned.*

Adults also succumb to pressure and coercion and give false confessions (or at least self-incriminatory confessions in violation of their civil rights). In October of 1987, Ronald Jones confessed to the rape and murder of Debra Smith. He later recanted his confession, claiming he'd been beaten and coerced into giving it. Nevertheless, Jones was convicted and sentenced to die for the crime. After serving several years on death row Jones was released from prison when DNA testing revealed he was not the perpetrator of the crime.

---

*Although his murder conviction was overturned, Pardue wasn't released from prison. During the twenty-four years he was incarcerated, Pardue escaped and was recaptured three times. Escape from prison is a felony, even if the escapee was wrongfully convicted. Under Alabama's habitual offender law Pardue received a life sentence without parole.

TWO BODIES, NO NAMES, NO SUSPECTS

Dietz was unhappy. He had two dead bodies (or, more accurately, one dead body and one partial skeleton), but he had no names for them and no good suspects.

Jeff Hadden had looked promising for a while, and Dietz still considered him a suspect. He'd "discovered" the skeleton, after all. And stayed behind to "guard" it when his buddy Tony Wingate had gone to notify the police. But Jane Doe #2 had been dead for only a week to ten days—and it appeared Hadden had been in Minnesota on a fishing trip at the time she died. At least that's what Hadden claimed. There was no denying somebody had used his credit card to buy gasoline as well as some supplies from a bait-and-tackle shop in Ely, Minnesota. Dietz had faxed a photograph of Hadden to the Minnesota State Police for them to show around, but it seemed a long shot.

The physical evidence at the scene wasn't very helpful. They'd collected a lot of stuff—some cigarette butts, a few candy wrappers and empty potato chip bags, an old baseball cap, a couple of beer bottles—but that would only be useful if they had a suspect to match it to. Even then most of it would turn out to be trash.

The knife had turned out to be a cheap hunting knife with a loose guard and a cracked handle. There was no blood on it, human or otherwise. It had probably belonged to some kid who tossed it away in disgust.

Besides, Jane Doe #2 hadn't been stabbed. According to the medical examiner she'd been manually strangled. Death by intentional compression injury. The human neck, Dietz considered, is almost designed for strangling . . . small diameter; no bony protection; the close proximity of the airway, spinal cord, and major blood vessels. It's even easier to strangle somebody if they're incapable of resisting; the M.E. found traces of the drug Rohypnol in Jane Doe #2's system. And he'd found semen in her vagina. Samples had been taken for DNA comparison—if they ever found a suspect.

The way Jane Doe #2 died was no mystery. Drugged, raped, and strangled. Jane Doe #1, however, was a different story. The medical examiner had no idea how she'd died. Even though about 70 percent of the skeleton had eventually been recovered there was virtually no soft tissue left to determine if she'd been drugged, raped, and strangled like Jane Doe #2. Nor was there any sign of physical trauma to the skeleton; no nicks or breaks that could be attributed to stabbing, gunshot, or blunt force trauma.

In fact, the medical examiner wouldn't even guarantee Jane Doe #1 was a woman. Most of the pelvic bones had been found, but even so, the M.E. would say he was only about 90 percent certain of the gender. Enough long bones had been recovered to estimate she was between five-foot-seven and five-ten. They could only estimate her weight based on the average weight for a woman of that height, which meant they could guess her weight within fifty, sixty pounds . . . assuming she wasn't exceptionally thin or heavy. No help at all, really. The bones of the right arm were larger than those of the left, indicating she was almost certainly right-handed.

They were waiting for a forensic anthropologist to determine approximately how long Jane Doe #1 had been in the woods of Marshtown Park. The medical examiner's office had started a pool. The estimates ranged from six to thirty months. Dietz had kicked in a buck and guessed eight months.

At least, Dietz thought, they knew more about Jane Doe #2. She'd been around five-foot-nine and 145 pounds. Mid-twenties. Blonde hair. They weren't sure about her eyes; soft tissues like eyes are among the first things insects and small animals go for. She wore an inexpensive brand of make-up and nail polish, but had obviously cared about her appearance. There were some fibers in her hair—from upholstery, probably, and some from a blanket. She'd had her appendix removed and had a very slight scar just above her pubic hair, which she'd kept closely trimmed. And then there was the tattoo on her right shoulder.

That was their best lead for an identification. Dietz and some uniformed officers had been visiting the tattoo shops in Stormont, showing a photo of the tattoo around. It was an unusual tattoo and maybe some tattoo artist would recognize it as their work. Assuming, of course, Jane Doe #2 had been tattooed in Stormont. Or Calhoun County. Or even in that state.

Glenda Woodward had been searching missing person reports—both for a recent report and for reports as far back as thirty months. Maybe there would be a description that matched. Or maybe they'd get a match based on dental records. Fortunately, both Jane Does had had dental work done. Maybe, maybe, maybe.

Both Dietz and Woodward had canvassed the homes near Marshtown Park, asking if anybody had ever seen anything that might be considered even remotely suspicious. No luck. The park wasn't used much except on weekends and in the summer. There was a nicer park with a pond just a few miles west, it seemed, and Marshtown Park was neglected.

Two bodies, no names, no suspects.

It stayed that way for two days. Then Woodward got a call from Missing Persons. The parents of one Carla Ann Willis had called to report their twenty-four-year-old daughter had been missing for a couple of weeks. Blonde, five-nine and a half, around one-fifty. With a tattoo of a snake-woman on her right shoulder.

"When was the last time you saw your daughter?" Dietz asked.

"Two, maybe three weeks ago," Mrs. Willis said. "But we usually talk on the phone every Sunday. I didn't worry too much that first day. But when Carla didn't call again the next Sunday I began to get scared."

The Willis home reminded Dietz of his grandmother's house—small, cluttered, too dark, odd smells coming from the kitchen. Mr. and Mrs. Willis even looked a little like his grandparents. They seemed too old to have a twenty-four-year-old daughter.

"I made Dan drive me to her apartment," Mrs. Willis said. "Course, he was worried too."

Mr. Willis nodded. "I was," he said.

"We knocked and knocked, but nobody answered," Mrs. Willis continued. "So we went to the apartment manager, and he let us in. We could tell right away she hadn't been there for a while. The garbage smelled and the food in the fridge had gone bad. And her fish, her fish were all dead and floating in the aquarium. Carla was always careful of them fish."

"Fed 'em every day," Mr. Willis agreed.

"So we called the police."

And now we're here, Dietz thought. And I'd rather be almost anyplace else. "You told the officer you spoke to on the telephone that just before your daughter disappeared she'd said she was having some pictures taken, is that right?"

"It sounded like one of her scatterbrained ideas," Mrs. Willis said. "She was always talking about something . . . becoming a decorator, acting lessons, studying design. I'm just a simple old woman. In my day we got married and raised a family. We didn't study design. I don't even know what design is."

Dietz let her talk for a while. She needed to get some of the anxiety and anger out of her system.

"Back to these pictures," he said after a few moments. "She'd met some-body who was going to take her picture?"

"A photographer," Mrs. Willis said. "She said she met him at some bar and he liked her bones. Liked her bones . . . what sort of talk is that? What does that even mean? Anyway, he offered to take some pictures of her. She thought she was going to get her picture in a magazine."

"Did your daughter tell you the name of this photographer?"

Mrs. Willis shook her head.

"Do you know the name of the bar where she met him?"

She looked at her husband, who shook his head. "No," she said. She looked at Dietz. "It's been two weeks now," she said. "You don't think . . . do you think there's a chance she's. . . ."

It was time to get it over with, Dietz thought. "Mrs. Willis, you said your daughter had a tattoo. Could you describe it for us?"

"Oh, it was a horrible thing," Mrs. Willis said. "She got it a couple years ago when she went to visit our son. He was stationed in San Diego. I hated it."

"Could you describe it?" Dietz asked again, patiently.

"It was a snake-woman," Mr. Willis said. "Part snake and part woman."

"I'm going to show you a photograph," Dietz said. "Tell me if this looks like your daughter's tattoo." He slid the photo out of a manila envelope and put it on the table in front of the Willises.

"Oh God," Mrs. Willis said. "Oh dear God."

Dietz put the photo back in the envelope. Two bodies, one name, no suspects.

....

The grim and doleful business of identifying the body of their daughter left the Willises too stunned to be very helpful—which was why Dietz had asked as many questions as he could beforehand. Even so, Mrs. Willis collected herself enough to provide Dietz with a photo of Carla and the names of some of her friends.

Dietz spent the rest of that day and evening interviewing Carla's friends. Most of her friends were unable to provide any information about the photographer—indeed, few of them believed the story. They thought it sounded like something Carla might have concocted to tell her mother. Carla, they said, wasn't really pretty enough to model for anybody.

The sole exception was April McDowell, who told Dietz that Carla had said she'd met a photographer named Collins. This Collins was going to take some racy pictures of her and send them to some magazine, McDowell said.

"No nudies," she said. "Just short shorts and tight halters. That sort of thing. I don't think Carla would have done nudies. I don't think."

McDowell and the others also provided Dietz with the names of the bars Carla frequented.

While Dietz was interviewing Carla's friends, Det. Glenda Woodward was going through Carla's apartment, looking for any clue or hint that might indicate how she wound up dead in Marshtown Park. Carla, however, kept no journal or diary. She had no appointment book or calendar. Nor did she keep an address book with telephone numbers. Beside the telephone, though, Woodward found several scraps of paper with telephone numbers scribbled down. Some had names, most didn't. She tipped them all into an evidence bag to sort through later.

The following day Woodward gave the telephone numbers collected from beside Carla Willis's phone to another detective and asked him to find out who the numbers belonged to. She then began a long and eventually fruitless search for a photographer named Collins, focusing on camera and photo supply stores that catered to professional photographers and serious amateurs. Woodward also contacted local photography clubs, professional photographers' associations, and modeling agencies—all to no avail.

In the meantime Dietz began to canvass the bars Carla frequented, showing the photograph given to him by her mother. Several of the bartenders and wait staff recognized her. A pleasant person, they said, who rarely got rowdy or drunk. Not really a party girl, but not a wallflower either. None of them knew of a photographer named Collins.

Jimmy Kaminsky, the bartender at T-Bone's Saloon, recognized Carla's photo as well. When questioned, Kaminsky told Dietz he didn't know any photographer named Collins . . . but there was a guy named Colin who drank there occasionally. Colin said he was a photographer, but Kaminsky just assumed it was a line he used on women.

"You know his last name?" Dietz asked.

Kaminsky shook his head. "He in some kind of trouble?" Kaminsky asked.

"We just need to ask him a few questions," Dietz said. "He may have some information that could help us. You ever see this Colin and Carla Willis together?"

"I might have. I'm not sure. It seems like I saw them together, but that might just be because now I've got them associated in my mind."

Kaminsky agreed to call Dietz the next time Colin was in the bar.

The case began to break the following morning. As so often happens, the breaks came from unexpected directions. Mrs. Willis called Dietz to see if her daughter's car had been found. Dietz hadn't been aware that Carla had a car, but said he'd check on it. A few quick telephone calls revealed the car had been towed from the parking lot of Tom's Diner. Dietz sent an evidence tech to the impound lot to go over the car.

The other break came as Dietz and Woodward sat at her desk going over their plans for the day. As they talked, Woodward sorted through the contents of her in-box. There she found a brief report from the detective to whom she'd given the telephone numbers. He'd managed to attach names and addresses to most of the numbers.

Among the names was Colin Brooks. Brooks's address was listed as 4220 Becker Street—only a few blocks from Tom's Diner, where Carla Willis's car had been abandoned.

Dietz grinned. Two bodies, one name, one suspect. Things were looking up. It was a grand way to start the day.

100

THE ARREST

After the authority to use deadly force, the most formidable weapon in the arsenal of police officers is the discretionary power to stop, detain, and arrest. We take the police power to arrest for granted, but consider it for a moment. Think upon the fact that if a police officer decides to arrest you as you walk down the street to mail a package, there is nothing you can do to prevent it. It doesn't matter who you are, who you know, where you work, how much money you make, where you went to school. It doesn't even matter that you did nothing wrong and can prove it if given a moment. There is no immediate appeal to a higher authority; it does no good to ask to speak to the officer's supervisor. If you resist the arrest, you are committing a crime—for which you may be legally arrested. You may be released later if you can show you did nothing wrong, but at the moment the officer decides to arrest you, your legal options are severely limited.

I have painted a bleak and frightening picture. Fortunately, the police generally do not abuse their authority to arrest. It's not an absolute and unrestricted authority. The law—at least in the United States—places a high value on individual freedom and liberty, and before the police can deprive a person of those treasured rights, the courts have provided some

Police Stop and Detention

According to the law a police officer is allowed to stop, briefly detain, and question a person if the officer has specific facts that suggest the person may be (or may have been, or may become) engaged in criminal conduct. There are two critical points. First, the officer must have *specific facts* before a stop can be legally made. A hunch is not good enough. Nor is an educated guess. The officer must be able to clearly articulate specific reasons for the stop. If the officer can't identify those facts, the stop is illegal and any evidence that might be discovered during the stop may be inadmissible in court. At least that's the theory. In reality the courts allow police officers very wide leeway when it comes to reasons for a stop.

Once the individual has been stopped, the officer can inquire about the individual's name and address. The officer can also require an explanation of the individual's actions. In addition, the officer can detain the individual long enough for a witness to a crime to come to the scene and view him. In some jurisdictions the police are also authorized to transport a stopped subject a short distance to be identified by witnesses.

The second important point is that the detention must be *brief.* It should be no longer than is reasonably necessary to achieve the purpose of the stop. The term "brief" is deliberately vague, of course. The courts are understandably reluctant to place an absolute time limit on a police stop. Nonetheless, at some undefined moment the police stop crosses a line and becomes an arrest. The rules regarding arrest, as will soon be discussed, are more stringent than those covering a stop.

If the stop involves a motor vehicle (a traffic stop), the officer has the authority to order the individual(s) out of the vehicle. The courts have upheld this practice as a reasonable precaution for the officer's safety.

If during the course of the stop the officer can find no probable cause for an arrest (a concept discussed later), then the officer must let the individual go.

Stop and Frisk

An officer has the authority to frisk an individual if the officer reasonably suspects the individual is a threat to the officer, to another individual, or to the general public safety. A stop and frisk can be done even if there isn't sufficient cause to arrest the individual.

The power to stop and frisk suspicious individuals has been used extensively and effectively as a weapon against street crime. However, critics of the practice point out that residents of inner city minority neighborhoods are subjected to stop and frisk at a much higher rate than other citizens. The odds are the majority of the people who read this book will never have been subjected to a stop and frisk—unless you are an African American or Latino living in the inner city.

Arrest

An arrest is more formal and more serious than a stop and, accordingly, is covered by more restrictive rules. An arrest can be made either after a warrant has been issued by a judge or, under certain conditions, without a warrant. In either case, in order to make a legal arrest the police are required to have some reliable evidentiary basis that the person arrested has engaged in a criminal act. The standard for that basis is known as probable cause.

Probable Cause

Probable cause has been defined by the Supreme Court as "a reasonable ground for belief, less than evidence justifying a conviction, but more than bare suspicion. Probable cause concerns circumstances in which a person of reasonable caution would believe an offense has been or is being committed." As stated earlier, a hunch—even an educated guess—is not enough for a police officer to effect an arrest. There must be some substantive evidence suggesting the suspect committed the crime.

Probable cause can come from a number of sources. We've discussed a few of them in earlier chapters—witnesses, evidence found at the crime scene, evidence revealed through forensic examination. There are a variety of other means of establishing probable cause.

Personal Observation

A police officer can make an arrest without a warrant if he or she has a reasonable belief a crime has been committed in the officer's presence. In other words, an officer can make an arrest if the officer sees an act take place and believes that act violates a law. An officer who observes an individual snatching a woman's purse and running away, obviously, can arrest that individual.

Circumstantial Evidence

An officer can make an arrest without a warrant based on reasonable inferences that a crime has been committed. For example, an officer on patrol who hears a burglar alarm at 3 A.M. and observes a shattered window in a musical instrument store can stop an individual seen hurrying from the area carrying a guitar case. If that individual tries to flee or can't provide a good explanation for his presence and conduct, the officer can arrest him. The officer may not have observed the commission of a crime but can reasonably infer from the circumstance that the individual probably was involved in a burglary.

Reliable Information from Other Persons

Police officers get information from a number of sources, including fellow officers, snitches, anonymous tips, witnesses, and radio reports. If the officer deems the information reliable he can stop an individual for questioning. If the person's answers aren't satisfactory, the officer can effect an arrest. For example, a witness might give an officer a description of a man who robbed a convenience store. That description would be broadcast over police radio. Another officer, seeing an individual who matches that description, can stop the person and, depending on the person's behavior, arrest him.

Official Reports

At the beginning of every shift, police officers are provided with information on various criminal events of which they should be aware. This includes such information as the names and descriptions of suspects wanted for questioning, vehicles thought to be stolen, and complaints of increases in certain crimes in certain neighborhoods. For example, the afternoon watch is informed of a man who has been exposing himself to young mothers in various parks around their precinct. An officer who observes an individual known to be a paroled sex offender idly wandering around a park in an overcoat would probably be justified in arresting that person on suspicion of indecent exposure.

An arrest can also be made by any officer if a warrant for an individual has been issued by a judge or magistrate.

Arrest Warrant

It isn't uncommon for police officers to arrive at a domestic murder scene and find the murderer waiting there to be arrested. Obviously, in such cases no warrant is necessary. However, in many murder cases the police will be unable or unwilling to arrest the suspect until they have gathered a great deal of evidence. Once enough evidence has been gathered, an arrest warrant may be applied for.

A warrant is a document issued by a judge or magistrate authorizing the police to exercise extremely intrusive powers, specifically the power to arrest or search someone's property. In order to obtain a warrant, an officer must present evidence to the judge or magistrate, either verbally or in a sworn affidavit, that there is probable cause to believe a crime has taken place and that the person named in the affidavit is criminally responsible for that crime. If the judge or magistrate finds the officer's arguments compelling, the warrant will be issued.

An arrest warrant must clearly identify the person to be arrested and the crime with which he or she is to be charged. The warrant directs all law enforcement officers of the state to arrest the person named. This might seem an unnecessarily complicated process, but it serves to protect the rights of all citizens under the Fifth Amendment, the right not to be "deprived of life, liberty or property, without due process of law."

Search Warrant

As just stated, the Fifth Amendment protects an individual's property as well as his liberty. In addition, the Fourth Amendment protects us from unwarranted search and seizure. The process of obtaining a search warrant is very similar to that of obtaining an arrest warrant. An officer must present a sworn affirmation to a judge or magistrate that there is probable cause to believe a crime has been committed and that specific evidence of that crime can reasonably be expected in a specified location.

The language of a search warrant and its supporting affidavit must be very precise both in terms of the location to be searched and the material sought in the search. For example, John Doe is suspected by the police of having enticed his young neighbor Jane Roe into his apartment, where they think he sexually assaulted and killed her, after which he disposed of her body in the Dumpster behind the apartment house. The police can't simply kick in John Doe's door and search the apartment. They have to get a search warrant, and that warrant would need to clearly state the nature of the crime, the reasons Doe is thought to be responsible for the crime, the specific address and number of Doe's apartment, as well as items thought to be inside the apartment, such as hair or undergarments belonging to Jane Roe.

This is done not just to protect John Doe, but to protect every citizen from police mistakes. We must recognize the fact that the police are as fallible as the rest of us. They must be very certain of their facts before they are allowed to enter a private dwelling and start looking around.

Search Incident to Arrest

Police officers are granted some leeway in regard to searching when making an arrest of a suspect. In order to ensure the officer's safety, the officer is legally permitted to search both the subject and an area within arm's reach of the subject without obtaining a search warrant. Any evidence of a crime found in such a search, such as illegal weapons or drugs, is generally admissible.

If the arrest takes place inside a dwelling place or building, the officers making the arrest are allowed to make a protective sweep of the rooms (and spaces a person might likely hide, such as closets) without a warrant. This isn't technically considered a "search"; it's merely a quick visual sweep of the area to protect the officers. However, if the officers see evidence of criminal activity in plain view during their protective sweep, that evidence may be used as the basis for a search warrant. For example, the police arrest John Doe in the living room of his apartment. During the protective sweep of the premises they observe child pornography in plain view in the bedroom. The officers are not allowed to immediately seize the pornography as evidence, but they may use their observation as the basis for obtaining another warrant to search Doe's apartment for pornographic material.

REAL LIFE VS. TELEVISION

It's not uncommon in television police dramas for the chief of detectives to order a suspect to be brought down to the station for questioning. The police, of course, have no right or authority to roust a citizen of the United States and deliver them to a police station against their will. Unless that citizen is a material witness to a crime.

A material witness is a person whose testimony is considered crucial. A Nebraska court once described a material witness as "an innocent citizen whose right to the full enjoyment of liberty is threatened solely because of his potential usefulness as a witness for the government...." In other words, a material witness is somebody who happened to be in the wrong place at the wrong time.

The police can take a material witness into custody if an officer has probable cause to believe that a crime has been committed, that the witness has information material to the prosecution of that crime, and that the witness will refuse to cooperate with the officer in the investigation of that crime.

Arrest Based on Legal Proceedings

It's very rare that police officers actually witness a murder and arrest the offender based on direct observation. Most murder arrests take place either after a confession (given at the scene or under interrogation) or after convincing evidence has been presented to a grand jury or a judge who determines the evidence is convincing enough to merit a trial.

Grand Jury

A grand jury is traditionally composed of twenty-three citizens* selected from a standard jury pool (jury selection is discussed in a later chapter). A grand jury is, in effect, two standard juries of twelve citizens minus one juror to prevent a tie vote.

Prosecutors wanting to arrest a suspect present evidence of a criminal act obtained through investigation to the members of the jury. It's the function of the grand jury to determine if there is enough evidence to believe that a crime has been committed, that the accused probably committed it, and that the accused should stand trial for the crime. Grand juries do not consider the actual guilt of the suspect—they merely weigh the evidence to determine whether the matter should go forward.

If the grand jury believes there is enough evidence to warrant a trial, they issue what is known as a true bill of indictment. Once an indictment has been issued, the accused may be formally arrested.

A grand jury is a secret, one-sided proceeding. It isn't open to the public. The accused has no right to be present during the procedure. Nor does the accused have the right to appear, testify, or present evidence in his own behalf to the grand jury. Indeed, the accused may not even be aware he is under investigation, although that is rarely so in murder cases.

While suspects have no right to testify before a grand jury, it isn't uncommon for a suspect to be subpoenaed to testify. In such cases the suspect is considered as a witness. Although the suspect/witness has the constitutional

---

*Some jurisdictions require only sixteen grand jurors.

right to refuse to answer any questions that might incriminate him (a right guaranteed under the Fifth Amendment), he isn't allowed to have a lawyer present in the grand jury room. The suspect/witness may, however, leave the room to consult with a lawyer before answering a question.

Any witness, including one suspected of criminal activity, may be compelled to testify under a grant of immunity. Immunity, in essence, is a pledge made by the prosecutor to partially or fully protect a witness from being prosecuted based on the testimony given. Failure to testify under a grant of immunity can lead to immediate imprisonment for contempt.

The secret and unilateral nature of grand juries makes them easily abused. Some prosecutors—most notoriously, special prosecutors appointed by the federal government to investigate corruption—have used them inappropriately for political purposes or as a means of harassing suspects. Too often grand juries act merely as a "rubber stamp" for prosecutors, issuing indictments based on scant evidence on criminal

GRAND JURY CONTEMPT

Perhaps the most well known modern instance of a witness refusing to cooperate with a grand jury investigation is the case of Susan McDougal. In 1996 McDougal, a former business partner to President Clinton, refused to answer questions put to her by prosecutors investigating the Whitewater scandal. McDougal told the grand jury she didn't believe the prosecutors were unbiased and so refused to answer their questions despite having been granted immunity. She was found to be in civil contempt and forced to spend eighteen months in prison.

On her release, McDougal continued to refuse to answer the questions put to her by the Whitewater investigators. In 1998 special prosecutor Kenneth Starr had the grand jury indict Ms. McDougal on two counts of criminal contempt and one count of obstruction of justice. Unlike the civil contempt charge, under which she could be incarcerated simply for her refusal to cooperate, a criminal contempt charge requires a jury trial. At the trial Ms. McDougal was able to present her reasons for refusing to cooperate with Starr's prosecutors. She was found not guilty and released.

cases that have little chance of being successfully prosecuted. The indictment then provides the prosecutor with a bargaining chip with which he or she can compel the indicted person to testify in another matter or to agree to plead guilty to a lesser crime.

Many states have scrapped the grand jury system in exchange for a preliminary hearing system.

Preliminary Hearing

A preliminary hearing serves the same basic function as a grand jury—it's a legal proceding held to determine whether or not there is enough evidence against an accused criminal to merit taking that person to trial. There are, however, significant differences between a grand jury and a preliminary hearing.

The most obvious difference is that there is no jury in a preliminary hearing; a judge listens to the evidence and makes the determination whether it warrants a trial. Second, unlike a grand jury, a preliminary hearing is a public proceeding; the public can attend and observe. In addition, a preliminary hearing is an adversarial proceeding. The accused offender has the right to be present during the hearing and to be represented by an attorney who can question the prosecution witnesses. Preliminary hearings, it must be obvious, are more fair and impartial proceedings.

If the judge determines there is enough evidence to warrant continued prosecution he or she returns a document known as an *information*. This serves the same purpose as an indictment. It's a formal, written accusation charging an individual with a crime.

Once an accused criminal has been indicted or a preliminary hearing information has been signed, a warrant may be issued for his or her arrest.

Booking and Arraignment

After being arrested, the suspect is passed from the police/investigative arena into the court/legal arena. This change of arena begins with "booking," the process by which a suspect is formally brought into the criminal justice system. This involves fingerprinting the accused offender, taking his photograph, and taking the standard personal information—name, date of birth, address, etc.

The accused must be brought before a judge within forty-eight hours after arrest to be arraigned. The time period is shorter in some states, though the Supreme Court only requires a suspect arrested without a warrant be brought before a judge within forty-eight hours so the judge may determine whether there was probable cause for the arrest.

At this point the status of the accused offender has changed. The accused has been transformed from the "suspect" to the "defendant." He must now defend himself against the charges made by the State.

At the arraignment, the charges against the defendant are read, an attorney is appointed if the defendant isn't already represented, and a plea of "guilty" or "not guilty" is entered. If the defendant pleads not guilty, a court date is set. If the defendant refuses to enter a plea, the judge will enter a plea of not guilty on his behalf. If the defendant pleads guilty, the judge may sentence him on the spot. In major felony cases, however, it isn't uncommon for a judge to refuse to accept a guilty plea at arraignment. Even in misdemeanor cases the judge will carefully question the defendant to be certain he understands the consequences of the plea and to determine if he is making the plea voluntarily.

NOLO CONTENDERE

Under some circumstances a defendant may enter a plea of "nolo contendere," or "no contest." With this plea the defendant isn't admitting guilt, but stating he does not wish to contest the charges made against him. This plea may be the choice of a defendant who insists on his factual innocence but recognizes that the prosecutor and police have amassed enough evidence to convince a jury that he is guilty.

More commonly a nolo plea is used as a strategy to reduce the potential of being found liable in a subsequent civil suit. Unlike a guilty plea, a plea of no contest can't be used as evidence if the defendant is later civilly sued for damages by the victim or the victim's family.

There is no immediate effect of a nolo plea, however. The defendant is sentenced as if he had pled guilty.

Murder Clearance Rates

There is another immediate and practical effect of an arrest. It clears a case. A crime is generally considered cleared (or solved) when at least one person has been arrested, charged with the commission of the offense, and turned over to the court for prosecution. Law enforcement agencies sometimes also clear a crime by atypical means—a case might be cleared if a person known to have committed a crime is killed during apprehension or commits suicide.

Television viewers who have watched the police drama *Homicide: Life on the Streets* are familiar with the ritual of clearing a case. On the show, the name of the victim is written in red while the case is open. It's erased and rewritten in black when the case is closed.

Clearing a case doesn't necessarily stop the investigation—there is often a great deal of investigative work still to do in order to prepare the case for trial. Nonetheless, once an arrest is made, the case is considered cleared for statistical and accounting purposes.

Murder, as has been noted, is generally considered the most serious crime. Homicide detectives are generally considered the best detectives. Murders receive more police and investigative resources than other crimes. Therefore it's not surprising to learn that murder has the highest clearance rate of all serious crimes.

However, the percentage of cleared murders has steadily decreased for at least two decades (see Table 4). In 1976 there were 18,780 murders in the United States. More than three-quarters (79 percent) of them were cleared. Twenty years later, in 1996, there were 19,650 murders; only two-thirds (66 percent) of them were cleared.

Why is this so? Largely because the nature of murder has changed over time. Traditionally most murders involved an argument between intimates, friends, or acquaintances, usually fueled by alcohol or drugs, which simply got out of hand. One of the factors that has long distinguished a murder from a first degree assault is the lethality of the weapon used in an argument. A murder is often nothing more than an argument with somebody who has quick access to a firearm. An offender can kill a person with

TABLE 4

Percent of homicides cleared by arrest

Year	Clearance rate (percent)
1976	79
1977	76
1978	76
1979	73
1980	72
1981	72
1982	74
1983	76
1984	74
1985	72
1986	70
1987	70
1988	70
1989	68
1990	67
1991	67
1992	65
1993	66
1994	64
1995	65
1996	67
1997	66

Source: FBI, Crime in the United States, 1976–97

TABLE 5

Homicides by circumstance*

Year	Felony	Argument	Gang	Other	Unknown
1976	3,327	9,106	129	4,630	1,588
1977	3,189	8,929	180	4,112	2,709
1978	3,262	8,950	194	4,447	2,706
1979	3,623	9,237	264	4,534	3,803
1980	4,070	10,299	221	4,963	3,486
1981	3,882	9,519	280	4,835	4,005
1982	3,721	8,612	238	4,322	4,116
1983	3,478	8,470	260	3,058	4,045
1984	3,382	8,211	223	2,708	4,166
1985	3,389	8,285	288	2,689	4,330
1986	3,992	8,602	357	3,015	4,644
1987	3,935	8,087	395	2,678	5,005
1988	3,932	7,872	428	3,010	5,437
1989	4,593	8,433	678	2,709	5,086
1990	4,867	8,988	905	2,867	5,812
1991	5,283	8,806	1,192	3,027	6,393
1992	5,143	7,950	994	3,110	6,563
1993	4,721	8,309	1,362	3,403	6,735
1994	4,303	7,529	1,340	3,622	6,536
1995	3,810	6,756	1,338	3,450	6,256
1996	3,688	6,621	1,091	2,330	5,919
1997	3,459	6,051	1,026	1,847	5,827

Source: Homicide Trends in the United States, 1976–97, Bureau of Justice Statistics

*Arguments include brawls due to the influence of narcotics or alcohol, disagreements about money or property, and other arguments. Felony types include homicides committed during rape, robbery, burglary, theft, motor vehicle theft, arson, and violations of prostitution and commercial vice laws, other sex offenses, narcotic drug laws, and gambling laws. Gang homicides include gangland killings and juvenile gang killings.

a baseball bat or a frying pan, but it's more difficult—both physically and psychologically. It's simply easier to exert two pounds of pressure on a trigger from across the room than to grapple at close range with your opponent and repeatedly strike him in the head with a blunt object.

Although the number of such murders has slightly declined, this is still the most common type of murder. However, two other types of murders have increased dramatically. Murders in which the circumstances of the crime are unknown have more than doubled since 1976 (see Table 5). Murders committed as a result of gang violence have increased sevenfold.

Many of the murders of unknown circumstance are very likely drug-related murders. In such crimes the victim and the perpetrator probably have little or no relationship, making it more difficult for detectives to find a link between them. In addition, witnesses are less likely to volunteer information, either about the offender or the victim. Similarly, witnesses to gang-related murders are unlikely to come forward. And while detectives may be aware of animosity between gangs, that isn't enough information to make an arrest.

The reduced murder clearance rate, in other words, is related to the rise of impersonal drug and gang violence, and is exacerbated by the increased lethality of the firepower available to street criminals.

TWO BODIES, ONE NAME, ONE SUSPECT

A suspect breathes new life into an investigation. It gives the investigation direction and focus.

Detectives Dietz and Woodward resisted the urge to immediately interview Colin Brooks, or pull him in for interrogation. They wanted more facts, more information about their man before they approached him.

Over the next few days Dietz and Woodward slowly began to build a circumstantial case against Brooks. A criminal record search was negative; Brooks had never been arrested before. He had, however, been married and divorced. Dietz made a note to interview Brooks's ex-wife, but it was a low priority.

Dietz obtained a copy of Brooks's driver's licence photo from the Department of Motor Vehicles and showed it to Jimmy Kaminsky, the bartender at T-Bone's Saloon. Kaminsky identified the photo as the man he knew as Colin, the man he was increasingly certain he'd seen talking with Carla Willis before she disappeared.

He also showed the photos of both Brooks and Willis to the wait staff and checkout girl at Tom's Diner. The waitresses recognized Brooks as a fairly frequent breakfast customer. He usually ate alone, reading the newspaper. One of the waitresses seemed to recall Brooks having breakfast recently with a woman . . . and it might have been the woman in the photograph, but she couldn't be positive.

Another waitress knew Brooks to be a photographer; he'd told her she had nice bones and asked her to consider posing for him. She'd declined.

From the DMV the detectives also learned that Brooks had two vehicles registered in his name—a Toyota Camry and a small recreational vehicle. Detective Woodward contacted an RV salesroom and procured a sales brochure showing an RV identical to the one owned by Brooks. She showed the brochure to the people who lived near Marshtown Park, asking if they'd ever seen a vehicle like this at the park. A few stated they had, in fact, occasionally seen a small camper similar to the one in the brochure, in the parking area of the park. Always during the day, always during the week.

Woodward made the rounds of the better camera and photo supply stores again, asking about Colin Brooks. She learned that Brooks was known as a competent and moderately successful photographer. The store clerks and other photographers, however, tended to laugh at him behind his back. Brooks liked to describe himself as a portrait photographer; in fact, he mostly shot weddings and T&A shots for the cheesier skin magazines. Woodward also learned that Brooks used his small RV as a mobile photo studio.

The next morning Dietz filed an affidavit in which he affirmed he was a detective with the State Police and was vested with the authority to investigate criminal offenses, including that of murder. In the affidavit Dietz stated that during the investigation of the murder of one Carla Ann Willis he had received information (which he listed) indicating there was probable cause to believe that Colin Brooks of 4220 Becker Street was involved. Dietz requested a warrant be issued to authorize him to search Brooks's home, recreational vehicle, and automobile and to seize evidence pertaining to the murder, specifically any camera equipment, unprocessed exposed film, processed negatives, transparencies, and prints, credit card and gasoline purchase receipts, and fiber samples.

Dietz and Woodward met with Judge David Landrigan to discuss the affidavit.

"It's too broad," Judge Landrigan said. "This isn't an affidavit for a search warrant; it's an affidavit for a fishing expedition. Credit card and gasoline purchase receipts?"

"To show he ate at Tom's Diner," Dietz said. "Where Carla's car was found.

And maybe to show he bought gas near Marshtown Park."

The judge shook his head, unconvinced. "And all this camera equipment. You say the man's a professional photographer and you want to seize the tools of his trade. How's he supposed to make a living?"

"How about if we change to only include exposed film inside any cameras?" Woodward asked. "We think there's a chance he might have taken photographs of the victim before or after killing her."

"Have you even talked to this guy?" Judge Landrigan asked. "Have you asked him about the victim?"

Dietz shook his head. "We didn't want to alert him that he was under investigation. That would give him the chance to destroy any evidence."

"Then you don't even know if he has a simple explanation for all this," the judge said. "The fact that he seems to have wanted to photograph her and may have had breakfast with her on the morning she disappeared doesn't mean he killed her."

"It's probable cause," Dietz said. "It shows he was probably involved."

Judge Landrigan raised an eyebrow. "Detective, I'm the one who decides whether or not it's probable cause. And I've decided you just don't have enough yet for a search warrant. Get me a more solid link between Brooks and the victim, and I'll get you your search warrant. But right now you just don't have enough."

....

"Now what?" Woodward asked, after they left the courthouse.

"Now we go talk to the sonofabitch," Dietz said. "We talk to him at his home. We start off easy. 'Just a few questions, Mr. Brooks, about Carla Willis.' We let him talk for a bit, then we haul him downtown and toss him into the box. And go after him. Maybe we'll get something that'll convince Landrigan to give us a warrant."

"You sure this is wise?" Woodward asked.

Dietz shrugged. "What else are we gonna do?"

"Then let's go talk to the sonofabitch," Woodward said.

....

Colin Brooks was in his home office when the doorbell rang. He was on the telephone talking to the new bride whose wedding he'd pho-

117

tographed the weekend before. He'd dropped off the proofs of the photos to let her pick the ones she wanted enlarged for the wedding book. She liked the photographs, she said, but some of the candid shots showed her mother with a cigarette in her hand. She wanted to know if there was some way to alter the pictures so the cigarette wouldn't show.

"I can take care of that," Brooks told her. "But it'll cost a bit more. I'll have to use an airbrush and some special darkroom techniques." Brooks figured he made an extra couple of thousand dollars a year by making sure some of the candid shots included somebody in the wedding party smoking.

The doorbell rang again. "Got to go," he said. "Another customer is here."

He opened the door to find Detectives Dietz and Woodward. They both gave him a friendly smile and showed him their badges.

"Colin Brooks?" Dietz asked.

"Yes?"

"I'm Detective Dietz, this is Detective Woodward . . . we're sorry to bother you but we need to ask you a few questions."

"What about?" Brooks asked.

"Mind if we come in?" Dietz asked. He loved asking that question. Nobody wants to let a cop into their house, he knew that. But nobody wants to refuse to let a cop into their house—he knew that as well. Very few people refused.

Brooks let them in. The two detectives sat in the living room and made themselves comfortable.

"What's this about?" Brooks asked.

"Carla Willis," Dietz said.

Brooks frowned. "Carla Willis?"

Dietz nodded.

"What about her?"

"You know her then," Dietz said.

"I know somebody named Carla," Brooks said. "Her last name might be Willis."

"Blond, five-nine, a-hundred-and-forty-five pounds," Dietz said. "Twenty-four years old."

Brooks shrugged.

"Does that sound like the Carla you know?"

"Sort of, yes," Brooks said.

"Tattoo on her right shoulder."

Brooks shrugged again.

"You mind if I use your restroom?" Woodward asked.

"Uh . . . sure," Brooks said. "Just down the hall there. On the right."

"Thanks." Woodward walked down the hall, looking into each room as she passed. She found the bathroom, but stepped beyond it to the last room on the hallway. Brooks's office. A desk cluttered with papers and photographs and camera equipment. A bulletin board over the desk with notes and photographs tacked to it. A bookshelf with the books arranged according to height.

Woodward stepped into the bathroom, closed the door, and washed her hands. She thought for a moment, dried her hands, then went back to the door leading into Brooks's office. One of the photographs tacked to the bulletin board over the desk was a picture of a woman standing in front of a gazebo. It was the gazebo she'd seen in the picnic area at Marshtown Park.

She walked into the office and leaned over the desk to examine the picture more closely. The woman in the picture was blond. It looked like Carla Willis.

Woodward returned to the living room. Dietz was showing Brooks the photo Mrs. Willis had given them.

"That could be Carla," Brooks said. "That looks like a high school graduation photo. It's hard to say. The face looks right, but the hair is all wrong."

"I need to step out to the car for a moment," Woodward said. "Excuse me."

Outside Woodward called Judge Landrigan and told him she was with Detective Dietz at the home of the suspect. "I received permission to use the suspect's restroom, which is near his office," she said. "In the office I observed a photograph taken at the murder scene. The photo appears to be the victim."

Judge Landrigan said he'd sign the warrant and have a court officer deliver it to her at Brooks's residence. Woodward then called headquarters and asked for a few uniformed officers to come to the scene and help with the search. That done she went back inside.

"I can't believe she's dead," Brooks said. "Was it a drug overdose?"

Dietz gave Brooks a look. "She was murdered," he said. "Would we be here asking questions if she died of a drug overdose?"

"You don't think I had anything to do with it," Brooks said.

"We just want to know what you know," Dietz said. "And you're telling me you don't know jack. You're telling me maybe you know Carla Willis, maybe you don't. Maybe you had breakfast with her at Tom's Diner, maybe you didn't. Maybe you offered to shoot some pictures of her, maybe you didn't."

"I offer to take photos of lots of women," Brooks said. "I can't possibly remember them all."

"How many of those women end up dead?" Dietz asked.

"What sort of question is that?"

"Tell me about Marshtown Park," Dietz said.

"What?"

"Marshtown Park. You know where it is, don't you."

Brooks nodded. "Just south of town. What about it?"

The doorbell rang. Brooks started to get up.

"I'll get it," Woodward said. She opened the door. A bailiff in a burgundy court blazer handed her the search warrant. Four uniformed Stormont P.D. officers were standing behind him.

Woodward handed the warrant to Brooks. "Mr. Brooks, we have a warrant to search your home and recreational vehicle." She turned to the officers. "Let's get started."

Dietz continued to interview Brooks at the scene until Woodward walked into the living room. She was wearing gloves to avoid tainting any evidence during the search. In one gloved hand she held a plastic bag containing a sheet of paper. It was a model release form signed by Carla Ann Willis.

Dietz grinned at Brooks. "Didn't I just hear you telling me you weren't sure if you knew Carla Willis? Maybe this will help your memory a bit."

Brooks sat quietly, apparently unable to say anything.

"I think we should continue this down at the station," Dietz said to Brooks.

"Am I under arrest?" Brooks asked.

"Do you want to be?"

Brooks shook his head.

"Then come down to the station voluntarily," Dietz said. "It'll show you're interested in cooperating."

Brooks continued to shake his head. "I'm not going anywhere," he said. "Not while all these cops are in my house."

Dietz nodded. He put his hand on Brooks's shoulder. "Colin Brooks, I'm arresting you for the murder of Carla Willis," he said. He pulled out a pair of handcuffs and cuffed Brooks's hands behind his back.

"Let's go," Dietz said.

PART THREE

The Legal Process

PROSECUTION VERSUS DEFENSE

Ours is an adversarial justice system. Our courts are grounded in the notion that the best hope for arriving at a fair and just verdict is through a trial in which two equally matched opponents (the prosecution and the defense) present evidence and question witnesses before an impartial jury and under the eye of an objective judge.

Obviously this notion presupposes a great deal. In fact the prosecution and defense are rarely equally matched; the prosecution usually has far more resources than the defense. Truly impartial juries are rare, and judges—many of whom are elected—often consider the political ramifications of their decisions. Nevertheless, our courts still usually manage to achieve something approximating justice. It's a remarkable achievement.

It's in the courtroom that the distinctions between the prosecution and the defense are most obvious. Each side has different duties, obligations and roles. The prosecution has a mandate to find the truth (although it isn't uncommon for them to forget this). The defense, on the other hand, is charged only with the duty to protect the rights of the accused and defend him within the bounds of the law (although it isn't uncommon for them to forget this). When the two sides meet and struggle before the bar of the court, some rough form of justice usually gets done.

The Prosecution

After the police investigate a crime and arrest the person suspected of having committed it, the case becomes the property of the prosecutor. The chief prosecutor, called the district attorney or county attorney, is a government official elected or appointed to represent the People (or the State or Commonwealth, depending on the jurisdiction). The district attorney hires other lawyers to assist in prosecuting accused criminals. The size of a DA's office depends largely on the size of the community represented. Rural counties with a small population may be represented by a part-time prosecutor; large metropolitan communities, on the other hand, will have several assistant district attorneys and a staff of investigators (who work independently of the police detectives).

Prosecutorial Role

The Supreme Court, in the 1935 case *Burger v. U.S.*, stated, "A prosecutor's proper interest is not that he shall win a case, but that justice shall be done." This is worth repeating. Prosecutors should be more concerned with doing justice than with winning convictions.

Although most prosecutors try to fulfill this role, it can be difficult—for two primary reasons. First and most important, the office of district attorney is an inherently political office. It's subject to all the pressures and vagaries of politics. The district attorney, as noted earlier, is usually an elected official. This means the DA serves at the pleasure of the people who elected him or her and must be periodically re-elected. In order to get re-elected a DA needs to get convictions, especially in high profile cases. And since the office of district attorney is often used as a stepping stone to higher political office, a failure to get convictions may mean the loss of a political career. It isn't surprising, therefore, that some criminal cases—especially high publicity cases—become tinged with political motives.

The second obstacle in the DA's search for justice instead of convictions is the fact that the people attracted to trial work are usually intensely competitive. This is generally a good thing, in that it means both sides will vigorously present their cases. However, some district attorneys have such a driving desire to win that it can occasionally blind them to their duties.

As we discuss prosecutorial functions, continue to bear in mind the contradictory tides that pull at a prosecutor. The job is to do justice, not win cases . . . and yet there is great public, political, and personal pressure to win cases. It's not an easy job.

Prosecutorial Discretion

When reviewing the evidence obtained by the police during their investigation the district attorney decides if the accused should be formally charged with a crime and what that charge should be. This isn't always a clear decision. The prosecutor has to weigh a number of issues in making such a decision, including:

- the likelihood of obtaining a conviction
- the need to protect the public by making certain an offender is taken off the streets
- the resources available to devote to the prosecution
- the attitude of the public in regard to the crime committed, the victim, or the accused

Consider the following case brought to a prosecutor: a high school senior is accused of killing his father, an alcoholic with a bad temper who had often been arrested for beating his wife. The young man claims the shooting was an accident; he was sitting down preparing to clean a shotgun when it went off, striking his father in the chest. He claims not to have known it was loaded. The angle of the dead man's wounds, however, suggests that the father was shot by somebody standing. The autopsy also revealed the victim was intoxicated when he died. The police and the prosecutor suspect the young man intentionally killed his father, possibly to protect his mother. However, it would be difficult to prove the young man had the necessary level of intent needed to convict him on first or second degree murder (refer to the section on legal definitions of murder). Nor is the young man a probable danger to society. Finally, there is considerable community support for the young man. The prosecutor, therefore, decides to charge the young man with negligent homicide.

The power to decide on an appropriate criminal charge is also sometimes used to over-charge a defendant in the hope of securing a plea bargain (which will be discussed in a later chapter).

Prosecutors can also refuse to charge a suspect if it appears a conviction or a plea bargain is unlikely. This is known as *nolle prosequi,* a refusal to prosecute. This can take place at any time, including during trial. Most often, though, prosecutors dismiss charges long before they begin to prepare for a trial.

Prosecutors also act as the ultimate gatekeeper of the State's evidence and witnesses. They control the paperwork—the forensic test reports, the statements taken from witnesses, the police reports. Technically, the law determines what information must be provided to the defense lawyers—but in practice, the prosecutors often decide what they get and when they get it.

Burden of Proof

Every criminal defendant in every courtroom in every state, county, and city in the United States enters that courtroom as an innocent person. Our legal system operates under a *presumption of innocence.* This means the defendant must be considered innocent until *proven* to be guilty of the crimes with which he or she is charged. It doesn't matter if the defendant committed a blatant act of murder on the pitcher's mound of Yankee Stadium in front of a live crowd of 50,000 baseball fans and a television audience in the millions—he walks into the courtroom an innocent man and must still be proven guilty.

The burden of that proof lies with the prosecution since it's the State that formally makes the accusation against the defendant. The defendant is under no obligation to prove anything. Placing the burden of proof on the State makes it more difficult for innocent people to be wrongfully convicted.

In addition, the State has the burden to prove every element of the crime. Even a simple crime, such as vandalism, usually contains several elements. If vandalism is legally defined as "willful and malicious damage or destruction of property valued at over $50" then the prosecutor has to

BEYOND A REASONABLE DOUBT

Any legal matter that requires a judgment or verdict is governed by a standard of proof. This refers to the level of certainty and the degree of evidence necessary to establish the truth of a legal argument in a criminal or civil court proceeding. In U.S. courts we have three basic standards of proof: the preponderance of evidence, clear and convincing evidence, and beyond a reasonable doubt.

Preponderance of evidence is the least demanding standard of proof. It means the party having the burden of proof must present evidence that is more credible and convincing than that presented by the other party. In other words, the allegations made are more likely true than not. There is more evidence to support the allegations than to disprove them. Preponderance of evidence is used primarily in civil actions, although it's also the standard used in some criminal defenses (such as insanity).

Clear and convincing evidence is a somewhat more exacting standard. It means the party bearing the burden of proof has to demonstrate that the truth of their allegations is *highly* probable. There must be a great deal of evidence to support the allegations made. This is the standard of proof required for some civil cases and some motions.

The most demanding standard of proof is that of **beyond a reasonable doubt**. This is the standard used in criminal trials. A reasonable doubt exists when, based on the evidence presented, a reasonable person would hesitate before acting in a matter of importance. Beyond a reasonable doubt requires a moral certainty. It does not mean beyond *any* doubt. If a juror does not have a compelling belief based on the evidence presented in court that the defendant is guilty, then reasonable doubt exists and the juror must vote "not guilty."

Thomas Jefferson wrote, "The sword of the law should never fall but on those whose guilt is so apparent as to be pronounced by their friends as well as their foes."

prove (1) that the property was damaged or destroyed, (2) that it was damaged or destroyed by the defendant, (3) that it was worth more than fifty dollars, (4) that the defendant fully intended to damage or destroy the property, and (5) that the defendant was acting out of malicious intent. Failure to prove *any* of those five elements beyond a reasonable doubt should result in the defendant being acquitted. If the value of the property destroyed was only forty-five dollars, then the defendant walks free. That isn't a technicality; it's the law.

The burden of proof is weighty, but to offset its burden the State has considerable resources at its command—uniformed police officers, detectives, forensic laboratories, and a large budget. In contrast, most defendants have only one lawyer, perhaps aided by a single investigator.

The Defense

Whereas prosecutors represent the interests of the State and argue on behalf of the People, criminal defense lawyers represent the interests of the defendant and argue only on his or her behalf. It's the defense lawyer's job to *force* the State to prove its case against the accused. The defense has an obligation to protect the civil liberties of the most despised segments of society. Because of the nature of their work, defense lawyers are not always held in high esteem by the public.

One of the defining characteristics of a society is how it treats its accused criminals. Comparatively, the United States does remarkably well. Remember, not everybody accused of a crime is guilty. Nor are all criminals evil. Martin Luther King was a criminal. Gandhi was a criminal. Jesus was a criminal. By vigorously defending the meanest street punk—by forcing the State to prove its case every single time—defense lawyers make it more difficult for the State to convict another Gandhi. It's not pretty work, but it's vitally important.

The Right to Counsel

In the United States, any person charged with a crime that could lead to incarceration has an absolute right to be represented by a lawyer. This wasn't always the case. The right of an accused person to be represented by a lawyer has been established through a long series of court cases, most notably the 1963 case of *Gideon v. Wainwright.*

Clarence Gideon was charged with breaking and entering into a pool hall. At his trial he asked the judge to appoint a lawyer to represent him, a right, he pointed out to the court, that was guaranteed to him under the Sixth Amendment of the Constitution. Florida law at that time, however, only permitted the appointment of counsel in capital cases. The judge therefore denied Gideon's request.

Gideon defended himself at trial. Not surprisingly, he lost and was sentenced to a term of five years in prison. From his prison cell Gideon appealed his case to the Supreme Court. The Court agreed to hear his case and in a unanimous decision they ruled that a defendant facing a felony charge was entitled to be represented by a lawyer. In 1972 this right was expanded to include any defendant accused of any crime that could be punished by incarceration, including misdemeanors (*Argersinger v. Hamlin*). A person facing criminal charges without a lawyer, it has been said, cannot truly obtain justice.

Assigned Counsel

When an accused criminal is indigent (lacking the financial means to hire a lawyer), an attorney can be appointed by the State. Defense lawyers assigned by the State operate from one of four basic appointed counsel systems: the public defender system, the assigned counsel system, the contract system, and a mixed system.

Public defenders represent the majority of indigent defendants. Public defender programs are, in effect, nonprofit law firms devoted exclusively to defending lower income people who have been accused of crimes. They take no other cases, represent no other types of clients. Unlike defense lawyers in private practice, however, they can't refuse a client unless there is a conflict of interest.*

There is a tendency for the general public to assume public defenders

---

*A conflict of interest most commonly occurs in cases involving co-defendants. Obviously, one attorney (or one law firm) can't represent two individuals who may be attempting to place the blame on each other.

are incompetent. This assumption is based on three main factors. First, public defenders are paid relatively low salaries. A good lawyer, the reasoning goes, would be in private practice making significantly more money. And, in truth, many public defenders could earn a higher salary in private practice. However, public defender programs tend to attract idealistic lawyers who are more interested in civil liberties than in salary.

The second reason public defenders are viewed as incompetent is because the staff of public defender offices tends to be young. The lawyers are often hired directly out of law school and have little or no experience. New attorneys, however, always work under the supervision of more experienced public defenders. A new lawyer working for a public defender program also gains much more courtroom experience than a new lawyer working for a private law firm. Despite their relative youth, public defenders quickly become courtroom veterans.

Finally, public defenders are perceived as incompetent because they lose most of their cases. This, however, is due less to the skill of the attorneys than to the fact that most of the clients represented by public defenders are, in fact, blatantly guilty. In addition, unlike lawyers in private practice, public defenders can't refuse a case if it appears to have little chance of success. Given the types of cases they accept and the nature of the clients they represent, the fact that public defenders win any cases at all is proof of their skill.

Under an *assigned counsel system,* lawyers in private practice are appointed by the court to represent indigent defendants. The court maintains a list of licensed attorneys, and when an indigent case arises, the next lawyer on the list is appointed. The fee the appointed lawyer is allowed to charge is usually dictated in advance, and it's almost always significantly lower than the fee the lawyer normally charges a client. This, of course, makes indigent cases unpopular; not only must a lawyer accept a lower fee, but the time spent preparing the indigent case represents billable hours taken away from better-paying clients.

Under assigned counsel systems, indigent defendants often receive short shrift. The quality of the appointed counsel varies greatly. Some appointed lawyers will have done little or no criminal work prior to their assignment. In addition, due to the predetermined low fee schedule, many lawyers simply can't afford to spend much time preparing indigent cases.

Under a *contract system,* lawyers accept some form of block grant. The type of grant varies from state to state, county to county. In some areas contracted lawyers agree to represent a certain number of indigent clients for a fixed fee. In other jurisdiction the contracted lawyer is given a sum of money and agrees to represent any assigned indigent clients over a certain period of time (three months, six months, or twelve months). Under either arrangement the lawyers who accept contracts do so freely, unlike those appointed under an assigned counsel system.

Most jurisdictions operate under a *mixed system*, using both public defenders and one of the other appointed counsel systems. In those jurisdictions, public defenders supply the legal services for the vast majority of indigent defendants. Contract or assigned counsel are used primarily to resolve conflicts of interest and overflow cases. A mixed system generally offers the best representation for indigent defendants.

The Defense Role

The function of the prosecutor, as stated, is to see that justice is done. The function of the defense attorney is both more simple and more morally ambiguous. A defense attorney's job in a criminal case is to vigorously represent the client, using any legal means available without regard to the consequences. This usually means criminal defense lawyers seek an acquittal for their client, even if the client is guilty.

This may sound despicable to many readers. However, it has long been a basic tenet of our judicial system that it's better for a guilty person to go free than for an innocent person to be wrongfully imprisoned. All the laws, codes of legal conduct, and ethical standards that surround and shape a criminal trial are grounded on protecting the civil rights of the innocent. In order to protect the innocent, we must also protect the guilty—because, as we have so often seen, mistakes are made.

A study conducted in the early 1990s estimated that 0.5 percent of all the persons arrested for violent crimes are factually innocent.* This is a conservative estimate; many experts feel the percentage is higher, perhaps as high as 2.5 percent. Now consider that more than 717,000 arrests were made for

---

*"Factually" innocent means the accused actually did not commit the crime, as opposed to "technically" innocent, which means the defendant has either not been convicted or escapes conviction based on a legal rather than a factual basis.

serious violent crimes (homicide, forcible rape, robbery, and aggravated assault) in 1997. Even using the most conservative estimate that only one half of one percent of those arrested were factually innocent, nearly 36,000 innocent people that year were arrested and faced serious felony charges. Criminal defense lawyers represent the last, best hope for the innocent.

Defense lawyers serve their clients in two main ways: as advocates and as advisers. As an advocate the lawyer deals primarily with past conduct— the criminal activity of which the client is accused. When acting as an advocate the defense lawyer must accept the facts as they are and must give the client the benefit of the doubt in regard to those facts. If a client accused of theft insists the property was given to him, the lawyer is required to act on that story and present the best possible defense. An advocate argues for the client.

As an adviser the defense lawyer counsels the client in regard to present and future courses of action. In such instances the lawyer provides a professional opinion as to the legal consequences of the client's behavior. If a client accused of theft suggests the matter could be settled if he met with the alleged victim alone, the lawyer is obligated to inform the client of the potential legal risks involved in that course of action. An adviser counsels the best course of action.

Ethical Considerations

Both prosecutors and defense lawyers are bound by rather strict ethical guidelines and professional standards. They have an obligation to represent their clients (the State for prosecutors, the accused for defense lawyers) to the best of their abilities *within the limits of the law.*

Both prosecutors and defense lawyers are prohibited from:

- **Knowingly using perjured testimony or false evidence.** If, for example, a defendant confesses his guilt to his lawyer, the lawyer *cannot* put the defendant on the stand to testify that he is innocent. Neither can a prosecutor put on a witness if the prosecutor knows that witness isn't telling the truth.

- **Knowingly making a false statement of law or fact.** For example, if the prosecutor or defense lawyer knows a dark stain appearing in a crime scene photograph is red paint, he or she can't tell or suggest to the members of the jury it's blood.

- **Concealing or intentionally failing to disclose information the lawyer is required by law to reveal.** A prosecutor, for example, is required to inform the defense of exculpatory evidence (evidence that points to the defendant's innocence). Similarly, a defense lawyer who comes into possession of evidence of criminal activity must, as an officer of the court, inform the police. The lawyer need not say how he or she came into possession of the evidence if that would violate the lawyer-client privilege, but the evidence must be turned over nonetheless.

- **Participating in the creation or preservation of evidence the lawyer knows to be false.** For example, if a prosecutor knows a weapon found at or near a crime scene is unrelated to that crime, the prosecutor can't make any representation that the weapon is evidence in the crime.

A defense lawyer or prosecutor who becomes aware that a witness has perpetrated a fraud upon the court is required to reveal the fraud to the court. If the person who has perpetrated the fraud is the defendant, the defense lawyer is obligated to ask the defendant to rectify the situation. If the client refuses or is unable to repair the fraud, the defense lawyer is required to reveal the fraud—unless the information is protected as a lawyer-client confidence.

Although the ethical constraints apply to prosecutors and defense lawyers alike, prosecutors—whose function, remember, is to seek justice, not merely to get a conviction—have some additional responsibilities. Prosecutors are required to make timely disclosure to the defense of evidence that tends to negate the guilt of the defendant, or that might mitigate the degree of the offense, or that could reduce the punishment if the defendant is convicted. Further, prosecutors are enjoined not to inten-tionally avoid pursuit of evidence merely because it might damage the prosecutor's case or aid the accused.

Prosecutorial Misconduct

The office of the prosecutor, like any position of power and discretion, is vulnerable to abuse. This vulnerability is exacerbated by the political and public pressure for prosecutors to win trials, get convictions, and thereby increase the odds of re-election.

We have no clear idea how common a problem is prosecutorial miscon-duct. However, the *Chicago Tribune* recently examined the issue. They con-ducted a nationwide examination of court records, appellate rulings, and lawyer disciplinary records. They discovered 381 cases since 1963 in which homicide convictions were reversed due to prosecutorial misconduct. That averages more than ten murder cases every year. The *Tribune*'s study focused exclusively on murder cases in which prosecutorial misconduct was discov-ered. It's highly improbable that every act of misconduct was uncovered.

Most often, prosecutors commit misconduct either by concealing evi-dence that indicates the defendant may be innocent or by presenting evidence they know to be false or misleading. Both of these acts are, of course, strictly prohibited by the legal canons that all lawyers are sworn to uphold. In the same 1935 case mentioned earlier, the Supreme Court stated that a prosecutor "may strike hard blows [but] he is not at liberty to strike foul ones. It is as much his duty to refrain from improper meth-ods calculated to produce a wrongful conviction as it is to use every legitimate means to bring about a just one."

One factor that contributes to prosecutorial misconduct is the fact that those found to have engaged in such behavior are almost never punished. Of the prosecutors involved in the 381 cases studied by the *Chicago Tribune*, none was charged with a crime or disbarred from legal practice. Indeed, many were eventually elected district attorney or appointed to the judge's bench.*

---

*By contrast, the 381 wrongfully convicted defendants went to prison; 67 went to death row. All served at least five years in prison before their cases were overturned; one served twenty-six years.

Not only are the prosecutors rarely punished, convictions obtained through prosecutorial misconduct are frequently upheld in court. According to *Brady v. U.S.* the court must reverse a conviction *only* if the evidence concealed or falsified by prosecutors was so compelling that its disclosure would have created a "reasonable probability" of a different verdict. Courts often uphold convictions based on the idea that the prosecutor's behavior, although reprehensible, probably did not affect the outcome of the trial. The courts are in effect stating that while the prosecutors cheated, the defendant probably would have lost anyway.

There is, in fact, very little to discourage prosecutorial misconduct other than the personal integrity of the individual holding the office. Consider the case of New Mexico prosecutor Virginia Ferrara. In a murder case, Ferrara failed to reveal evidence of the existence of another suspect in the case—a clear violation of prosecutorial ethics. The conviction was eventually overturned. Ferrara, however, no longer worked as a prosecutor. She had become chief counsel for the agency that oversees and regulates misconduct charges against lawyers in New Mexico.

On the very rare occasions law enforcement officials are called to account for misconduct charges, they receive little, if any, punishment. As this is being written, the case of the DuPage 7 has just been resolved. Three former prosecutors and four sheriff's deputies were charged with perjury and obstruction of justice for fabricating a confession and suppressing exculpatory evidence in order to secure a rape/murder conviction against Rolando Cruz.

Cruz had been charged in the kidnaping, rape, and murder of ten-year-old Jeanine Nicarico. An anonymous tip led police to investigate a man named Alejandro Hernandez. Cruz, an acquaintance of Hernandez, was interviewed during the investigation. Cruz is said to have told police investigators he'd had some sort of "dream vision" about the crime. Cruz later reported he'd made the entire thing up in an attempt to get some portion of a ten-thousand-dollar reward for information leading to Nicarico's killer. The investigators were alleged to have turned that "dream vision" into a confession. Cruz and two other men were charged with rape and murder. After a trial, they were all convicted. Cruz was sentenced to death.

Over the next decade Cruz appealed his conviction twice. During that time two DuPage County investigators quit their jobs over their belief that justice was being compromised. An assistant Illinois attorney general, after reviewing the case, resigned rather than argue to uphold Cruz's conviction and death sentence. Witnesses testified they were intimidated by investigators. Defense attorneys accused prosecutors of concealing evidence. During the appeal process a convicted child rapist and murderer who was serving a sentence for the murder of a seven-year-old girl admitted murdering Nicarico. The prosecutors, made aware of the confession, did not inform Cruz's lawyer. They also apparently destroyed their notes on the confession.

Cruz's death sentence was affirmed on appeal. It was only after DNA testing a decade later revealed Cruz could not have committed the crime that he was released. The four sheriff's investigators and the three prosecutors were charged with perjury and obstruction of justice.

Prior to the trial, the charges against two of the seven defendants were dismissed. The other five were found not guilty at trial. After the verdict the jurors and the defendants all went to a bar where DuPage County politicians, police, and lawyers hang out. They all partied together until the early-morning hours.

Most prosecutorial misconduct goes undiscovered. When discovered it's improbable there will be any serious investigation. When there is an investigation it's highly unlikely anybody will be charged with a crime. If a prosecutor is charged with a crime, the odds are against conviction. Although we continue to see the occasional innocent person freed from prison, we give virtually no consideration to how they got there.

Ineffective Assistance of Counsel

The most egregious and common ethical transgression committed by prosecutors is an overzealous prosecution; the most egregious and common ethical transgression committed by defense lawyers is an underzealous defense. Like prosecutorial misconduct, ineffective assistance of counsel is difficult to prove in court. And as with prosecutorial misconduct, ineffective assistance of counsel rarely carries much of a consequence for the lawyer involved. Both prosecutorial misconduct and ineffective assistance of counsel, however, can have the same result: an innocent person in prison.

In order to be considered ineffective, a defense lawyer's performance has to fall below an objective standard of reasonableness, and that poor performance must have prejudiced the client's defense. Ineffective assistance of counsel is a common grounds for an appeal.

In 1983, James Patrasso went on trial for two counts of attempted murder. During a dispute with his employers (a pair of drug dealers), Patrasso was assaulted with a blackjack. He pulled a pistol and when it appeared the two drug dealers were reaching for their weapons, he shot them (both survived and were later indicted for a variety of federal crimes). Patrasso stated he was acting in self-defense when he shot the pair.

At trial Patrasso was represented by attorney Patrick Muldowney, who had not tried a felony case in ten years. Muldowney did virtually nothing to prepare for trial; he did no investigation, did not interview witnesses, did not read the police files, did not ask Patrasso for his version of the incident. He did not discuss the potential of arguing self-defense with Patrasso, did not prepare cross-examination questions for the State's witnesses, did not prepare his client to testify. Muldowney based the entire defense on a single technical error: although the crime took place on February 13, 1982, all the court documents—the indictment, the bill of particulars, the grand jury testimony—alleged that the crime took place a year later on February 13, 1983. On that date Patrasso was in jail, awaiting trial.

During the trial Muldowney made no opening argument. Since he'd prepared no questions, his cross-examination of the State's witnesses was indifferent. He put his client on the stand and asked him only one question. Finally, Muldowney gave a two-sentence closing argument—and then only in response to the court's urging.

Patrasso was, of course, convicted. At sentencing Muldowney offered no arguments for a light sentence. The judge encouraged him to offer some mitigating evidence, but Muldowney informed the court he had nothing to say. Patrasso was sentenced to serve sixty years in prison.

He appealed his case claiming ineffective assistance of counsel. However, it requires more than merely bad lawyering for such an appeal to be successful. The appellate court has to be convinced that the lawyer was so ineffective that it affected the outcome of the trial. If the court believes the evidence presented against the defendant would have been enough to convict despite a vigorous defense, the appeal will fail. In

Patrasso's case, the court felt he would probably have been convicted even if he'd been represented by a better attorney.

The case of Dale Tippins demonstrates just how difficult it is for a claim of ineffective assistance of counsel to succeed. Tippins was on trial in 1986 for buying cocaine from an undercover police officer. Tippins was indigent, so was assigned counsel—a lawyer named Louis Tirelli. Tirelli fell asleep in court during the trial. Not just once; he fell asleep in court every day during the six-week trial. This did not go unnoticed. The prosecutor observed it, as did the jurors and the court reporter. So, in fact, did the judge—the Honorable William Nelson of the Rockland County Court in New York.

After being convicted and sentenced to eighteen years to life, Tippins appealed, asking the court to vacate the verdict on the ground of ineffective assistance of counsel. During the hearing, the prosecutor, court reporter, and a juror all testified that Tirelli slept through the trial. Judge Nelson testified to the same thing. Nelson also stated his opinion that, despite his lawyer's tendency to nap during trial, Tippin received a fair trial. Nelson also stated he believed Tirelli was not ineffective.

The court agreed and Tippin's conviction was affirmed. It took nine years and a Federal Appeals Court before Tippin found somebody who agreed that a sleeping attorney is not an effective attorney. In fact, only one circuit court has ever ruled that it's a *per se* denial of effective assistance of counsel for an attorney to sleep during trial.

The Right to Self-Representation

It has been said that a person who represents himself in court has a fool for a client. The law is intricate and courtroom procedures are often confusing. It's exceedingly difficult for a layman to competently represent himself. Nonetheless, defendants have a constitutional right to represent themselves in court. In order to avail themselves of that right, however, a defendant must willingly, knowingly, and competently waive the right to counsel.

In recent years a number of high profile defendants have chosen to represent themselves in court, among them mass murderer Colin Ferguson, serial killer Ted Bundy, and euthanasia advocate Jack Kevorkian. All are currently serving prison terms.

The Judge

Jean Giraudoux, the French playwright and novelist, once said, "No poet ever interpreted nature as freely as a lawyer interprets the truth." As we've seen, lawyers sometimes get carried away with their work. Throughout the trial process it's the judge who is expected to remain the impartial, disinterested arbiter of the law. The judge decides what evidence the jury will be allowed to see, which witnesses the jury will be allowed to hear, and what testimony those witnesses will be allowed to give. The judge also rules on all questions of law and procedure that might arise during the course of the trial. When the trial is over the judge is responsible for instructing the jury in regard to their obligations in considering a verdict. Finally, the judge hands down the sentence if the defendant is convicted. We'll examine the various duties of the judge in more detail in later chapters.

SECOND THOUGHTS

"You've been charged with a single count of first degree murder," attorney Liza Walsh told Colin Brooks. "There may eventually be other charges."

"I don't know anything about—"

Walsh held up a hand, silencing Brooks. "Don't say anything yet," she said. "Right now I don't want to talk about your role in this . . . if you have one. I'm just letting you know what's going on."

They sat in a tiny conference room at the county jail. Brooks had gone through the booking process of being fingerprinted and photographed. The moment he'd been arrested he'd demanded a lawyer and had refused to answer any more questions. After he was booked he was allowed to make a phone call. He called the lawyer who had handled the legal details involved in incorporating his photography business. The lawyer told Brooks he didn't do criminal work, but offered to send another lawyer from the firm, one who specialized in criminal defense.

"There may be some future charges stemming from the same victim," Walsh said. "I'm hearing some discussion of a rape charge. It seems there's toxicological evidence that the victim was drugged, raped, and then killed. And there may be another murder charge. They've found two bodies in the same location. They apparently haven't identified the other one yet."

Liza Walsh had entered private practice after spending six years as a lawyer in the public defender program. Although she'd expanded her trial practice to include personal injury cases, her primary interest remained criminal defense work. When another lawyer in the firm said he had a client who'd been arrested on a murder charge, Walsh happily set aside the motion she was working on and headed to the county jail. Anything is better than writing another motion.

"That's the situation facing you," she told Brooks. "We'll discuss it all in more detail later. First things first. And the first thing is bail. We'll have a hearing tomorrow and I'll make a motion for reasonable bail . . . but you need to know it's almost certainly going to fail. Even if the judge sets bail, it'll be impossibly high. That means you need to start considering the possibility that you're going to be in custody for a while."

Brooks looked stunned. Walsh had seen that look many times before. It's a difficult adjustment to make; one moment you're a free citizen and the next you're a suspected criminal locked into an impersonal, monstrously noisy jailhouse, surrounded by hostile and suspicious strangers and without the support of your family and friends. It's no wonder, she thought, that suicide rates are so high in jails.

"Next there'll be an arraignment in which we'll enter a plea," she told Brooks. "I strongly recommend we enter a plea of not guilty, regardless of the facts. You can always withdraw the plea later if you want to, but for now it will give us the time to start our own investigation and find out whether or not there are any holes in the prosecutor's case. Do you have any questions about bail or your arraignment?"

Brooks shook his head.

"You'll probably have some later," Walsh said. "If you do, call me. Now, tell me what happened today. You don't need to tell me anything that happened in the past. I just want to know what happened to you today."

Walsh took notes as Brooks told her how Detectives Dietz and Woodward had come to his home, asked him questions, and arrested him.

"They didn't read me my rights," Brooks said. "Not until they put the handcuffs on me and put me in the police car."

Walsh nodded. "Doesn't matter," she said. "You weren't under arrest. You invited them into your house and you were answering the questions voluntarily. They don't need to read you your rights until you're in custody. What's interesting is that they didn't serve you with the warrant when they first arrived. Tell me that part again."

"The woman detective went to use the bathroom," Brooks said. "When she was done she went out to the car. And fifteen minutes after she returned there was a knock on the door and—"

"And the woman detective answered the door?"

Brooks nodded. "Like she was expecting it. And then somebody handed her the warrant and she handed it to me. Then the cops started going through my house."

"That's odd," Walsh said. "That's very odd. We'll look into that. Maybe we can do something with that."

Walsh scribbled furiously on a legal pad for a moment. "Now," she said, "I'm going to ask you a few specific questions. I want you to listen to the questions and answer only what I ask you. Okay?"

"Okay."

"Right," Walsh said. "First, did you know Carla Willis?"

Brooks nodded. "I'd met her a few times in different bars," he said. "She wanted to be a model and asked me if I'd shoot some photos of her. I was reluctant. She just didn't have what it takes to be a model. But she kept asking and I eventually agreed. I had her sign a model release form. But that's as far as it went. I never followed through on it."

Walsh nodded. "The police have seized some film from your home. They're not going to find any pictures of Carla Willis then?"

Brooks hesitated. "I shouldn't have lied to you," he said. "I took her photos. I was afraid if I admitted that, then I'd look guilty. You haven't even asked if I'm guilty."

"I don't care if you're guilty," Walsh said. "I'm your lawyer. Is there anything about the pictures I should know about? Anything unusual or kinky?"

Brooks shook his head. "They were just standard cheesecake shots. No nudity, even. Just a lot of short shorts and tight tank tops."

"When was the last time you saw Carla Willis?"

"The day I shot the photos."

"And she was okay when you last saw her?" Walsh asked.

Brooks nodded.

"Did you have sex with her?"

"No," Brooks said. "Of course not."

"The police apparently found sperm in her vagina," Walsh said. "They'll ask the court to require you to give up a DNA sample and the court will order it. I just want to make sure about this. You're saying I don't have to worry about DNA evidence, that when they test the sperm from Carla Willis's body it's not going to match yours. Right?"

Brooks sighed. "I had sex with her," he said.

"Voluntary?" Walsh asked. "She consented?"

"Yes."

"And was she alive the last time you saw her?"

"Yes."

She stood up. "Okay, that's enough for now. I'm going to head back to the office and start working on bail arguments. You have any questions?"

Brooks shook his head.

"Good," Walsh said. "In the next few days the prosecutor will have to share the police files with me. Once we know what they know, we can really get to work. Until then there's only one thing I want you to do."

"What's that?" Brooks asked.

"I want you to keep quiet," Walsh said. "I don't want you talking to anybody about the case—do you understand?"

Brooks said he did.

"Nobody," Walsh said. "Not the police, not the jailers, not the other people here in jail, not your family, not the pope. Don't say anything about the case and don't write anything. Don't write your parents about it, don't write your girlfriend if you have one, don't write Santa Claus. Don't say or write anything about the case to anybody. Right now there's nobody you can trust except me. Do you understand that?"

"I understand," Brooks said. "What's going to happen to me?"

"It's too soon to say," Walsh said. "I know this isn't much help, but try not to think too much about the future. Or the past. Just get through each hour of the next few days the best you can."

On the drive back to her office Liza Walsh found herself thinking about Carla Willis, dead at age twenty-four. At twenty-four Walsh had been in her first year of law school. At twenty-four she'd had boundless energy and enthusiasm; she'd been able to attend her classes, do her research and homework, go to parties, drink too much, stay up too late, and get up the next day and do it all again. At twenty-four her world had seemed to hold limitless possibilities.

At twenty-four Carla Ann Willis was dumped naked and dead into the woods, stripped of her dignity, of her clothing, of her life.

And Liza Walsh was going to do everything she could within the law to see that the man accused of the crime would walk free.

It's a big old goofy world, she thought. I hope I'm really doing the right thing.

Assistant County Attorney David Van Buskirk had gone to work for the Calhoun County Attorney's Office directly out of law school. He'd worked his way up through the ranks—from prosecuting misdemeanors to felonies to major felonies. The Brooks case would be his fifth murder trial. If his boss agreed that they should seek the death penalty, this would be his first capital case.

Van Buskirk believed in the death penalty. He admitted it wasn't a deterrent to crime. He admitted it was expensive and that occasional mistakes were made. But he felt some crimes were simply so heinous that they cried out for vengeance, for retribution. Raping and murdering a twenty-four-year-old woman while she was drugged unconscious was just that sort of crime.

Still, Van Buskirk's support for the death penalty had always been essentially philosophical. It had always been an academic question, something to debate over a few beers with his colleagues. Up to now. Now he might be personally responsible for getting a man executed. Now he was feeling a few qualms.

Van Buskirk carefully went through the investigation reports. The murder investigation hadn't ended with the arrest of Colin Brooks. In fact, it had accelerated. Detectives Dietz and Woodward and a team of investigators were going over Brooks's life with a microscope. If there were two bodies, perhaps there were three. Maybe more. Colin Brooks might be a serial killer. There could be bodies dumped in other places. The detectives had begun looking for a connection between Brooks and any bodies of young women found in isolated sites in a six-county area.

Detective Woodward had pulled another coup. She'd interviewed Anita Arbonne, the defendant's former wife. Arbonne had said that she'd divorced Brooks for several reasons, but the thing that first began to "creep her out" was her discovery that Brooks was having sex with her while she was asleep. Arbonne suffered from insomnia and often resorted to using a strong sleeping pill in order to sleep. She began to notice that the mornings after she took a sleeping pill, she'd wake up with semen in her or on her. She asked Brooks about it and he'd readily admitted to having sex with her while she was unconscious. He'd told her he found it incredibly erotic. He began to suggest she take her sleeping meds more often.

Knowing that Carla Willis had been drugged with Rohypnol before being raped and strangled, Woodward thought this might be a pattern for Brooks. If he'd done it to his wife and to Willis, he'd probably done it to others. As a photographer, he'd had a ready supply of potential victims. Woodward began to track down models who'd posed for Brooks.

So far she'd found four who thought Brooks might have drugged them and had sex with them.

As Van Buskirk reviewed the file the telephone rang. It was Detective Dietz.

"Good news," he said. "We've identified the other victim. She's a twenty-nine-year-old woman named Bernice Sayers. Her live-in boyfriend filed a missing persons report on her nine months ago."

"What's her connection to Brooks?" Van Buskirk asked.

"Don't know yet," Dietz said. "But we're working on it. If there's a connection, we'll find it."

"Well done," Van Buskirk said.

Two murders committed around nine months apart, Dietz thought to himself. That will almost certainly make this a death penalty case. I sure hope I'm doing the right thing.

THE DEFENSE INVESTIGATION

As we have seen, prosecuting attorneys often have a small army of uniformed police officers, detectives, criminalists, and experts at their disposal. Defense lawyers, by contrast, generally count themselves lucky to have one full-time professional investigator. A large proportion of the investigations conducted by the defense are done by law students working part-time as interns. Only wealthy defendants can afford to hire enough lawyers and investigators to even begin to approach parity with the prosecution. The O. J. Simpson defense team probably had more lawyers and investigators than any single criminal defense team in history—perhaps as many as ten percent of the prosecution team.

Professional criminal defense investigators are usually licensed private investigators.* Many are former police officers or police detectives. Former law enforcement personnel offer advantages and disadvantages to the defense team. The advantage is that they are familiar with the way the police and prosecution work and know how to look for errors in the State's investigation. The disadvantages are twofold: first, former police officers have a tendency to retain the police perspective. They may not be emotionally capable of conducting a vigorous investigation that might lead to a guilty person walking free. They may consciously or subconsciously sab-

---

*Not all professional criminal defense investigators are licensed private investigators, in part because not all states have P.I. licensing agencies. Some states license private investigators at a municipal or county level. Some states do not license private investigators at all.

otage the investigation in order to see that "justice" is done. Second, former police officers sometimes find it difficult to adjust to the fact that they are no longer in a position of authority. Private investigators are merely private citizens who have been licensed and bonded to conduct investigations for a fee. Unlike police officers, private detectives have no inherent power to compel witnesses and potential witnesses to cooperate; they must instead rely on their own personal ability to get witnesses to talk to them.

The defense investigation always gets a late start—days, weeks, possibly even months after the crime has been committed. This is necessarily so, since there can be no defense team until after there is a defendant—and there is no defendant until somebody has been arrested and charged with the crime. By the time the defense investigation begins, the prosecution's investigation has been underway for some time and may even be completed. The defense begins its investigation with a cold trail.

Discovery

Our legal system frowns on the practice of trial by ambush. Both the prosecution and the defense have an obligation to inform the other about certain types of evidence. The process by which this information is shared is called *discovery*.

The greatest burden of discovery lies with the prosecution. In a 1963 case (*Brady v. Maryland*), the Supreme Court ruled it was a violation of the defendant's right to due process when the prosecution suppressed evidence favorable to the accused. Although discovery laws vary widely in different jurisdictions, defendants generally have the right to obtain:

- Copies of his or her own written or recorded statements or confessions
- Relevant police reports
- Copies of arrest and search warrants
- Results of any forensic tests conducted by the crime lab
- Any evidence to be given by expert witnesses
- The names and addresses of witnesses scheduled to be called at trial

The defendant also has the right to view any physical evidence seized by the police,* as well as other relevant documents, photographs, or other objects.

The defense, in contrast, is generally required to reveal much less of its evidence. In most jurisdictions, however, the defense is required to reveal the list of witnesses it intends to call, including expert witnesses and the results of any examinations or tests conducted by expert witnesses. In many states the defense is also required to notify the prosecution if it intends to offer an affirmative defense (which will be discussed later).

The Search for Reasonable Doubt

The defense team, remember, has a radically different objective than the prosecution. The prosecution, ideally, is involved in a search for the Truth. The defense, on the other hand, seeks only to defend the accused—to protect the defendant's civil rights and to force the State to prove its accusations beyond a reasonable doubt. Because its goal is different, the defense approach to the investigation is different. The defense investigation may be described as a search for reasonable doubt.

This search follows two main paths. The first is to attack the prosecution's case. The second is for the defense to construct a case of its own.

Attack on the Prosecution's Case

Through the discovery process, the defense is able to determine the basic outline of the case against the defendant. This allows the defense to begin to search for holes, gaps, and errors in the prosecution's case. Such flaws are usually found in three areas: witnesses, evidence collection, and police/prosecution misconduct.

Witnesses

The defense investigation often begins with an investigator re-interviewing the witnesses who were interviewed by the police. This is done primarily to determine if the police reports accurately reflect the witnesses' statements.

*The defense may ask for independent testing of evidence seized by the police.

149

The police have been known to write their reports in ways that are helpful to their case. They may not actually misrepresent what a witness says, but may cast the statement in a light that is more favorable to the prosecution.

Defense investigators may also investigate individual witnesses to determine their credibility, honesty, and impartiality. They may try to discover if a witness has a reason to lie about the defendant. This doesn't mean the defense can smear or slander the witness; it merely means that if there is any evidence that the witness may not be entirely trustworthy, the jury has the right to know it.

For example, if the defendant had sold the witness some bad drugs in the past, the witness might have a motive to harm the defendant.

Evidence Collection

The defense routinely reviews the manner in which the police collect, process, and store physical evidence. Physical evidence, as we noted, can be delicate. If proper procedures weren't followed, the evidence may be unreliable. If the chain of custody protocol was broken at any point, the evidence may be unreliable. Unreliable evidence should not be allowed to convict a person.

One of the most devastating attacks on police evidence collection techniques took place during the O. J. Simpson trial. According to Simpson jurors, one of the primary reasons they voted for acquittal was due to the sloppy evidence collection and testing procedures. Following the Simpson verdict crime labs across the nation reviewed their evidence collection and testing policies.

Police/Prosecution Misconduct

We've already discussed prosecutorial misconduct. The defense team also searches for evidence of police misconduct, including illegal arrests and illegal searches. Any evidence that the police obtained in willful violation of the law, any evidence falsely manufactured by the police, and any evidence altered by the police can usually be excluded during a trial. There is a legal concept referred to as "fruit of the poisonous tree." The underlying idea is that fruit that comes from a poisonous tree is itself poisonous and should be discarded. Evidence obtained in violation of the law, even damning evidence, is also tainted and should also be discarded.

For example, the police arrest John Doe in the living room of his apartment on a charge of burglary. They make a protective sweep of the apartment, keeping an eye out for any evidence in plain sight as well. One officer, however, opens a shoe box he finds beside the bed. In the shoe box he finds drugs and seizes them and the shoe box. The search of the shoe box in another room was *not* justified during a protective sweep of the apartment. Any evidence found in the shoe box was obtained illegally and must therefore be excluded at trial. It is fruit of the poisonous tree.

Construction of a Defense Case

In addition to finding and revealing errors in the prosecution's case, the defense sometimes also builds a case of its own. Remember, the defense is under no obligation to prove anything to a jury; they have only to establish reasonable doubt. However, juries sometimes find it easier to accept reasonable doubt if they are offered an alternative explanation for the evidence.

The defense team, therefore, often attempts to build a case of its own. This is done in a variety of ways, but the two most common are to develop new suspects and to offer an affirmative defense.

Developing New Suspects

Once the police decide on a prime suspect they have a tendency to focus all their investigative resources on gathering evidence to prove that suspect is guilty. This tactic is very effective in terms of time and resources, but it means other potential suspects are often overlooked. To the credit of the police, they're usually right. But when they're wrong it means they've wasted a great deal of time and resources. This is one reason the police are so reluctant to admit when they've made a mistake.

The defense team often takes advantage of the tendency of the police to concentrate on a single line of investigation. Defense investigators regularly attempt to find evidence that suggests the crime was, or could have been, committed by somebody other than the defendant. When interviewing witnesses, defense investigators generally ask if anybody else might have had a reason to commit the crime. The investigators will then conduct a cursory investigation to determine if any of the potential suspects named could possibly have committed the crime. The investigation is cursory because the defense needn't prove somebody else is guilty of the crime; they merely have to raise reasonable doubt.

At trial defense lawyers can then reveal avenues of investigation that the police ignored. To a jury this suggests sloppy police work, which can lead to reasonable doubt, which leads to acquittal.

Affirmative Defenses

An affirmative defense is a claim put forward by the defendant that must be supported by evidence. It is, in essence, an alternative explanation for the criminal act that posits the defendant is not guilty—for a specific reason. The most common affirmative defenses used in murder cases are self-defense, alibi, and insanity.

Self-Defense

In essence, a defendant who pleads self-defense in a murder case admits killing the victim but claims the killing was done to protect himself from imminent harm. A person has the right to use force—even lethal force—to defend against immediate impending injury or death.

As with all affirmative defenses, the defendant needs to offer evidence to support the claim of self-defense. However, the burden of proof remains with the prosecution; they must prove the act was *not* self-defense. In order to be successful, however, the defendant has to offer evidence that the force used in self-defense was necessary, reasonable, and proportionate. A claim of self-defense does not justify a violent over-reaction. Some states also require the defendant to have attempted to avoid the use of force, perhaps by attempting to leave the scene or by defusing the situation. Finally, the defendant also has to show that the danger was imminent. In other words, the defendant is required to demonstrate that he had no choice but to use force to protect himself.

The final decision on whether the defendant acted in self-defense belongs to the jury. Juries in some states tend to have more liberal interpretations of self-defense. In Texas, which is notoriously lenient in self-defense cases, a man recently argued he acted in self-defense in a quadruple murder case. The defendant, Narit Burin Bunchien, had been in an altercation with two of the victims a few weeks prior to the incident. Bunchien had allegedly referred to a fifteen-year-old girl as a "prostitute." On the night of the shooting, the young girl and three friends went to Bunchien's home, pounded on the door, and demanded he come out and apologize. Bunchien told the jury he agreed to apologize, but when he opened the door one of the four struck him. At that point Bunchien pulled a pistol. According to Bunchien, somebody called for the fifteen-year-old girl to run to their car and get a gun. At that point, Bunchien chased all four people into his driveway and opened fire. Each of the victims, including the fifteen-year-old girl, was shot four to seven times. None of them was armed. No guns were found in the car. Nonetheless, the jury accepted Bunchien's argument that he was frightened for his life and was acting in self-defense. He was acquitted.

Some states allow a variation on self-defense known as *imperfect self-defense*. This defense suggests that the defendant honestly, but mistakenly, believed he was facing imminent danger when the force was used. Imperfect self-defense is more commonly a factor during the sentencing phase of the trial after the defendant has been found guilty. The most well known case relying on an imperfect self-defense argument involved Lyle and Eric Menendez. The two brothers maintained they killed their parents after years of abuse by their father in the erroneous belief that the father was planning to kill them. The first trial ended in a hung jury. At their second trial the brothers were convicted.

An affirmative defense related to self-defense is the *battered woman's defense*. This argument states that the defendant's use of force was a justified response to long-term physical and emotional abuse. Some of the traditional elements of self-defense are absent in the battered woman's defense, notably the requirement that the defendant attempt to avoid the dangerous situation and that the danger be imminent. The nature of abusive relationships is often such that the abused person may feel emotionally or financially unable to leave her abuser. In addition, it's not uncommon for a battered spouse to strike down her abuser when the abuser is most vulnerable (and therefore least capable of responding violently), such as while he is asleep.

The battered woman's defense has met with inconsistent success. All fifty

153

states allow expert testimony regarding the psychological effects of battering, but few make any concession in regard to the elements of self-defense. Some states continue to insist a battered spouse may only justify the use of force when facing immediate danger. Some states also assert a battered woman cannot use lethal force if retreating would eliminate the need for it.

Alibi Defense

Contrary to the belief of many people, the term "alibi" does not mean a lie. The word comes from the Latin root *alius,* meaning "other." The same root also gives us the word "alien." An alibi is simply a statement by the accused that he was at some other place when the crime was committed and is therefore innocent. Although many alibis are false, the term itself refers only to the claim that the defendant was elsewhere.

Again, the defendant is required to offer some evidence—physical evidence and/or testimony—to support his claim that he was not present at the time the crime was committed. For example, if the defendant claims he was at the hardware store buying two gallons of blue latex paint at the time of the murder, the defense investigator will attempt to locate the clerk at the store who waited on the defendant. The investigator will also try to obtain the credit card receipt showing the date and time the purchase was made.

In most states the defense is required to notify the prosecution prior to offering an alibi defense. This is part of the discovery process. The prosecution then has the opportunity to verify or discredit the defendant's claim.

Insanity Defense

The insanity defense is certainly the most misunderstood of all defense strategies. Many people are unaware of the distinction between a medical diagnosis of mental illness and a legal definition of insanity. The two may overlap on occasion, but they are not synonymous. A defendant may be mentally ill but not legally insane. In fact, the vast majority of people suffering from mental illness are not legally insane.

Early in this book we discussed how the offender's intent determines the severity of the criminal act. A death that results from negligence is understood to be less severe than a death that results from reckless behavior, which is less severe than a death that was deliberate and calculated. We have a separate justice system for juveniles in part because society recognizes that the capacity of a child to form intent is less sophisticated than that of an adult.

Intent matters. So does control. A person who is unable to control his behavior is generally considered less culpable than a person who can but chooses not to. The insanity defense is grounded in the notion that a legally insane person has an imperfect capacity to form intent and is unable to control his or her behavior. As early as 1723 English law recognized that people who were "totally deprived of reason so as to be as an infant [or a] wild beast" could not be held morally liable for their behavior.

The legal definition of insanity varies in different jurisdictions. What is insane in one courtroom may not be insane in another. However, most definitions of insanity generally rely on two primary elements:

> • At the time the crime was committed, the defendant must have been incapable of distinguishing right from wrong. A person who cannot appreciate that killing is wrong is less culpable than a person who does understand it and kills anyway.
> • At the time the crime was committed, the defendant must have been in the grip of an irresistible impulse. A person may know right from wrong, but the person who is incapable of controlling his behavior is less culpable than a person who can.

Intent and control matter. Other indications of mental illness generally do not. A defendant may suffer from visual and auditory hallucinations, may "speak in tongues," may be delusional—but so long as he understands the difference between right and wrong and can control his behavior, he is not legally insane. A defendant who believes she is Queen of the Nine Universes, and who receives communications from her Celestial Guardians through bright flashes of light to kill transgressors on this plane of existence, would be considered legally sane so long as she understood it was wrong to kill and she had the capacity to resist the suggestions of the Celestial Guardians.

As with the other affirmative defenses discussed, the defendant has to offer evidence to support the claim of insanity. This usually involves the

155

expert testimony of a psychiatrist who has examined and tested the defendant, as well as the testimony of friends, family members, and others who may have witnessed the defendant's behavior.

Unlike the other affirmative defenses, however, the burden of proof in an insanity case temporarily shifts to the defense. The defense must prove the defendant was legally insane at the time the crime was committed. The standard of proof (see the sidebar on page 127) required in most jurisdictions is a preponderance of evidence. A few jurisdictions demand the more exacting standard of proof of clear and convincing evidence.

Despite what we see on television, the insanity defense is infrequently employed. A successful insanity defense is a very rare event. Research suggests it's used in less than 1 percent of cases scheduled for trial. In three out of four cases, the jury rejects the defense and the defendant is found guilty. In the majority (approximately 80 percent) of the very few cases in which an insanity defense is successful, the prosecution and defense both agree the defendant was insane and arrange a plea bargain.

What happens when a person is found not guilty by reason of insanity? As with so many legal issues, it depends on the jurisdiction. However, nobody acquitted due to insanity (or found "guilty but mentally ill," a related verdict) is simply released back into the community. In most jurisdictions, the person is immediately confined for treatment in a secure psychiatric hospital. Periodically the person is granted a hearing before a review board to determine if he or she remains a danger to self or others. It not, the person becomes eligible to be released. On average, however, defendants found not guilty by reason of insanity are confined as long as, or longer than, defendants who are convicted of the same crime.

....

There is an old criminal defense aphorism: If the facts are against you, bang on the law. If the law is against you, bang on the facts. If both the law and the facts are against you, bang on the table. This is the essence of criminal defense work. The criminal defense team has an obligation to use every legal stratagem at its disposal to defend the client. It doesn't matter how guilty the client is, it doesn't matter how reprehensible the crime is, it doesn't matter how the defense team feels about it. The defense team *must* bang on the law, bang on the facts, and bang on the table.

JUST THE FACTS

Mark Denton had become a private investigator almost by accident. He'd picked up a bachelor's degree in criminal justice, but learned along the way that he didn't have the right personality to be a police officer. The thought of wearing a uniform every day made him shudder. Probation and parole officers did important work, but it struck him essentially as a form of sophisticated baby-sitting. Private security work offered a lot of potential for advancement for anybody holding a degree—but that seemed to be mostly about protecting the property of the upper middle class, and Denton thought they already owned too much of the property.

As he neared graduation he'd answered an advertisement posted on the criminal justice departmental bulletin board. The ad was for an investigator for the public defender. He had no desire to help defend criminals, but it seemed the least offensive alternative. It would do until he figured out what he really wanted to do with his life.

He was surprised to discover that he loved the work and had a knack for it. He liked the absurd odds—he and a lawyer up against the full array of the State. He liked the strange hours—criminals and folks who associate with them don't work nine to five, which meant he often found himself out on the streets in the wee hours. He liked the uncertainty and ambiguity of it—having to make difficult and critical decisions based on woefully inadequate information, without any time to spare for consideration.

157

He also liked and respected the lawyers with whom he worked. Criminal defense work, he learned, isn't really about defending criminals. It's about defending the Constitution. They should call it constitutional defense, he told his friends, not criminal defense. The criminal was incidental. What was important was defending civil liberties. Four years of college and a degree in criminal justice, and yet he'd never really understood that. Not until he'd seen the justice system in action.

After he'd worked a few years for the public defender, Denton had been lured away by a private law firm. The private firm offered more money and greater diversity in the work. Best of all, the lawyers had the right to refuse to accept cases that were stone losers. They didn't always refuse them, of course. Which explained why Denton was working on the Brooks case.

This wasn't a case they could win on the facts, Attorney Liza Walsh had told him. The facts in this case hurt the defense. It would have to be won on the law—and any facts they'd need would be facts that backed up the law. This would be a case of trying to show how the police had made mistakes.

"The place to start," Walsh had told him, "is where the police started. Go to the park, make sure the police photos and sketches are accurate. Go re-interview the witnesses, make sure the police interview statements are accurate. Go over every aspect of the police file and. . . ."

"And make sure they're accurate," Denton had said. "I get it."

"I know you do," she said. "But the stakes are now as high as they can go. They've charged Brooks with capital murder. If we lose, our boy gets the needle."

That took a lot of the fun out of the work. Denton rarely gave much thought to the sentence faced by the defendant. That wasn't his responsibility. That was the lawyer's worry. All he had to do was gather the facts and give them to the defense lawyer. He didn't differentiate between "good" facts and "bad" facts. He just reported what he found. Just the facts.

But suddenly he found the weight of Brooks's life settling on his shoulders. He couldn't afford—in fact, nobody could afford—to make any mistakes in this case. He'd have to be doubly, triply careful and thorough.

And that's exactly what he'd done. He'd started at the beginning and followed the police investigation step by step. He found a few discrepancies between police reports and the statements the witnesses gave him, but nothing substantial. And he noted some problems in the way evidence had been collected at the crime scene. But he found nothing that would make Liza Walsh a happy lawyer. Not until he began to look into the search warrant.

Walsh had been curious about the warrant. Through the discovery process she'd learned the police detectives had asked for the warrant after finding a photograph of the victim in the defendant's home office. According to the application for the warrant, the photo was in plain view; it was seen by Detective Woodward as she went to use the defendant's bathroom.

Denton was just being thorough when he'd gone to Brooks's house. He hadn't expected to find anything out of the ordinary. But he noticed that Brooks's office was farther down the hallway leading to the bathroom. It was unlikely Woodward would have just "happened" to miss the bathroom and wind up in Brooks's office. And the bulletin board on which the photo had been tacked was over the desk at the other end of the room. It seemed improbable that Woodward could have recognized the woman in the picture as Carla Willis from all the way across the room. Unless it was a really large photograph.

Denton decided to take a look at the photo. After sketching the floorplan and photographing the hallway he called Walsh on his cellular phone and had her arrange for him to look at the evidence seized from Brooks's home.

Although he generally enjoyed his work, there were a number of aspects Denton disliked. Dealing with the victims and the victims' families, for example. It's a fine thing to know you're defending the Constitution, but that knowledge is thin armor when you have to face the people who have suffered. The victims and their families, though, tended to be decent about it—as though they understood he was only doing his job. Dealing with the police, though, was different. The police usually saw him as the enemy and treated him as such.

Denton didn't think of himself as the enemy. It was his feeling that both the police and defense investigators were necessary evils. The police were there to prevent abuse by the citizenry; defense investigators were there to prevent abuse by the police. The tension between the police, the prosecutor, the defense investigator, and the defense made civil freedom possible. Besides, there would be no point in having only one side. A fair contest requires two sides. You can't have the Boston Red Sox without the New York Yankees.

At the evidence control room Denton was treated with formal chilliness.

"You can look at the stuff," the evidence control officer told him. "Everything is in evidence bags. You can't open any of the bags. You can take notes, but you can't photocopy anything. You can't take pictures of anything. I'll be with you while you look at the stuff."

Denton looked carefully at each piece of evidence that had been seized from Brooks's home—partly because he was being thorough and partly because he didn't want the evidence control officer to know he was looking for something specific. The photograph of the woman and the gazebo turned out to be a five-by-seven-inch enlargement. Not nearly big enough for Woodward to identify the woman as Carla Willis, not from clear across the room. She'd misinformed the judge when she applied for the search warrant.

Just as he was putting the photo aside to move on to the next piece of evidence, Denton noticed something even more startling. The woman in the picture wasn't Carla Willis.

PART FOUR

The Trial

PRETRIAL EVENTS

Long before the trial begins, the prosecution and the defense start maneuvering for an advantage. Their pretrial gambits and stratagems will shape the eventual course and outcome of the trial itself. In fact, the vast majority of criminal cases are resolved at this stage and never come to trial at all. Trials, after all, are expensive and chancy affairs. Most trial lawyers would prefer to arrange the outcome of the case among themselves without having to put the matter before a jury. Nobody ever knows what a jury will do.

The first pretrial consideration is the defendant's liberty.

Bail Hearing

The Eighth Amendment of the Constitution guarantees the right of a criminal defendant to obtain a reasonable bail. It's important to remember that all accused criminals are just that—accused. As noted earlier, they are presumed to be innocent until they have been proven guilty in court. Because of that presumption, there must be a very good reason to deprive a citizen of his liberty before he has been convicted of a crime. Additionally, the courts recognize that an accused criminal has the right to assist in his own defense. That is hard to do when incarcerated.

As soon as possible after arrest, the defendant must be granted a bail hearing. Bail refers to an arrangement between the defendant and the court (and sometimes with a bail bondsman) that allows the defendant to remain free from custody while awaiting trial. The defendant (or a bondsman or other interested party) may be allowed to post a sum of money, or property worth a sum of money, as a guarantee that he will be present in court at a later date.

Most metropolitan areas maintain a standardized bail schedule that sets the amount of bail based on the crime with which the defendant is charged. However, both the prosecutor and the defense attorney may argue for higher or lower bail. In a murder case it's not uncommon for the prosecution to ask that the defendant be held without bail.

When setting bail a judge will generally take the following into account:

- the defendant's criminal record
- the gravity of the current charge(s)
- the potential risk of flight from the jurisdiction
- the risk to the community if the defendant is released
- the defendant's financial status

The purpose of bail, it must be remembered, is to ensure the defendant will appear in court as required. If the defendant fails to appear, the bail deposit is forfeited to the State and a warrant for the defendant's arrest is issued.

Plea Bargain

The vast majority of criminal cases, over 90 percent in many jurisdictions, are resolved through a plea bargain. A plea bargain (also referred to as a plea arrangement, a negotiated plea, or a "deal") is an agreement between the prosecutor, the defendant's attorney, and the defendant. Plea bargains fall into two categories: sentence bargains and charge bargains. A sentence bargain is one in which the defendant agrees to plead guilty (or no contest) in exchange for the recommendation of a lighter sentence by the prosecutor. Since mandatory sentencing guidelines have gone into effect in so many jurisdictions, sentence bargaining is less common.

There are three types of charge bargains:

- **The defendant agrees to plead guilty to a lesser charge.** For example, a defendant might agree to plead guilty to manslaughter rather than face trial on the charge of second degree murder.
- **The defendant agrees to plead guilty in exchange for having the number of charges reduced.** A defendant facing multiple counts of a crime might agree to plead guilty to a single count.
- **The defendant agrees to plead guilty to a less socially unacceptable charge.** For example, a pedophile might agree to plead guilty to a charge of sexual assault rather than face trial on the charge of sexual assault on a minor.

Federal criminal cases usually require plea agreements to be made in writing. In state cases, however, plea bargains are generally not written. Despite the fact that they are oral agreements, it's rare that they are not honored.

Although plea bargaining is a routine process, it has a bad reputation among the general public. Many people interpret plea bargaining as a boon for criminals, a way for guilty people to avoid the punishment they deserve. In fact, the plea bargain process benefits prosecutors, defendants, defense attorneys, and the taxpayers. The criminal courts have become more crowded as politicians, wanting to position themselves as "tough on crime," pass new laws and demand harsher penalties. Those same politicians, wanting to appear fiscally conservative, also want to limit or reduce the size of the government. In the end that means increased workloads for judges and prosecutors. In order to keep court dockets from becoming hopelessly jammed, plea bargains are necessary. In addition, trials are time-consuming and expensive. Plea bargains are time-effective and inexpensive. A trial may last days, weeks, or months and can involve witness fees, juror expenses, police overtime, and expert witness costs. The more important the trial, the longer it takes and the more it costs; the O. J. Simpson trial, for example, cost taxpayers around $9 million. A plea bargain, by contrast, can often be worked out in a very short time. The Simpson trial exemplifies another reason plea bargains are attractive—trials are unpredictable. A plea bargain offers the prosecution and the defense much more control over the outcome.

In most jurisdictions plea bargains can take place at any point after the accused is arrested and before a jury returns a verdict. Plea negotiations have even been arranged while a jury is deliberating. In trials resulting in a hung jury, prosecutors and defense lawyers often work out a plea bargain rather than go through the time and expense of another trial.

Pretrial Motions

There is a great deal of legal arguing done by the defense attorney and the prosecutor before the trial actually begins. These pretrial motions are critical; they can shape the course of the trial and influence the eventual outcome—they can even resolve the case before the trial begins. The variety, scope, and number of pretrial motions is staggering. Each motion has to be argued before the judge and ruled on. The following is a small sampling, including the most important potential pretrial motions.

Motion to Dismiss

Defense lawyers routinely file motions to dismiss some or all of the charges pending against the defendant. Motions to dismiss are based on a defect in the prosecution's case. If the evidence was illegally obtained, if the arrest was invalid, if a search was based on a flawed warrant, if the indictment is overly vague, if the trial has consistently been delayed without cause (see below), if the defense believes there is insufficient evidence to go forward to trial—any flaw in the prosecution's case is grounds for a motion to dismiss. These motions, however, rarely succeed.

Motion for a Speedy Trial

The Sixth Amendment guarantees all accused criminals the right to a speedy trial. It's a right derived from the Magna Carta, and is intended to ensure a defendant can't be held in custody indefinitely on the pretext of a pending trial. The right to a speedy trial is also designed to minimize the anxiety that accompanies a public accusation of criminal activity and to limit the potential problems that might arise from a long delay between the accusation and the resolution of the matter.

The right to a speedy trial, like all the rights guaranteed in the Constitution, exists to protect the innocent. However, it's uncommon for the defense to file a motion for a speedy trial. Since a large proportion of criminal defendants are factually guilty, a long delay is usually beneficial to the defense case. Over time the memories of witnesses begin to fade, there is an increased chance that evidence will be lost or damaged, witnesses may move away and become difficult to locate. In some cases, however, the defense can gain a tactical advantage by pressing the case before the prosecution is fully prepared.

Motion to Suppress Evidence

This is one of the most common pretrial motions. We have discussed the Fourth Amendment right to be free from unreasonable searches and seizures, as well as the concept of the "fruit of the poisonous tree." It's through motions to suppress that defense lawyers attempt to exclude such illegally obtained evidence. It's just as accurate to say it is through motions to suppress that the defense attempts to force the police to obey Constitutional constraints. The concept of excluding illegally obtained evidence is known as the *exclusionary rule.*

The exclusionary rule has been around in one form or another since 1886. It exists in part because the courts recognize there is no other effective measure to compel the police to follow evidentiary laws. A police officer, for example, who commits an illegal search may be subject to arrest and prosecution—but in reality, prosecution is so unlikely that it can be discounted as an enforcement tool. Similarly, an officer who commits an illegal search has very likely violated departmental policies and might be subject to internal departmental discipline—but, again, enforcement is highly improbable. Finally, it's possible for the victim of an illegal search to sue the officer(s) responsible for damages under a civil rights statute in federal courts. However, the people who are usually the victims of illegally obtained evidence are very often disreputable persons toward whom juries are unsympathetic, or they are poor and unable to afford a civil suit against the government. The only viable punishment for violating a defendant's civil rights, therefore, is to suppress illegally obtained evidence from use at trial.

There are, of course, always exceptions to any rule. In regard to illegal searches and seizures there is the *good faith exception*. Evidence obtained by the police using a defective search warrant (one based on inaccurate or mistaken information supplied by the police) can still be used in court if the officers conducting the search were operating on good faith. Although officers have been known to stretch the truth when asking a judge or magistrate for a search warrant, few officers will tell a direct lie to obtain a warrant.

The most common examples of evidence that defense attorneys seek to suppress are coerced confessions and illegally obtained physical evidence. In some cases, the suppression of evidence allows the guilty to go free. However, as Justice Cardozo said, "The criminal goes free, if he must, but it is the law that sets him free. Nothing can destroy a government more quickly than its failure to observe its own laws."

Motion for a Change of Venue

Generally a criminal proceeding takes place in the county in which the alleged crime took place. On occasion, however, the defense will ask the judge to move the trial to a different location. This is referred to as a change of venue.

The most common reason for requesting a change of venue is pre-trial publicity. In a high publicity case it may be difficult to find jurors who haven't been influenced by reports in the newspapers or on the evening news. Not only might potential jurors form an opinion as to the defendant's guilt or innocence before they've heard any evidence, they may also hear about evidence that would be suppressed during trial. It would be difficult for such a juror to decide on a verdict based solely on what was heard in court and not what was heard before the trial began.

There are, of course, attendant risks for both the prosecution and the defense when a change of venue has been granted. The defense risks the fact that the new venue may be even more biased against the defendant. But generally the risk is far greater for the prosecution. This was the case in the trial of the four police officers for the beating of Rodney King. The trial was moved from Los Angeles to Simi Valley, a more conservative community with a large proportion of retired law enforcement officers— a jury pool that would be more sympathetic to white police officers accused of assaulting a black ex-convict motorist.

Motion to Close the Courtroom

This is one of the rare pretrial motions filed by the prosecution. The motion is filed when evidence is to be given by a confidential informant (referred to as the CI). The CI may be an undercover police officer who is still in the field or a witness whose safety might be at stake if his identity is revealed. Defense attorneys routinely oppose such a motion, arguing that the defendant has a right to confront his accusers and to a public trial. As with other motions, the decision rests with the judge.

Jury Selection

A jury, the poet Robert Frost once said, consists of twelve persons chosen to decide who has the better lawyer. There is some truth to that, if only in that the better lawyer generally picks a better jury—a better jury being one that will be more sympathetic to the lawyer's arguments.

The jury is the true trier of fact. The judge decides what evidence the jury may hear and instructs the jury on how to consider its verdict, but the jury alone decides which facts they will pay attention to. Jury deliberations will be discussed in more detail in a later chapter.

Most criminal juries consist of twelve jurors and a few alternates (in case one or more jurors is unable to finish the trial). The Constitution, however, does not specifically require a twelve person jury, and the Supreme Court has held that a smaller jury does not deprive a defendant of a fair trial. Every state, however, uses a jury of twelve to decide murder cases.

In most states the pool of potential jurors (called a *venire* or jury array) is drawn from lists of registered voters and/or lists of licensed drivers. Potential jurors are selected from these lists by a random process. The size of the venire varies in different jurisdictions, but it's generally around 120 people.

Voir Dire

When the potential jurors report for jury duty, a smaller group of around fifteen (twelve jurors and three alternates) is called into the courtroom, where they are questioned. This process is known as *voir dire* (French for "speak the truth"). In some jurisdictions the voir dire is conducted by the judge, in others the prosecutor and defense attorney take turns questioning the potential jurors.

The purpose of voir dire is to determine if the potential juror can be fair, impartial, and unbiased. In addition to generic questions regarding age, education, marital status, employment, etc., the juror will likely be asked questions such as the following:

- Does the juror know any of the parties involved in the case—the defendant, the lawyers, or the witnesses?
- Is anybody in the juror's family a police officer, a lawyer, or a court officer?
- Has the juror ever been arrested for any crime?
- Has the juror ever been a victim of a crime?
- Does the juror have any physical or medical condition that might make it difficult to serve as a juror?

The number and types of questions asked of the jurors is determined by the presiding judge. In the O. J. Simpson case potential jurors were given a questionnaire of over 300 detailed questions.

Jury Challenges

The prosecutor and the defense attorney are both given the opportunity to challenge a juror and strike him or her from the jury. There are two types of juror challenges: challenges for cause and peremptory challenges. A challenge for cause is based on the attorney's belief that the juror is unsuitable for a specific reason. The reason could possibly prejudice the juror in favor of the defense or the prosecution. A juror who had been the victim of a crime might be unwilling or unable to put aside a personal antipathy toward the defendant. A juror who had been the victim of police violence might feel hostility and suspicion toward the police. The attorney challenging the potential juror for cause must convince the judge of the juror's unsuitability. There are generally no limits on the number of challenges for cause.

Peremptory challenges, in contrast, do not require any basis. Either the prosecution or the defense attorney may strike a potential juror for an undisclosed reason, or for no particular reason at all.* The number of peremptory challenges available to each lawyer varies in different jurisdictions and, in some cases, may vary based on the type of crime. In murder trials both attorneys are often permitted more peremptory challenges.

Bench Trial

Not all trials are held before juries. In some instances the judge will be the sole trier of fact. Such trials are known as *bench trials.* Bench trials tend to be quicker and less expensive; they eliminate the time and expense necessary to impanel a jury, they remove the expense of daily juror fees (and the potential cost of sequestration, which is discussed in a later chapter), and they save time spent arguing points of law outside the jury's hearing.

The decision to have a bench trial rests with the defendant, although in some jurisdictions the prosecution needs to consent to the request. In most cases, defendants benefit from a jury trial; all the defense needs to do is raise a reasonable doubt in the mind of one juror to escape conviction. However, in very complex cases that rely on highly technical evidence or esoteric points of law the defense may feel better served by a bench trial. Weighed against this is the fact that research indicates that judges are nearly twice as likely as juries to pass a verdict of guilty.

---

*It should be noted, however, that the Supreme Court has held that neither prosecutors nor defense lawyers can use peremptory challenges to strike potential jurors based on race.

Death Qualification

Juries in capital cases are different from standard criminal juries. A jury in a capital case must be *death-qualified*. Death qualification simply means the members of the jury must be willing to impose the death sentence if the defendant is convicted. Any juror who is morally or philosophically opposed to the use of capital punishment is eliminated during voir dire.*

An unintended effect of death qualification, however, is to impanel a jury with a predisposition to convict and to sentence a convicted murderer to death. Social science research has shown that proponents of the death penalty are more likely to believe a defendant who exercises his Fifth Amendment right to not testify at trial is guilty, generally have less concern about wrongful convictions, and tend to distrust defense attorneys. A death-qualified jury, therefore, is a jury stacked against the defendant. Nonetheless, the Supreme Court has upheld the use of death-qualified juries.†

---

*Potential jurors who oppose the death penalty are challenged and dismissed for cause.

†The Supreme Court has consistently shown itself skeptical about social science research. This is due partly because of inherent differences between legal and scientific reasoning. We briefly discussed these different approaches in the first chapter. Social scientists study fact patterns and attempt to come up with generalized conclusions. Legal thinkers, on the other hand, apply general rules of law to specific fact patterns. Social scientists deal in generalities, such as: "Proponents of the death penalty are more likely to distrust defense attorneys and therefore less likely to give credence to defense arguments, making them more likely to vote for conviction." Legal reasoning deals in specifics, such as: "Is there evidence to indicate that a particular juror is biased?" Legal reasoning might accept the concept that death-qualified juries tend to be prone to convict, but requires specific evidence that a specific jury or juror is biased before accepting that a specific defendant was unfairly convicted.

172

MOTION TO SUPPRESS

County Attorney David Van Buskirk (right on time) arrived for the motion hearings before Judge Nancy Keegan. Attorney Liza Walsh was sitting at the defense table with her client, Colin Brooks. Van Buskirk gave her a professional smile.

He was ready to argue the pretrial motions. In fact, he was ready to prosecute Colin Brooks. If the judge put me in front of a jury this afternoon, he thought, I'd be ready. He was as well prepared as he could possibly be. He knew the case file and the facts of the crime intimately. He knew the strengths and the weaknesses of his case—and he was satisfied the strengths far outweighed the weaknesses.

There had been disappointments, of course—there always were. Despite the best efforts of the detectives they'd been unable to find any solid link between Brooks and Bernice Sayers, the skeletonized victim. Sayers had been known to spend time in some of the same bars as Brooks and Willis, but nobody could say whether or not they knew each other. On the day she'd disappeared, Sayers had told her boyfriend that she had an appointment, but she wouldn't say what sort of appointment. Sayers had told her boyfriend that it was a surprise, but that he would be happy about it. It was possible, he thought, that she was going to have some photographs taken for his birthday . . . but he didn't know. A girlfriend of Sayers told investigators that Sayers had talked on at least one occasion, about giving her boyfriend some racy photographs of herself, but didn't know if Sayers had ever followed through on the idea. The boyfriend went out of town on business every six weeks or so, and she'd thought the pictures would keep his mind focused on her while he was away.

Van Buskirk had decided not to charge Brooks with Sayers murder. There simply wasn't enough evidence to convict. As far as that went, Van Buskirk had to admit there wasn't even enough evidence to show that Sayers had been murdered. It just seemed more likely than not.

On a more positive note, Detectives Dietz and Woodward had located eleven women who had modeled for Colin Brooks and suspected him of having drugged them and raped them while they were unconscious. Van Buskirk had charged Brooks with eleven counts of aggravated rape—the aggravating factor being that the victims were helpless to resist and unable to give consent. He knew he'd never get convictions on them all . . . but he'd thought it might serve to shake the Brooks defense.

Liza Walsh was considerably less happy with her case. Her client's story had changed too many times. First he didn't know the victim. Then he admitted he did know her, but said he never took her picture. Then he admitted taking her picture, but said he didn't have sex with her. Then he admitted the sex, but said it was consensual. Now he was saying that Carla Willis had become agitated and angry after the sex. She took some sort of pill to calm herself down, and then stormed out of his camper—and that was the last time he saw her. It wasn't a good story and she hated to put it in front of a jury.

If all goes well today, she thought, maybe I won't have to.

Judge Keegan rapped her gavel twice and called the court to order. "We have three motions before us this afternoon," she said. "The defendant's motion to sever, motion to dismiss, and motion to suppress. Let's deal with the motion to sever first."

Walsh had asked the court to try the murder charge separately from the rape charges, and for each rape charge to be tried independent of the others. In other words, she asked for twelve different trials—which would be prohibitively expensive for the prosecution and defense alike. Walsh knew the eleven counts of rape were just a trial tactic, just as Van Buskirk knew the request for twelve separate trials was a tactic. It was all part of jockeying for position.

"I'm inclined to grant the motion to sever in reference to the murder charge," Judge Keegan said. "However, I'll reserve judgment on severing the eleven related rape counts." She looked at Walsh. "If you wish to argue that aspect of the motion, counselor, you may. But I suspect you won't like the result."

"I have no desire to argue that aspect at this time, your honor," Walsh said.

Judge Keegan nodded. "Good. Now, as to this motion to dismiss . . . defendant asserts the search of his premises was illegal. That's the same assertion made in the motion to suppress, isn't it?"

"It is, your honor," Walsh said. "Obviously, I'd prefer the motion to dismiss, but in case that's denied I'd like to—"

"It seems to me we're getting ahead of ourselves," Judge Keegan said. "Let's first determine if the evidence was gathered legally; then we can entertain the motions to dismiss and suppress. Mr. Van Buskirk, are you prepared to address this issue?"

"I am, your honor."

"Then let's get to it," Judge Keegan said. "Please call your witness, Mr. Van Buskirk."

"Call Detective Glenda Woodward, your honor."

The bailiff swore in Detective Woodward, and Van Buskirk asked her to state her name, occupation, and length of service as a law enforcement officer. Van Buskirk led Woodward through the events of that afternoon—the arrival at Brooks's house, the interview, her trip to the bathroom and subsequent observation of the photograph.

"Detective Woodward," Van Buskirk said, "when walking down the hallway in the defendant's house would you encounter the bathroom first or the office?"

"The bathroom," she said. "The office is one room beyond the bathroom."

"Then how did you find yourself looking in the defendant's office?"

It was a common trial lawyer's tactic. When faced with information that presents a witness in a bad light it's better for the lawyer to bring it out rather than wait for the opposing party to do it. Otherwise it looks like an attempt to hide something, and that never plays well with a judge or jury.

"I'd looked in each room as I passed it," Woodward said. "I wanted to make sure there was nobody else in the defendant's house. At that point in time Mr. Brooks was a suspect in a violent crime. I was making a visual sweep of the area. I've been a police officer for nine years—it's second nature to me to want to know who's behind me."

"And when you looked into the defendant's office what did you see?" Van Buskirk asked.

"I saw a picture pinned to a bulletin board," Woodward said. "At first I thought nothing of it. Like I said, I was just making a visual sweep of the area. But while I was in the bathroom the picture remained in my mind. I kept thinking about it. And then it occurred to me that the picture included the gazebo in Marshtown Park."

"The park where the victim's body was found?"

"That's correct."

"And then what did you do?"

"When I finished in the bathroom I returned to the defendant's office and examined the picture more closely."

"And what did you learn?"

"It appeared to be a picture of the victim," Woodward said. "A picture of the victim taken at the same location where her body was found."

Liza Walsh sighed. She realized the police had discovered the photograph wasn't Carla Willis. Her ambush had been undermined.

"What did you learn about that picture later?" Van Buskirk asked.

"I learned it was not, in fact, a picture of the victim."

Van Buskirk nodded. "But at that moment in time you believed it truly was the victim, correct?"

"Objection, your honor," Walsh said. "Leading the witness."

"Sustained," Judge Keegan said quietly.

Van Buskirk nodded. "Detective Woodward, what was your belief at the time you first saw the picture?"

"At the time I first observed the picture it was my belief that it was of Carla Ann Willis, the victim in this crime."

"And when you requested the search warrant you were acting on your belief that the woman in the picture was Carla Ann Willis?"

"That's correct," Detective Woodword said.

"I have no further questions, your honor."

"Attorney Walsh?" Judge Keegan indicated it was her turn.

She stood up and approached the lawyer's podium. "Detective Woodward, you stated earlier that my client was a suspect in the case."

"That's correct."

"Was he your only suspect?"

"Objection, your honor," Van Buskirk said. "The question is irrelevant and immaterial. This is a hearing on the legality of the search; whether or not there were other suspects is completely and utterly irrelevant."

"Sustained," Judge Keegan said. She motioned Walsh to continue with another question.

"You'd attempted to get a search warrant for Mr. Brooks earlier that same day, hadn't you?" Walsh said.

"Yes," Woodward said.

"But the judge denied the warrant, didn't he?"

"Yes, that's correct."

"Because there wasn't enough evidence to support a search warrant."

"The judge wanted to see a more—"

"Yes or no, Detective," Walsh said. "The warrant was denied because there wasn't enough evidence to support it?"

"Objection, your honor," Van Buskirk said. "The witness is trying to answer the question. She should be given the opportunity to finish her comments."

"Answer yes or no, Detective," Judge Keegan said.

"No," Woodward said. "There wasn't enough evidence to support it."

"And after you were denied that warrant you went to Mr. Brooks's house anyway."

"That's correct," Woodward said. "To interview him."

"You went there, Detective Woodward, with the intent to find something that might possibly help you get the warrant denied earlier, isn't that so?"

"We went to the defendant's house to interview him," Woodward insisted. "But a good detective always keeps her eyes open."

Woodward's testimony went on for another twenty minutes, after which she was excused from the witness stand. Van Buskirk and Walsh then took turns trying to convince the judge of the strength of their respective positions. Walsh argued that the search warrant was based on intentionally misleading information. The warrant was, therefore, defective, and any evidence seized from the defendant's house was obtained illegally.

Van Buskirk argued that Detective Woodward was operating in good faith and had made a simple, honest mistake. From a distance, he said, the woman in the photograph did bear some resemblance to Carla Willis. Woodward's familiarity with the victim's face was based on viewing her decomposing body at the park where she'd been discovered and looking briefly at a high school photograph taken some six years before. There was no attempt to defraud the court, he argued.

"I'm inclined to agree," Judge Keegan said. "It seems to me Detective Woodward was acting in good faith. Attorney Walsh, I'm going to deny your motions to dismiss the case and suppress the evidence."

Judge Keegan looked at the two attorneys for a moment. "Are there any other motions we need to consider at this time?" she asked.

"No, your honor," both lawyers answered.

"Good." Judge Keegan nodded and almost smiled. This was moving right along. "Then let's take a ten-minute recess and get started on jury selection. And when I say ten minutes, I mean ten minutes. Not fifteen. And certainly not twenty. Am I understood?"

"Very clear, your honor," Liza Walsh said.

David Van Buskirk looked at the faces of the seventeen potential jurors and tried to look directly into their brains. What are they thinking? he asked himself. He watched them closely as the judge informed them they were being considered to sit in judgment on a capital murder case. He could almost see some of them flinch. Those were the ones who'd probably be eliminated simply because they were unalterably opposed to the death penalty.

"A death-qualified jury is the best jury in the world for a prosecutor," his boss had told him. "Whether they admit it or not, most of the jurors will be at least a little suspicious of whoever is sitting in the defendant's chair. If you took Mother Theresa out of her habit and dropped her in the defendant's chair, the only thing most of the folks on a death-qualified jury would see is a truculent, shifty-eyed old woman capable of almost any outrage. You gotta love a death-qualified jury."

Liza Walsh looked at the faces of the seventeen potential jurors and tried to look directly into their hearts. What are they feeling right now? she wondered. Some of them were clearly intimidated by the idea of sitting on a capital murder case. Some, on the other hand, looked almost grimly eager.

After the first round of seventeen potential jurors, eight of the group had been eliminated because they were morally and philosophically opposed to capital punishment. After voir dire Van Buskirk had challenged one; Walsh had challenged four. Four were approved.

More potential jurors were brought in, and they did it all again. And again and again that afternoon. And they did it again the following morning and afternoon. They did it until they had a jury of twelve (nine men, three women) and five alternates (three women, two men).

Van Buskirk was pleased. The jurors all seemed like solid, upstanding citizens willing to do their public duty. They'd follow the law, he felt certain. And that was all he asked.

Walsh was less than pleased, but felt the jury she had was as good as she was likely to get. The idea of twelve people whose knowledge of the law came primarily from TV crime shows, deciding whether her client would live or die filled her with dread and forboding. But . . . all she needed to do was convince one that there was reasonable doubt. Just one.

THE TRIAL

There is a rhythm and pattern to a trial. A trial moves according to very old, formal, almost ritualistic rules. The rules are not mandated by law but have grown organically through tradition. They are designed to ensure that everybody—the prosecution, the defense, and the judge—understands what should be done and when it should be done. There will undoubtedly be surprises or moments of confusion in a trial, but the framework of the trial process remains consistent—and consistent across jurisdictions. With very slight variations, a trial in California will follow the same generic pattern as a trial in Maine or Louisiana.

Think of the trial as an improvisational play. The actors know their cues. They know when to enter and when to exit each scene. They know the basic outline of the play. But the dialogue changes with each performance, and nobody knows how the final act will end.

With some minor variation every criminal trial in the United States follows this same basic pattern:

- Opening statements
- The prosecution case-in-chief:
  - swearing in of the witness
  - direct examination of the witness
  - cross-examination of the witness
  - redirect of the witness
- Prosecution rests its case

- Motion to dismiss
- The defense case-in-chief:
    - swearing in of the witness
    - direct examination of the witness
    - cross-examination of the witness
    - redirect of the witness
- Prosecution rebuttal
- Closing arguments
- Jury instructions
- Jury deliberations and verdict

We'll examine jury instructions and deliberations in a later chapter. For now we'll examine the body of the trial.

Opening Statements

The trial begins with opening statements by the prosecution and the defense. Opening statements are designed to inform the jury what they should expect to see from the evidence and hear from the witnesses throughout the trial. They are, in effect, previews of the prosecution and defense cases. Trials rarely run smoothly; they tend to run in fits and starts, and periodically they jerk to a halt. Giving the jury a preview of the evidence and testimony makes it easier for them to see the larger picture. It's easier to put together a jigsaw puzzle if you have an idea how the finished picture is supposed to appear.

Opening statements, however, are just that—statements by the opposing lawyers. They are not evidence. The judge reminds the jurors that they can't rely on facts mentioned during opening statements when deliberating their verdict. In his opening statement, a prosecutor might tell the jury that a certain witness will testify he observed the defendant at the scene of the crime. That fact does not become evidence until that witness actually gets on the witness stand and testifies that he did indeed see the defendant at the crime scene.

Opening statements aren't evidence and they're not meant to act as argument. Neither the prosecution nor the defense can use the opening statement to argue the strength or merits of their respective cases. For example, a defense lawyer can't claim the defense witnesses are more credible than the prosecution witnesses. Such a claim can be made during closing arguments, but an opening statement is used only as an overview of the evidence that will be presented.

The prosecution always makes its opening statement first. Most often the defense gives its opening statement directly after the prosecutor's opening. This has the advantage of reminding the jury that there are two sides to the story and that they should give both sides a fair hearing before deciding on the defendant's guilt. In some jurisdictions the defense also has the option to wait to give its opening statement until the prosecution rests its case. This allows the defense lawyer to know what evidence will be needed to counter that presented by the prosecution.

Prosecution Case-in-Chief

As with opening statements, the prosecution always presents its case first. This is both logical and fair. The prosecution case-in-chief is, in effect, a public accusation against the defendant and an attempt to prove that accusation. In order to be able to dispute that accusation, the defendant has to know what the accusation is and the evidence and testimony that exists to support it. That means the prosecution *has* to present its case first.

Swearing in

Each witness called to the stand to testify is required to solemnly swear or affirm that he or she will tell the truth, the whole truth, and nothing but the truth. In acknowledgment of the increasing religious diversity of the United States, witnesses in most jurisdictions are no longer required to place their hand on the Bible and swear, "so help me God." According to the federal rules of evidence, the oath or affirmation must be "administered in a form calculated to awaken the witness's conscience and impress the witness's mind with the duty to [testify truthfully]." Failure to tell the truth exposes the witness to a charge of perjury.

TESTILYING

It's an open secret among defense lawyers, prosecutors, and judges that police officers occasionally bend the truth while testifying. The practice is common enough that the term *testilying* has been coined to describe it. Testilying takes place when an officer molds the facts to better suit the prosecution case.

It's important to understand that the vast majority of police officers are decent, honest people. Many, however, see no problem in telling a "white lie" to help convict a guilty person. In effect, testilying is an attempt to frame a guilty person. Police officers are realists. They understand that trials are always chancy affairs and nobody can predict what a jury will do (which is how it should be; a trial in which conviction is assured is not a trial). Many officers see testilying merely as a means to enhance the odds of getting the "right" verdict. Their motives are understandable; it's frustrating to see a person you believe to be guilty walk out of court. It's understandable—but it doesn't make it right.

Testilying is difficult to prove. Many legal experts believe the detectives in the O. J. Simpson case were testilying when they claimed Simpson was not a suspect when they climbed over the fence onto his property. Anytime a woman is killed in a crime of rage (and the extreme violence done to Nicole Brown Simpson clearly indicated it was a crime of rage), the most obvious first suspect is the husband/boyfriend or former husband/boyfriend. If Simpson was not immediately a suspect, he should have been. However, if Simpson *had* been a suspect, then entering his property without his permission or without a search warrant would have been an illegal search. Any evidence that resulted from that illegal search (such as the bloody glove) would have been suppressed. It may be that the detectives were faced with the choice between admitting to an illegal search or falsely testifying that Simpson was not a suspect.

Although witnesses who lie under oath are vulnerable to a charge of perjury, the fact is such charges are rarely pursued. It's very difficult to prove that a witness had actual knowledge of the truth and deliberately lied. For the most part perjury charges are brought by prosecutors only as an attempt to coerce cooperation in another matter or in high publicity cases. Los Angeles detective Mark Fuhrman was charged with perjury as a result of his testimony in the 1995 Simpson murder trial. The basis for the charge was not his claim that he didn't view Simpson as a suspect when he climbed the wall onto Simpson's private property (see page 184), but his claim that he had not used the word "nigger" in the preceding ten years.

Direct Examination

After the witness is sworn in, the lawyer who called the witness begins the direct examination. A witness called by the prosecution is, of course, questioned first by the prosecution. Under direct examination, the witness reveals the facts thought to be supportive and pertinent to the case.

The testimony of the witness is limited to what the witness actually saw, heard, or did. With few exceptions witnesses are not allowed to speculate or give opinions. The exceptions are commonsense exceptions—a witness, for example, is usually permitted to testify to a person's apparent state of intoxication or to the general speed of a moving vehicle. Expert witnesses, once the judge is convinced of their expertise in a given field, are allowed to give opinions relevant to the case. For example, a psychiatrist may testify in regard to a defendant's mental state at the time of the crime.

For the most part, witnesses in direct examination may not be asked leading questions. A leading question is one in which the answer is suggested. For example, the prosecutor may ask a police officer, "What did you observe in the defendant's car?" This gives the officer the opportunity to state what he observed. But the prosecutor may *not* ask the officer, "You saw a gun on the floorboard of the defendant's car, didn't you?" This informs the officer how the prosecutor wants him to answer. A leading question is actually a statement posed as a question.

Leading the witness is grounds for objection (see page 190). As with nearly all legal issues, there are exceptions to the rule against asking leading questions during direct examination. For example, some leeway is granted when questioning children. The most common exception, however, is for hostile witnesses. A hostile witness (also called an adverse witness) is one who has information pertinent to the side calling the witness, but who may not want to cooperate with them. A prosecutor, for example, might call a close friend of the defendant to testify. If the friend is uncooperative on the stand, the prosecutor may ask the judge to declare him a hostile witness, thus permitting the use of leading questions.

Cross-examination

Once the prosecutor finishes the direct examination, the defense lawyer has the opportunity to question the witness. This is known as *cross-examination*. Cross-examination is intended to cast a different light on the information brought out during direct examination. For example, a witness might testify under direct examination that she clearly observed the defendant leaving the scene of the crime carrying the victim's purse. In cross-examination the defense lawyer will point out that the witness wears glasses, that the sunlight was in her eyes and shaded the face of the person she saw, that the person was actually carrying a gym bag rather than a purse, and that she assumed the person was the defendant because he was about the right height and weight. Cross-examination is designed to create an alternate image in the minds of the jury.

Unlike direct examination, leading questions are permitted on cross-examination. Leading questions allow the defense attorney to control the witness and the information revealed to the jury. It's a mistake, however, to believe that cross-examination is intended to discover information. Trial lawyers are trained never to ask a question they don't already know the answer to. Cross-examination is the attorney's chance to use the witness to present the defendant's side of the story.

Redirect Examination

After the defense has completed the cross-examination of the witness, the prosecution has another opportunity to ask questions. This is called *redirect examination*. The purpose of redirect is to rehabilitate the witness— to correct any misunderstandings and clarify any confusing points that might have been raised during cross-examination.

186

The scope of redirect, however, is limited. The prosecutor is required to restrict his questions to the testimony brought out in cross-examination. The prosecutor can't elicit any new information. For example, if the defense only cross-examined the witness in regard to her identification of the defendant, the prosecution can't use redirect to ask the witness about any earlier contacts with the defendant. That would exceed the scope of the cross-examination.

The defense may then re-cross-examine the witness about the information covered during the redirect. In theory this process could continue for several iterations, each more narrowly focused than the last. Trial lawyers, however, understand that juries may find such tactics more irritating than illuminating.

This process is the same for each witness called by the prosecution. It continues until the prosecution has presented all its evidence. At that point the prosecution rests its case.

Motion to Dismiss

At the end of the prosecution case, the defense routinely files a motion to dismiss the case.* The grounds for the motion may vary somewhat, but the motion usually asserts that the prosecution has failed to meet its burden, that the prosecution didn't prove one or more of the elements of the crime, and that there isn't enough evidence to merit continuing the case.

Although trial judges have the discretion to grant a motion to dismiss and free the defendant immediately, they are extremely reluctant to do so. The prosecution has to severely botch a trial or the evidence has to be extremely tainted in order for the judge to grant a dismissal before the defense case-in-chief. Even a judge who believes the evidence against the defendant is skimpy and unlikely to bring a conviction will generally allow the case to continue and go to the jury.

A dismissal during trial is legally equivalent to an acquittal. If the case against the defendant is dismissed, he is protected from facing trial on that same charge again.

•In some jurisdictions this is known as a Motion for a Directed Verdict.

DOUBLE JEOPARDY

Among the provisions of the Fifth Amendment of the Constitution is the following: no person shall "be subject for the same offence to be twice put in jeopardy of life or limb." This means a person accused of a crime and acquitted of that crime cannot be tried for the same crime again. The prosecution gets one attempt, and only one attempt, to prove its case. Knowing this, prosecutors may be reluctant to bring forward cases they don't believe they can win. They would generally prefer to dismiss a case before it becomes subject to jeopardy, hoping that new evidence might make it possible to try the accused at some point in the future.

The general rule is that jeopardy attaches when the trial begins. In most instances this takes place as soon as the first juror is sworn in. At any point up to that time the prosecution can dismiss the case without prejudice, leaving open the possibility of a future prosecution.

As with almost every legal issue, there are ways to get around double jeopardy. A person acquitted in a state court may still be charged under a different statute in a federal court. The Supreme Court has held that this is not a violation of the double jeopardy clause. This is what happened in the case of the four Los Angeles police officers accused of beating Rodney King. The officers were tried in a California court on charges of assault with a deadly weapon and the use of excessive force by a police officer. All four officers were acquitted. Later the four were charged with the federal crime of willfully depriving King of his civil rights. Even though the charge was based on the same exact events, this was seen as a separate crime tried in a different jurisdiction. In the federal case two of the four officers were convicted.

Another method of getting around the double jeopardy clause is for the victim or victim's family to file a civil lawsuit. Civil suits and criminal trials are entirely different creatures, and therefore not subject to double jeopardy. After O. J. Simpson was acquitted of the murder of his ex-wife and her friend, the families of the victims filed wrongful death lawsuits against him. Although the accusation was the same—that Simpson had caused the deaths of Nicole Brown Simpson and Ronald Goldman—the legal process and the potential sanctions were radically different. In the criminal case Simpson's freedom was at jeopardy; in the civil suit only his money was at risk.

Defense Case-in-Chief

After the prosecution has finished presenting its case (and assuming the defense motion to dismiss is rejected), the defense has the opportunity to present its case-in-chief. This mirrors the process just completed by the prosecution. The only difference is that now the defense conducts the direct and redirect examinations and the prosecution has the opportunity to cross-examine the defense witnesses. The defense lawyer is subject to the same restrictions against leading questions.

The defense case-in-chief has one distinct disadvantage: the witnesses called by the prosecution usually include uniformed police officers, police detectives, police evidence technicians, and expert witnesses. Each of these people will have received training on how to testify in court. Most of them will have had prior experience testifying. They will be less nervous and better able to phrase their answers to assist their side than will the defense witnesses. The vast majority of defense witnesses, by contrast, have never appeared in court.

The defense case generally takes less time to present. This is true primarily because the defense is under no obligation to prove anything. The prosecution has to prove every single element of their case beyond a reasonable doubt. The defense has only to establish uncertainty in the minds of the jurors. Because the defense has nothing to prove there are usually fewer defense witnesses.

Prosecution Rebuttal

After the defense has rested its case-in-chief, the prosecution normally has the opportunity to respond to the defense evidence. This is known as *rebuttal*. The scope of rebuttal is limited to the evidence presented by the defense. The prosecutor may attack that evidence, but isn't allowed to introduce new unrelated evidence. Nor can the prosecutor use rebuttal to re-examine the prosecution case-in-chief. The purpose of rebuttal is simply to respond to the evidence presented by the defense.

OBJECTIONS

A criminal trial is a contest. Trial lawyers, including both defense attorneys and prosecutors, are notoriously competitive. Each side attempts to get an edge on the other. Throughout the trial each side will occasionally object to the tactics, evidence introduced, or questions posed by their opponent.

The form in which objections are made has been molded by legal tradition. The attorney objects, giving the grounds for the objection. There may be a debate between the lawyers about the nature and merits of the objection. The judge will make a ruling either to sustain the objection and block the offending behavior or to overrule the objection and allow the opposing lawyer to continue. If the objection is overruled the objecting attorney will often request the objection be noted in the record, preserving it in case of an appeal.

The grounds for objection are manifold. The following are some of the more commonplace objections:

- **Relevance.** A lawyer may object if the evidence or testimony being offered is irrelevant to the case. For example, the fact that a witness is behind on his child support payments would not be relevant to his ability to identify the defendant as the person who committed the crime.
- **Materiality.** Evidence and testimony must be material to the case. In other words, it must be of some importance. A lawyer can object to evidence or testimony if it's immaterial. The prosecution, for example, might introduce a credit card receipt showing the defendant was in the vicinity of the crime scene around the time it was committed. However, an itemized list of what the defendant purchased may not be material.
- **Competence.** The witness must be competent to provide testimony. A lawyer can object to testimony the witness is incompetent to provide. The clerk who sold the defendant a box of rat poison, for example, isn't competent to testify how much rat poison it would take to kill the victim.
- **Hearsay.** A witness is generally not allowed to testify as to what another person said if that other person is available to

testify. There are many exceptions to the hearsay rule, however. Some of the more common exceptions are: a *dying declaration*—somebody who witnesses the final statements of a dying person (and that person must be aware he or she is dying) can testify to the person's dying declaration; a *defendant's admissions*—if the defendant makes a guilty admission to somebody that person may testify about the admission; an *assertion of state of mind*—a person hearing a statement made by the subject about his or her state of mind is usually allowed to testify as to that statement; *prior inconsistent statements*—a witness is to testify as to an inconsistent statement made by the defendant or another witness.

- **Foundation.** A lawyer is not allowed to introduce evidence until facts are presented in court establishing its authenticity. For example, before the prosecution can introduce photographs of the murder scene, the prosecutor must first have the photographer testify about taking the photographs.
- **Scope.** As already discussed, a lawyer is not allowed to ask questions beyond the scope of the previous examination.
- **Best evidence.** The best example of real evidence must, when possible, be introduced. A photocopy of an insurance policy, for example, would not be admissible if the original document is available.
- **Speculation.** A witness is not allowed to speculate, but only to testify as to what he or she saw, heard, or did. The witness who sold the defendant the box of rat poison, for example, is not allowed to surmise about what the defendant intended to do with the rat poison.
- **Argumentative.** A lawyer can object to the opposing counsel asking questions or making comments intended to provoke the witness rather than probe for information.

Objections are used strategically. In some instances the lawyers will offer an objection knowing it will be overruled simply to preserve the record for an appeal. At other times the lawyers will offer objections merely to disrupt the rhythm of their opponent.

For example, if the defense indicates that another person observed near the crime scene may have committed the crime, the prosecution is permitted to offer evidence to show the other person was in the area to attend a Bible study class and can account for his whereabouts at all times. However, the prosecutor would not be allowed to introduce a new witness who saw the defendant near the crime scene. That would be beyond the scope of the defense case.

Closing Arguments

After all the evidence has been introduced and all the witnesses have testified, the prosecutor and the defense attorney have one final opportunity to present their cases to the jury. These are the closing (or final) arguments. Like opening statements, closing arguments are not evidence. They are, rather, the attorney's interpretation of the evidence and are intended to persuade the jury to reach a certain verdict.

In many jurisdictions the prosecution, as the party with the burden of proof, is given the choice of giving its closing argument first or second. Understandably, the prosecution usually elects to have the last word.

Obviously, the prosecution will seek to convince the jury that they have met their burden—that they have proved beyond a reasonable doubt that the defendant committed all the elements of the crime with which he was charged. The prosecution will ask for a verdict of guilty. Just as obviously, the defense attorney will attempt to persuade the jury that the prosecution failed to meet its burden of proof—that reasonable doubt exists in regard to whether the defendant committed the crime, or in regard to the defendant's intent, or in regard to one or more elements of the crime. Each side will point out the merits of its own case and the weaknesses and defects of the opposing counsel's case. Each side will urge the jury to come to the "right" decision, even though they disagree what the "right" verdict is.

Closing arguments are often considered to be the most dramatic and critical part of the trial. It is, after all, the very last chance for the lawyers to sway the jury. However, research indicates that most jurors have their minds made up before closing arguments are made and relatively few change them as a result of the arguments.

THE WHOLE TRUTH

"... and nothing but the truth." Detective Dietz lowered his hand and took his place on the witness stand.

It was the afternoon of the first day of the trial. David Van Buskirk was delighted at how well it was going. It had been a little awkward at the beginning. He couldn't present the evidence in a logical fashion. The case had begun with the discovery of Ann Sayers's skeleton, but since Brooks wasn't on trial for killing Sayers—and hadn't even been charged with it—they couldn't discuss her skeleton. He'd had to put on Sgt. Wilton of the Calhoun County Sheriff's Department to state that while he and other officers were at Marshtown Park on another matter they'd discovered the body of Carla Willis.

There had also been a slight problem when Van Buskirk added a new witness to the list. Dennis Fazio. Liza Walsh had objected, of course, and called it trial by ambush . . . but the fact was they'd just discovered Fazio. He'd been arrested for possession of narcotics with intent to sell, but told the investigating officers he could provide some valuable information in a murder case . . . if they cut him a deal. Fazio told investigators he'd been selling Rohypnol to Colin Brooks for a couple of years.

Judge Keegan had hesitated, but decided to allow Fazio as a witness.

After that, the evidence had gone in as smooth as butter. And now Detective Dietz was ready to make the case. He was an old pro at this, Van Buskirk knew. Dietz had been testifying in capital murder cases for a decade or more. He was calm, quietly professional, and juries loved him.

Dietz was so good, in fact, that all Van Buskirk had to do was feed him simple questions. "What did you do next, Detective?" "And then what did you do, Detective?" "Were you able to draw any conclusions from that, Detective?"

Dietz's direct examination took up the rest of the afternoon. The court was recessed for the night; the following morning Liza Walsh began her cross-examination.

"Detective Dietz," she said, "you stated in your testimony yesterday that Mr. Brooks was a suspect even before you went to his home to interview him."

"That's correct, ma'am."

"But he wasn't your first suspect in the case, was he?"

Dietz hesitated. "No ma'am."

"There was another person you suspected of this crime, isn't that correct."

"Yes ma'am, that's correct," Dietz said. "But we were able to eliminate him as a suspect."

"You eliminated him as a suspect because he told you he was out of town at the time of the murder."

"Yes ma'am, because of that and because he was able to produce credit card receipts showing he was in Minnesota at the time the murder took place."

Walsh nodded. "It's not difficult for one person to use another person's credit card, is it Detective?"

"I'm not sure I understand your question."

"Let me give you an example," Walsh said. "If I had your wife's credit card, it wouldn't be difficult for me to go to . . . let's say New York—and use that credit card to buy a pair of gloves from Bloomingdale's."

"No, it wouldn't be difficult," Dietz admitted. Then he grinned. "But I'm sure I'd notice when I got my monthly statement. My wife doesn't spend that kind of money on gloves," he said. The jury chuckled.

"Perhaps I should take your wife shopping," Walsh said, getting a slightly bigger laugh. Two can play at charming the jury, she said to herself. "You mentioned the receipts . . . you didn't check the signature on the receipts to the signature of your original suspect, did you?"

Again Dietz hesitated. "I don't think we did; no ma'am."

"You can't say for certain that your original suspect was in Minnesota at the time of the murder, can you?"

"Not with one hundred percent certainty, no."

"Detective Dietz, do you normally dismiss a person as a suspect so casually?" Walsh asked.

"It wasn't a casual decision," Dietz said. "Nor was he a serious suspect. He was a suspect simply because he was the one who found the skeleton in the—"

"May we have a sidebar, your honor?" Walsh asked Judge Keegan.

The jury watched in confusion as Van Buskirk and Walsh huddled with the judge, whispering furiously. Judge Keegan held up a hand to silence them.

"We'll excuse the jury for a while," she said. And the jurors were hustled from the courtroom.

"Your honor, I have to move for an immediate mistrial," Liza Walsh said as soon as the door closed behind the jurors. "This jury has been tainted. The witness's reference to the skeleton of—"

"Nonsense, your honor," Van Buskirk interrupted. "It was at most a harmless error and a simple instruction to ignore the remark would suffice to—"

"Ignore the mention of a skeleton?" Walsh asked. "It's insane to expect a juror to wipe her mind clear of something like that. It would be—"

"I have more faith in the jury than you, it seems," Van Buskirk said. "I'm confident they can separate—"

Judge Keegan held up a hand for silence. "One at a time, please. Go ahead Ms. Walsh."

The judge sighed deeply. She nodded as each lawyer argued the point, but she only gave them part of her attention. She knew the arguments, and they were both compelling. She hated to make decisions like this. Had the jury been tainted? Or would they be able to overlook the comment? Did they even catch the reference to a skeleton? And even if they had, would they make the deduction that there was a second body in the park? Was it worth the trouble and expense of having to impanel a new jury?

Judge Keegan sighed again. "I've made my decision," she said. "Ms. Walsh, your motion for a mistrial is denied. I'll instruct the jury that the mention of the skeleton was inadvertent, that it is entirely and completely unrelated to this case, that they should forget they'd heard it, and that it most certainly should not be considered during deliberations."

"Your honor," Walsh said, "I have to obje—"

"Your objection is noted," Judge Keegan said. "Bailiff, bring the jury back in, please."

And so the trial went on. Each day new prosecution witnesses added more evidence. The lab techs, the DNA specialists, the people who had seen Brooks and Willis together at a bar, the waitress at the diner who had served breakfast to Willis and Brooks on the day Willis disappeared, the police photographers who developed and printed the pictures Brooks had taken of Willis on the last day of her life.

Each day Van Buskirk felt more confident, and each day Walsh felt more hopeless.

During a recess, Colin Brooks and Liza Walsh retired to a conference room. He asked her how she thought the trial was going.

"It's not going well," she said.

Brooks nodded. "I want to testify," he said.

"I don't think that would be a good idea," Walsh said.

"I want to tell the jury that I didn't do it."

Walsh nodded. "I understand," she said. "But it's very risky. Once you're on the witness stand you're pretty much on your own. I can't protect you very much. I strongly recommend against it."

"I want the jury to know my side of the story," Brooks said.

Walsh sighed. "And which version of your story did you want to tell them?" she asked. "The prosecutor would like nothing more than for you to get up on the witness stand. He'd go after you like a wolverine."

"You really think it's that bad an idea?" Brooks asked.

"Yes, I do," she said. "It's your decision to make, but I suggest you don't do it."

"I want to do it," he said.

Walsh nodded. "I'll put you on last, then," she said. "That will give you a bit more time to come to your senses and change your mind."

She started to leave the conference room, then stopped. "This is why I've never asked you if you're guilty," she said. "If you'd said yes, I wouldn't be able to put you on the stand."

....

Liza Walsh looked at the jurors, trying to gauge their feelings from their faces. There were a couple of potential doubters, she thought. I need to convince one of them, just one.

"Ladies and gentlemen, this is my last chance to talk to you," she said. "My last chance—Colin Brooks's last chance—to discuss the evidence of this case. The evidence, ladies and gentlemen; not the mass of speculation and supposition put forth by the prosecution.

"And what does the evidence really show? It shows Colin Brooks knew Carla Willis and that he took some photographs of her, as she requested. It shows Mr. Brooks and Ms. Willis had sexual intercourse. And that's it. Where's the crime in that?

"The prosecution claims the intercourse was forced—but there's no physical evidence to suggest that. There is none of the bruising and other trauma normally associated with rape. In fact, there is no evidence, physical or otherwise, that Mr. Brooks committed this crime. The prosecution's entire case rests on the supposition that simply because Mr. Brooks was the last person *known* to have seen Ms. Willis alive that he therefore must be the killer.

"You've heard Mr. Brooks testify. He didn't have to testify. He's not required to. But he wanted you to hear his side of the story. He wanted to get up on the witness stand and proclaim his innocence. Did he seem nervous to you? Of course he did. His life is at stake here, he's terrified. Who wouldn't be? Imagine yourself in a similar position. You do a favor for somebody, and afterward that person takes some type of drug and then begins to behave strangely. She rushes off . . . and is later found dead. You're the last known person to see her alive. Suspicion naturally falls on you. It's like a nightmare.

"Mr. Brooks is living that nightmare, ladies and gentlemen. Has he behaved like a killer? No, not at all. As you heard in the testimony, none of his friends noticed any change in his behavior after Carla Willis disappeared. Mr. Brooks even cooperated with the police. If he was guilty of this

197

crime, would he have invited them into his house? Would he have sat in his living room discussing it with them? Would he have allowed one of the detectives to go wandering willy-nilly around his home unsupervised? No, no, of course he wouldn't. Mr. Brooks cooperated with the police up until the moment they arrested him—and then he exercised his constitutional right to consult a lawyer.

Walsh paused a moment. "Ladies and gentlemen, I've told you that Mr. Brooks is not a criminal. That's not entirely true. Mr. Brooks has, on occasion, purchased drugs illegally. The prosecution put on a witness—Dennis Fazio, a drug dealer facing his own criminal charges, a drug dealer who agreed to testify against the defendant in exchange for a lighter sentence. This pusher testified that on occasion Mr. Brooks would purchase a few tablets of Rohypnol.

"Now, that does sound suspicious. But you heard Mr. Brooks testify as to why he bought those drugs. As a freelance photographer he has very limited health care insurance. He also suffers from occasional insomnia. Rohypnol is a sleeping pill. Now, he could go to a doctor and get a prescription for sleeping pills. It would only cost him, say, one hundred dollars to see the doctor and another twenty to thirty dollars to fill the prescription. Or he could go see Dennis Fazio and buy a few nights of sleep for a few dollars a pill. Now I'm not saying it's right, I'm not saying Mr. Brooks is justified in breaking the law—but I am saying it's understandable why he did it.

"And that's the entire case, ladies and gentlemen. A mixed bag of supposition, coincidence, and hocus pocus. This is a case built on a foundation of doubt.

"I want each of you, when you go into the deliberation room, to think about each separate element of this case. I want you to carefully weigh each bit of evidence for what it's really worth, not for what the prosecution says it's worth. And I want you to ask yourself the following question: Am I certain beyond any reasonable doubt that the prosecution has proven each and every one of these elements?

"I feel confident, if you answer that question, you'll reach the correct verdict. And I submit to you the only possible verdict in this case is not guilty."

David Van Buskirk stood slowly. "My learned colleague Ms. Walsh suggested you judge this case based on the evidence. I have to agree with her about that. I disagree with her, however, on what that evidence shows. She thinks her client is misunderstood, a hapless casualty of fate and freakish coincidence. She thinks he just happened to be in the wrong place at the wrong time, that he just happened to be the last person to see Carla Willis alive. She thinks he just happened to buy a few tabs of Rohypnol, a drug known as the "date rape drug," a few days before Carla Willis was murdered while she was unconscious. Ms. Walsh thinks Carla Willis just happened to have enough Rohypnol in her system to render her completely unconscious. Ms. Walsh thinks her client is a victim.

"Well, we know who the real victim is here," Van Buskirk said. "It's Carla Ann Willis. It's a young woman murdered in the prime of her life . . . drugged into oblivion, raped, and strangled. And despite what Ms. Walsh would have you believe, every iota of evidence points directly at her client, at Colin Brooks."

He turned and pointed directly at Brooks, holding the pose for a long moment. It was a nice trial move he'd learned from an old prosecutor. Anything the client does in response makes him look guilty. If he stares back while you're pointing at him he looks hostile and confrontational. If he looks away he appears to have a guilty conscience.

"This man denied to Detective Dietz that he knew Carla Willis, and yet all the while in his office he had four rolls of film with her photographs on them and a model release form signed by—"

"Objection, your honor," Walsh said. "That's not an accurate representation of the detective's testimony. The prosecutor is misleading the—"

"Misleading?" Van Buskirk. "How dare—"

"Quiet, please," Judge Keegan said. "The jury can use its own recollection of the testimony of Detective Dietz. And I'll take this opportunity to remind you, ladies and gentlemen of the jury, that what these lawyers say is not evidence. It's only argument. You may proceed now Mr. Van Buskirk."

It took a moment for Van Buskirk to collect his thoughts. Which was exactly what Liza Walsh had hoped. The objection was a legitimate one, but objections during closing arguments are rare. She'd objected in part to throw Van Buskirk off his stride.

It worked for a brief time, but Van Buskirk soon regained his pace and momentum. He covered the evidence point by point. Perhaps in too much detail, Walsh hoped. Maybe he'll bore the jury to the point that they'll vote for an acquital.

"Ladies and gentlemen, you have a great and terrible burden laid on you. You have to judge the guilt or innocence of one of your fellow citizens. When you enter the jury room you have the fate of Colin Brooks in your hands. While you're deliberating, I'll ask you to remember that Colin Brooks once held the fate of Carla Ann Willis in his hands. And we know what he did. I'll ask you to keep Carla Willis in your mind and in your hearts . . . and do the right thing. Find Colin Brooks guilty."

It was late in the afternoon. Judge Keegan decided to let the jury go home and return in the morning for instruction on deliberating. The jury filed out. The judge returned to her chambers. The sheriff's deputies escorted Brooks back to the county jail. The spectators departed. David Van Buskirk and Liza Walsh packed their briefcases and left the courtroom. The bailiff turned off the courtroom lights.

THE VERDICT

The jury system has existed in various forms since at least the fourth century B.C. The ancient Greeks used a singularly complex jury system that might require as many as twenty-five hundred jurors on an important case. Roman juries consisted of fifty-one jurors. Every town in ancient Israel with a population of more than one hundred and twenty used a twenty-three person *Sanhedrin* to judge criminal cases. In England in 1166 the Assize of Novel Disseizin set down the provision for "twelve good men and true" to hear and decide on property disputes.* The system worked so well that it was soon used in all manner of civil suits and, eventually, criminal cases. By some point in the fourteenth century, the twelve-person jury became fixed in tradition supreme court. Supreme Court Justice Byron White has referred to this as a "historical accident, unrelated to the great purpose which gave rise to the jury in the first place."

Juries are the wild card of the criminal justice system. After all the evidence and arguments, in the end it comes down to twelve common citizens chosen from the community, judging one of their own. Because the

---

*Following his conquest of England in 1066, William the Conqueror divided the land his army had wrested by force from the Saxons among various of his followers. Although they only held the land in the King's name, property disputes were common and bitterly argued. A hundred years after the Norman Conquest, the disputes were equally acrimonious but even more complex.

people who become jurors have all the flaws and idiosyncrasies of the general population, juries sometimes reach verdicts that are wildly out of sync with the facts. Sometimes they base their verdicts on singularly peculiar and meaningless scraps of information, or on some eccentric misinterpretation of the evidence. Juries are by no means perfect instruments of justice. And yet in the vast majority of cases they manage to cobble together a verdict that is remarkably close to justice.

Jury Instruction

A jury, it's been said, is composed of twelve people of average ignorance. This is as accurate as it is cynical. The fact is, most citizens of the United States don't have a good grasp on how our legal system works. Their understanding of juries and appropriate jury behavior is based largely on television and movies (in which juries tend to be either incompetent or filled with amateur detectives).

But to say a jury is ignorant of the law isn't to say jurors are stupid. Lawyers, after all, have to go through four years of intensive study and training in law school and then must pass a rigorous bar examination before they're allowed to practice law. The law is intricate and it's really asking too much to expect a jury of ordinary people to suddenly begin thinking like legal scholars.

Because of this the judge, before allowing the jury to deliberate, will instruct the jurors on the appropriate factors they should consider in reaching their verdict. This includes the matters of law the jury should keep in mind, the elements of the crime, the type of evidence required to prove each element beyond a reasonable doubt, a definition of that phrase, and a reminder about the burden of proof. Most jury instructions are standardized, often contained in books used by several different jurisdictions. In addition to the standard jury instructions, the judge may solicit further instructions from the prosecutor and defense attorney. The judge will read the jury instructions aloud to the jury (in a murder case this may take as long as two hours). In most jurisdictions the judge will also provide the jury with a written copy of the instructions.

Deliberations

Once the jury has been instructed by the court, the jurors move to the deliberation chamber. In some jurisdictions the judge will have appointed a jury foreperson, in others the first duty of the jury is to elect a foreperson.*

It's at this point that the jurors finally get to discuss the case. Prior to deliberations, jurors are repeatedly warned *not* to discuss the case with anybody—not with family, friends, or other jurors. This is to prevent the jurors from reaching conclusions before they've heard all the testimony and seen all the evidence. At every lunch break and at the end of every day of the trial the judge repeats the admonition for the jury not to talk about the case. If a juror is discovered to have discussed the case, that juror may be dismissed from the jury. If the breach is serious enough, a mistrial might be called and the prosecution will have to decide whether or not to re-try the case.

There are other rules a juror is required to follow or face dismissal. Jurors are required to:

- **Stay awake during the testimony.** This may sound comical, but a criminal trial can be mind-numbingly dull at times. Remember, before introducing some critical evidence, the attorney is required to lay a foundation. This often means the jury must listen to long, esoteric scientific explanations. As discussed in the section on attorney misconduct, it can even be difficult for the lawyers to remain awake.
- **Remain free from mind- or mood-altering substances.** Jurors who are taking some prescription medicines might be excluded from serving on the jury. In addition, jurors need to refrain from any recreational drink or drugs during the lunch breaks.

---

*In jurisdictions where the jury foreperson is elected by the jury members, the judge includes a jury instruction advising how the election should be conducted.

- **Refrain from discussion with either the defense attorney or the prosecutor.** A juror must remain impartial.
- **Refrain from conducting independent investigations.** The jury must rely only on the evidence and testimony presented in court. Jurors aren't allowed to investigate the crime on their own time. In one of the best jury movies ever made, *Twelve Angry Men*, the character played by Henry Fonda visits the neighborhood where the crime took place. While there he buys a knife similar to the one used in the crime. This might be good drama, but it's also juror misconduct. In a real trial Fonda would have been dismissed from the jury and the trial likely would have ended in a mistrial.
- **Refrain from conducting independent experiments.** Unscientific experiments might lead the jury to base its verdict on misleading and unreliable results. In a trial that hinged in part on how quickly bite marks on flesh fade, one juror actually agreed to be bitten on the arm by another juror. This experiment became known after the trial and on appeal the conviction was overturned based on this flawed attempt at research.

Discussion of testimony and evidence by the jury takes place only in the deliberation room—nowhere else. Not in the hallways, not in the restroom, not in the lunchroom. And deliberations requires the presence of all the jurors. If one leaves to use the restroom, deliberations are suspended. That's the theory, at any rate. Reality, as usual, is a lot less tidy.

The actual process of deliberation varies from jury to jury. There is no particular method imposed on the jury for reaching a verdict. Some begin by systematically discussing each of the elements of the crime to see if the prosecution has proven its case. Some vote immediately to see if there is any consensus, then debate the issues. Some cast open ballots, some prefer to keep the initial voting a secret.

Regardless of the method used, research shows that the vast majority of jurors take their work very seriously. They go about the business of justice with great deliberation (hence the name of the process).

Even though jurors in most jurisdictions are now allowed to take notes during the trial,* they often find they have different memories of the testimony given or the evidence introduced. On occasion, jurors also have conflicting notions about crucial points of law. When this happens, the foreperson can send the judge written questions or requests to examine evidence or have testimony read back to them.

There is no set time limit imposed on jury deliberations. Jurors are given as much time as needed to reach a *unanimous* verdict. All verdicts in criminal cases require unanimity. In order to convict a person of a crime—to label the defendant as a criminal and deprive him of his freedom—each of the twelve jurors must be convinced beyond a reasonable doubt of his guilt. So long as a jury is making progress toward reaching a verdict, the judge allows the deliberations to continue.

In many jurisdictions, judges have the power to issue what is known as an *Allen charge*† if the jury appears to become hopelessly deadlocked. An Allen charge is another jury instruction in which jurors are told they have an obligation to do everything possible to reach a unanimous verdict. It also states that, while each individual juror is expected to reach an independent decision regarding the defendant's guilt or innocence, a holdout juror may want to re-examine his or her opinion in light of the contrary majority opinion. This is a rather controversial charge, believed by many to be unduly coercive against holdout jurors.

Sequestration

Sequestration is the practice of keeping the members of the jury together and separating them from outside influences. Sequestration of the jury is increasingly rare. It's a tremendous burden on the jurors and their families. It's also exceedingly expensive to the State, which is responsible for the costs of sequestration. As noted earlier, it cost the government approximately $2.5 million to house and feed the jury during the O. J. Simpson trial.

---

*This is a rather recent development; traditionally jurors were discouraged or actually prohibited from taking notes. It was thought jurors would lose track of the testimony while they were busily scribbling comments to themselves. Most jurors, even those who don't take the opportunity to make notes, report feeling more confident about the process when they are allowed to do so.

†Named for the Supreme Court case *Allen v. U.S.*, which permitted the practice.

In the vast majority of murder cases, jurors are allowed to come to court in the morning and go home at the end of the working day, after being warned by the judge not to discuss the case. Given the serious nature of murder cases, however, many juries are sequestered during deliberations. However, in very high publicity murder cases—such as the Simpson case—jurors and alternate jurors are sequestered from the very start in order to prevent them from being inadvertently exposed to reports about the crime.

The Verdict

Jury deliberations have three possible outcomes: guilty, not guilty,* and deadlocked (also referred to as a hung jury). A hung jury, as has been noted, results in a mistrial.

Assuming a unanimous verdict is reached, the jury foreman fills out a verdict form and notifies the bailiff. The judge recalls the interested parties—the prosecutor, the defense attorney, the defendant—to the courtroom. The jury foreperson presents the verdict form to the bailiff, who gives it to the judge. The verdict is then read aloud.

After the reading of the verdict, the losing party generally requests that the jury be polled. The clerk of court will then ask each individual juror to state his or her verdict on each of the charges. This is to ensure that the verdict was, in fact, unanimous and that none of the jurors was coerced into voting with the majority.

Jury Nullification

On occasion a jury will ignore the evidence, ignore the testimony, ignore the judge's instructions concerning the law, and reach a verdict in accordance with their own notion of fairness. This is known as *jury nullification*. In effect, the jury acknowledges the defendant is, in fact, guilty of the crime but nonetheless returns a verdict of not guilty. The jury is, in effect, judging the law and not the defendant.

---

*Including "not guilty by reason of insanity" and "guilty but mentally ill."

The concept of jury nullification has been both vilified and celebrated by legal scholars. Clearly, it represents a violation of the juror's duty to the trial court and the criminal justice system. Just as clearly, it represents the right of the community to declare its opposition to laws it finds unjust.

Jury nullification has a long and noble history in English-speaking courts. As early as 1670 a jury in England refused to convict William Penn* of the subversive practice of preaching Quakerism. The government retaliated; the jurors were fined and one was actually imprisoned until another judge ruled jurors could not be punished for their verdicts. In 1735 in New York a jury acquitted newspaper publisher John Peter Zenger of seditious libel, a crime of which he was clearly guilty. Zenger had printed negative but truthful facts about William Cosby, the governor of New York. The law at the time, however, prohibited critical comments about the governor—even if they happened to be true. By refusing to convict Zenger, the jury helped to establish the principle of freedom of the press. We can see similar examples of jury nullification in regard to such volatile issues as slavery, prohibition, opposition to the war in Vietnam. At present we're seeing jury nullification used in "three-strike" cases when jurors learn that conviction for even a relatively minor criminal act will result in a mandatory life sentence.[†]

Verdicts in Capital Cases

In most jurisdictions capital cases are bifurcated; there are two separate stages. First is a guilt phase. This is the trial, the attempt to determine if the accused is guilty of the crime. If the defendant is found guilty the trial enters the second phase—the penalty or sentencing phase. In this stage the determination is made whether the defendant will receive a sentence of death or one of life imprisonment without the possibility of parole.

---

*Penn eventually emigrated to the American colonies and founded the State of Pennsylvania.

[†]Twenty-two states and the federal government have adopted legislation that makes a life sentence mandatory for any person convicted of a third felony, regardless of the nature or severity of the offenses involved. These laws are commonly known as the "three strikes" laws—three strikes and you're out.

In effect, the sentencing phase is a sort of mini-trial. The rules of evidence are considerably more relaxed in the penalty phase. Evidence that would be inadmissible during the guilt phase can be used to help determine the appropriate penalty. This includes a wide range of information about the defendant, the victim, and the nature of the offense itself. Remember, in the penalty phase the defendant has already been found guilty—the presumption of innocence, obviously, doesn't apply.

In some jurisdictions the sentence is determined by the judge, in others the same jury that convicted the defendant makes the determination. The decision whether or not to impose the death penalty is made by weighing aggravating and mitigating factors. Aggravating factors must be proven beyond a reasonable doubt; mitigating factors need only meet the lesser standard of a preponderance of the evidence. If the judge or a unanimous jury decides the aggravating factor(s) substantially outweigh the mitigating factor(s), the defendant is sentenced to die.

Aggravating Factors

An aggravating factor is a fact or circumstance relating to the crime that the prosecutor believes makes the crime more serious, and therefore more deserving of a sentence of death. Different jurisdictions consider different factors to be aggravating. Pennsylvania, for example, recognizes eighteen different aggravating circumstances, whereas Ohio identifies only eight.

Aggravating factors include, but are not limited to, the following:

- During the commission of the murder the defendant knowingly created a great risk of death to more than one person.
- Forced sexual penetration of the victim before, during, or immediately after the commission of the murder.
- The murder was committed for the purpose of avoiding or preventing a lawful arrest or prosecution.
- The defendant committed the murder for money or the promise of money, or hired another to commit the murder for money or the promise of money.

- The victim of the murder was a police officer or a prison guard and was killed in performance of his or her official duty.
- The murder was especially heinous, atrocious, or cruel.*

Victim Impact Statements

Most states give the family of the victim(s) an opportunity to address the court and the defendant during the sentencing phase. During these victim impact statements family members talk of the grief and suffering they've experienced because of the crime. Some states include the suffering of the family as an aggravating factor.

While everybody agrees that victim impact statements are good for the families of murder victims, critics maintain they should have no influence in sentencing. All murders are tragic, critics say, but the offender should not receive a harsher (or less harsh) sentence based on the family's ability to express its grief.

Mitigating Factors

A mitigating factor is any fact or circumstance that suggests a sentence other than death would be appropriate. It might pertain to the facts of the crime, to the defendant's state of mind or physical condition at the time of the crime, to the defendant's character or background—anything that makes the defendant's role in the crime seem less reprehensible or that inspires sympathy, compassion, or mercy for the defendant.

Mitigating factors don't excuse or justify the crime, nor do they reduce the degree of the defendant's blame for the crime. They simply suggest extenuating circumstances.

Mitigating factors include, but are not limited to, the following:

- The defendant had no history of prior criminal activity.
- The victim had at least some complicity in the defendant's conduct.

---

*"Especially heinous, atrocious, or cruel" generally refers to those crimes in which the victim was tortured or subjected to serious physical abuse prior to death.

- The defendant's capacity to appreciate the criminality of his conduct, or to conform his conduct to the requirements of law was impaired.
- The defendant's age.
- The defendant's childhood.

Unanimity

As in the guilt phase, the jury's decision in the penalty phase must be unanimous. Each individual juror must independently decide that the defendant deserves the death penalty—that the aggravating factors have been proven beyond a reasonable doubt and outweigh all the mitigating factors. If one or more jurors isn't convinced, then the jury can't impose a death sentence. Similarly, the decision to sentence the defendant to imprisonment for life without parole must also be unanimous. If one or more jurors doesn't agree the defendant should receive a sentence of life imprisonment without parole, then the jury can't impose a sentence of life imprisonment without parole.

If a jury is unable to reach a unanimous decision on either death or life without parole, the judge is required to impose a standard life sentence. This includes the possibility of parole. Clearly, this is an incentive for the jury to cooperate.

IF YOU FIND...

"Ladies and gentlemen of the jury," Judge Keegan said, "the defendant, Colin Brooks, is charged with the murder in the first degree of Carla Ann Willis on or about the twenty-second day of May, 1999, in Calhoun County."

Judge Keegan had read these same phrases, with slight variations, aloud to juries many times. Each time she was struck by their fragility. She was reminded that these same phrases had been said in courtrooms in English-speaking nations for five hundred years. She was part of a very long tradi-tion—and yet the words she spoke in her judicial voice seemed almost too feeble to express what was going on. A woman—perhaps two women—were dead. A man was on trial for his very life. And she was about to turn five centuries of legal tradition, a family's tragedy, and a man's freedom over to a dozen or so randomly selected citizens. It was a tremendous leap of faith.

"No person may be convicted of murder in the first degree unless the State has proved beyond a reasonable doubt each element of the crime," she read to the jury. "These elements are: first, the death of a human; sec-ond, the death was unlawful; third, the death was caused by the defendant; and fourth, the death was caused with malice aforethought.

"By malice aforethought we mean a deliberate intention to take away the life of a human being. It does not mean hatred, spite, or ill will. The deliberate intent to take a human life must be formed before the act and must exist at the time a homicidal act is committed. No particular length of time is required for formation of this deliberate intent. The intent may have been formed instantly before commission of the act."

She looked at the jury. Some were nodding. Some looked confused already.

"In addition the defendant has been charged with committing murder with an aggravating factor. An aggravating factor is a fact or circumstance relating to the crime that the prosecution has asked you to consider. In this instance the aggravating factor is that the death of Carla Ann Willis occurred as a result of an act or event that happened in the commission of a forcible rape. In order to accept the aggravating factor the prosecution must prove beyond a reasonable doubt that a forcible rape took place. A forcible rape occurs when sexual penetration takes place while the victim was incapable of giving legal consent or when force or violence was used against the victim or threatened against the victim and the defendant had the apparent power to carry out the threat of force or violence."

Judge Keegan was always amazed at how such formal language could suck the horror out of the act it described. And that was part of its purpose. The formality allowed the court to be very specific about the law and yet removed and distant from the crime. Legal decisions, especially those involving life and death, should not be based on emotion.

"If you find beyond a reasonable doubt that the defendant committed the crime of murder in the first degree, you shall return a verdict of guilty by marking the verdict form appropriately."

She looked at the jury and read the next part slowly. "If you have a reasonable doubt of the defendant's guilt to the charge, or if you find that the State has failed to prove each element of the charge beyond a reasonable doubt, you *must* return a verdict of not guilty by marking the verdict form appropriately."

She paused a moment, allowing it to sink in.

"The issue of punishment," she told the jury, "is not before you. Punishment will be determined by this court. You are only to concern yourselves with a determination of guilt."

And with that, the jury was taken into the deliberation room and turned loose to do its job.

....

"Well, here we are."

The jurors began to settle themselves around a long conference table.

"Now what?" somebody asked.

"I think we have a couple of options," the jury foreman said. "We can take a quick secret ballot just to see where we stand, or we can just start at the beginning and review the evidence. And then take a vote."

"Let's take a vote."

"Yeah, a vote."

"Very well," the foreman said. "Everybody take a sheet of paper, write the letter 'G' for guilty or 'N' for not guilty. Then fold the note in half and pass it forward to me."

The vote was eleven to one in favor of guilty.

"Well, that should make things easier," one of the jurors said.

"Who voted not guilty?"

"Shouldn't matter," one said. "The whole point of a secret ballot is that your vote is secret."

"I agree," the foreman said. "Why don't we just start reviewing the evidence and see if that helps clarify things."

After an hour of discussion they took a second secret vote. Again, the vote was eleven to one in favor of guilty.

"We're not getting anywhere," a juror said.

"Maybe the person who's voting not guilty could tell us why," another said.

"That would be putting a lot of pressure on that person," the foreman said.

"I don't mind," a middle-aged man said. "It's me. I'm not entirely convinced that this Brooks guy is guilty beyond a reasonable doubt."

"What do you mean, you're not convinced?"

"I mean I'm not convinced," the holdout said. "Maybe it was like his lawyer said. A coincidence."

"A coincidence," one scoffed.

"It could be," the holdout said. "I mean, nobody saw him strangle her. Who's to say it didn't happen like he said . . . they shot the pictures, she took some drugs and got a little weird and stormed off. That's possible, isn't it?"

"I suppose it's possible, but it's not very likely."

"It's possible yellow bats could fly out of my butt," a juror said.

"All I'm saying is that it's possible," the holdout said. "And if it's possible, then I got a reasonable doubt."

They asked the bailiff if the judge could define reasonable doubt for them again. With the definition in hand they went at it for another hour. Nobody changed their vote.

"Wait a minute, wait a minute," one juror said. He looked at the holdout. "You're saying . . . let me make sure I understand what you're saying. You're saying that it's reasonable to think that all this stuff, that all this evidence, could be on account of a coincidence, am I right?"

The holdout nodded.

"You're saying that maybe the drug the victim took made her loopy enough to run off and leave her only ride back from Marshtown Park to Stormont. Right?"

"Right."

The juror grinned. "Well here's the problem with that. One, we only got the defendant's word that he saw her take some sort of drug. And two, the only drug anybody has talked about finding in her system was this roofie stuff. And that's a sleeping pill. Ain't no sleeping pill gonna make you loopy enough to run off and leave your ride. Only thing a sleeping pill's gonna do is make you go to sleep. Am I right, or am I right?"

The holdout considered for a moment. "You're right," he said.

"Of course I'm right."

"Are you changing your vote then?" the foreman asked.

The holdout nodded.

"Everybody who is in favor of finding Brooks guilty, raise your hand," the foreman said.

All twelve jurors raised their hands.

Several jurors applauded.

"It's nothing to celebrate," one said. "We've just found a man guilty of a capital crime. He could get the death penalty."

....

Judge Keegan thanked the jury and sent them home. Now it fell on her to decide whether or not the crime merited the death penalty. This was the reason she disliked capital cases. This would probably be the reason she would eventually leave the bench. But the law was the law, and in her courtroom it was applied as fairly as it could possibly be. If the prosecution could show the aggravating factors outweighed the mitigating factors, she would have no alternative but to sentence Colin Brooks to death.

The penalty phase was wide open. Since the rules of evidence were relaxed, almost anything that pertained to sentencing was allowed. Judge Keegan heard about the skeletal remains of Bernice Sayers. She heard testimony from some of the eleven women who had accused Brooks of using Rohypnol to incapacitate them for sex. She heard Brooks's ex-wife testify as to his interest in sex with drugged and immobile women.

She also heard from Brooks's mother and sister, who testified that he was a good and decent man in his heart—a dutiful son and a supportive brother. She heard from a psychiatrist who described Brooks's sexual interests as a fairly harmless paraphilia that could be treated with various behavioral therapies.

And in the end Judge Keegan reluctantly had to admit the prosecution had met its burden. She had no choice but to follow the law.

"Colin Brooks, you have been found guilty of the crime of murder in the first degree in the murder of Carla Ann Willis. Based on the evidence presented to this court the aggravating factor of forcible rape has been proven. It is therefore the order of this court that you be taken into custody and held in prison until such time as you may be executed by lethal injection. May God have mercy on you and on this court."

PART FIVE

The Sentence

THE APPEALS PROCESS

It takes a long time to execute a prisoner condemned to death. From 1977 to 1997 the average length of time between sentencing and execution was slightly more than nine years.

The primary reason for the long interval between sentencing and execution is the appeals process. A criminal appeal is essentially a legal proceeding in which a convicted criminal accuses the trial court of having made an error and asks a higher court to correct it.

The U.S. judicial system is a multi-tiered system. Each branch of the judiciary (civil and criminal) contains several layers of courts. Courts hearing criminal cases range from those designed to hear and rule on such matters as municipal traffic offenses to the U.S. Supreme Court, which decides on constitutional issues.

In regard to capital murder cases, there are essentially four tiers of courts: the trial court, state appellate courts, federal appellate courts, and the Supreme Court.

Trial Courts

Murder trials, like the ones we've discussed, take place in trial courts. But there are a wide variety of trial courts. Courts of limited jurisdiction, also known as lower courts, hear less serious matters like traffic violations and simple misdemeanors. More serious criminal matters—aggravated misdemeanors and felonies—are heard in courts of general jurisdiction. Different states have different names for these courts; they are usually called superior courts, district courts, circuit courts, or courts of common pleas (in New York, for some reason, the court of general jurisdiction is known as the supreme court).

The vast majority of murder trials take place in state trial courts. There is a separate federal criminal court system. Federal murder trials are heard in U.S. district courts. However, federal capital murder trials are very rare. In an attempt to appear tough on crime, members of the U.S. Congress have enacted a number of federal capital crimes, but these crimes are seldom committed. Federal capital offenses include the following: murder related to the smuggling of aliens; murder committed at an airport serving international civil aviation; treason; mailing of injurious articles with intent to kill or resulting in death; and murder of a member of Congress, an important executive official, or a Supreme Court Justice.

State Appellate Courts

Since most murder trials take place in state trial courts, most appeals begin in the state appellate system. Again, each state has its own judicial structure. Most states have two levels of appellate courts—an intermediate appellate court and a court of final resort (usually called the state supreme court). A small number of states have no intermediate appellate courts; an appeal in these states goes directly to the state supreme court. A smaller number of states have two intermediate appellate courts.

A person making an appeal is called an appellant. The appeal process begins at the lowest intermediate appellate court. If that court rejects the appeal the appellant can then appeal to the next highest state appeals court. This continues until the appeal is either granted or has been rejected at every level of the state appellate system. At that point the appellant turns to the federal court system, which is discussed later.

The proceedings that take place in appellate courts are radically different from those in trial courts. A single judge oversees the process and makes all the rulings in a trial; appellate courts rely on a panel of judges ranging from three to nine members (there is always an odd number of judges to prevent tie votes). In a trial, the judge or jury bases the verdict on the credibility of the witness testimony and the physical evidence. Appellate courts, however, aren't interested in specific testimony or evidence. Their interest is only whether the trial court properly interpreted the law and used the correct procedure during the trial. This is critical, and deserves to be repeated: Appeal courts aren't interested in the evidence or the testimony; they are concerned only about law and procedure. Appellate judges make their decision after reviewing the trial transcript, reading prepared briefs (written arguments submitted in advance by the opposing parties and others who might have an interest in the outcome), and hearing oral arguments. They do not hear fact witnesses; they do not look at evidence. Appellate judges are not concerned about factual guilt or innocence.

Criminal appeals are generally based on one of two claims. They accuse the trial court of having made an error in regard to the defendant's conviction, or they accuse the trial court of erring in regard to the defendant's sentence.

Appeal of Conviction

When appealing the conviction, the defendant argues that the conviction was improperly or illegally obtained. There are a wide variety of grounds for such an appeal. The appellant may claim the police violated the law in obtaining evidence, or that improper evidence or testimony was put before the jury, or that evidence was hidden from the jury, or that the jury was not an impartial jury, or even that the jury failed in some way to follow the appropriate deliberation process. An appeal of a conviction is based on a flaw in the procedure by which the defendant was convicted.

Most of these claims and arguments would have been made during the trial or the pre-trial hearings. Indeed, the defense *must* object to illegal or improper evidence and testimony in order to make the objection part of the court record. Remember, the appeals court bases its decision primarily on what is reflected in the record. If the defense lawyer fails to make a good record for appeal the defendant's only hope for a review of the conviction might be based on the lawyer's incompetence.

If the court finds the conviction was flawed, it can order the defendant be given a new trial. For example, in 1988 Susie Mowbry went on trial in Texas for shooting her husband to death while he was asleep. The prosecution maintained the motive for the crime was $1.8 million in insurance money. Mowbry claimed her husband had killed himself because of financial difficulties. She was convicted and sentenced to life imprisonment. In her appeal Mowbry claimed the prosecutors concealed blood evidence that contradicted their murder theory. The appeals court agreed the evidence should have been revealed and ordered that Mowbry be given a new trial. Mowbry was acquitted at her second trial—but that's only important to Mowbry. What's important to notice is that the appeals court stated the flaw was in the procedure, not in the evidence itself. The appeals court didn't say anything about Mowbry's factual innocence or guilt; it merely said the procedure used by the trial court was in error and that Mowbry should be given a new trial using correct procedure. Mowbry, by the way, spent nine years in prison before her appeal was granted.

New Evidence of Innocence

As odd as it sounds, it's extremely rare for an appeals court to grant a new trial based on recently discovered evidence of a defendant's innocence. That's because appellate courts aren't about facts, they're about law and procedure.

For the most part the appellate court doesn't care if the appellant is factually guilty or innocent. The court only cares whether the appellant was legally convicted and properly sentenced. It doesn't matter to the appellate judges if the jury in the trial court believed a witness who lied or if another person has confessed to the crime for which the appellant was convicted. So long as the trial court applied the law properly and followed the appropriate procedure, the conviction is legal and stands.

Most states place time limits on the admissibility of new evidence discovered after a conviction. In many states the time allowed to discover and present new evidence is thirty days or less* after the verdict is rendered.

---

*It's thought this rule dates back to the colonial era. Trial courts would delay a final judgment in case there were witnesses traveling from more remote areas of the colony.

This is an exceedingly difficult deadline to meet when the convicted person is in prison and unable to afford a private investigator.

Time limits are only one of the barriers against the use of newly discovered evidence. In order to get a new trial based on newly discovered evidence, the appellant is required to demonstrate that:

- The new evidence was discovered after the trial.
- The failure to learn about the evidence before or during the trial wasn't the result of the defendant's lack of diligence.
- The new evidence is material to the issues at trial.
- The weight and quality of the new evidence would likely result in an acquittal.

Appeals courts are reluctant to overturn a conviction. The vast majority of appeals of convictions are denied. Trial judges are granted a great deal of leeway in the way they handle their trials. An appellate court needs a compelling reason to overrule a decision made by the trial court. The fact is, no criminal defendant is guaranteed a perfect trial—merely a fair one.

Appeal of Sentence

Some appeals do not dispute the process by which the conviction was obtained. Instead they argue that the sentence imposed on the defendant was unfair or too harsh. If the appeals court agrees, the defendant is returned to court to be re-sentenced.

Appeals of sentence generally have more success than appeals of convictions. To my knowledge, no research has been done on why this is so, but I suspect it's due to three reasons. First, an order to re-sentence the defendant doesn't invalidate the verdict reached by a jury. Second, an appeal of sentence is less of a rejection of the trial judge's rulings. Finally, an appeal of sentence is less of a burden on the judicial and criminal justice system. A new trial costs a great deal of money and involves a lot of time and effort.

Although the following is a federal case rather than a state case, it's a good example of an appeal of a sentence. Remember, the appeals court

223

isn't interested in right or wrong, guilt or innocence; the court is concerned only that the proper law and procedures are followed.

In 1995, Michael Fortier pled guilty to various crimes related to the bombing of the Federal Building in Oklahoma City (which killed 168 people and injured more than 500 others). Specifically, Fortier pled guilty to failing to alert authorities about the bombing plot, to helping convicted bombers Timothy McVeigh and Terry Nichols sell stolen weapons, and to lying to the FBI. Fortier was sentenced to serve twelve years in prison. Fortier appealed his sentence, claiming the judge had used the wrong sentencing guidelines and that the sentence imposed on him was therefore too harsh. In sentencing Fortier the judge had used the guidelines for first-degree murder sentences. Fortier argued those guidelines should be used only if evidence demonstrated Fortier acted with malice or if the crime fell under felony murder rules, neither of which applied in his case. Instead, Fortier argued, he should have been sentenced under the more lenient involuntary manslaughter guidelines. Under those guidelines Fortier's sentence should have been a maximum of four years. The appeals court agreed and ordered Fortier to be returned to court and re-sentenced under the appropriate guidelines.*

Writ of Habeus Corpus

If the appellant loses the appeal at the state level, the next step is to file a habeas corpus petition in the state court. *Habeus corpus* is Latin for "you have the body." This petition is essentially a civil suit filed by a person who is incarcerated against the person incarcerating him, usually a warden or the director of the state's department of corrections.† In a writ of habeas corpus the prisoner claims the government (in the form of the warden) is illegally holding him prisoner and asks the court to force the State to prove otherwise.

Because it has the power to force the government to produce an inmate

---

*McVeigh was convicted of murder, conspiracy, and weapons counts; he is appealing his death sentence. Nichols, convicted of involuntary manslaughter and conspiracy, was sentenced to life; he is appealing his conviction.

†For example, in the landmark right to counsel case *Gideon v. Wainwright,* Wainwright was the corrections director of Florida—the person incarcerating Gideon.

in court, a writ of habeas corpus is also known as the Great Writ. An appeals court does not take it lightly. A prisoner has only a single chance to use habeas corpus at the state level. Although prisoners can file a second habeas corpus petition, the petitions will be summarily dismissed unless there is a *very* good reason the issues raised weren't included in the original petition.

Federal Appellate Courts

The appellant, after exhausting all the options at the state level, may then turn to the federal appellate courts* for relief. Although there are federal trial courts in all fifty states (there are, in fact, over ninety federal trial courts), the federal appellate courts are divided into large districts, each of which covers more than one state. There are thirteen federal appellate courts, which are called Circuit Courts of Appeal.

All federal judges are nominated by the president of the United States and are confirmed by the U.S. Senate. Once confirmed, federal judges sit for life; they can be removed from office only by impeachment.

The federal appeals courts perform the same basic function as the state courts of appeals. Panels of judges examine the trial record to determine if the trial court applied the law properly and followed the appropriate judicial procedures. As in the state appeals courts, federal appellate judges don't base their decisions on facts, evidence, or testimony—only on points of law and procedure.

U.S. Supreme Court

The United States Supreme Court is the highest court in the land and the court of last resort for any criminal or civil case tried in any court in any U.S. jurisdiction. When the Supreme Court makes a ruling, it becomes a precedent that must be followed by all lower courts—which means every court in the United States.

*A person convicted of a crime by a federal trial court rather than a state trial court begins the appeal process in the federal system.

Writ of Certiorari

Because their decisions have such far-reaching implications, the nine Supreme Court justices are very selective about the cases they choose to hear. Of the approximately five thousand appeals sent to the Supreme Court each year they elect to hear about three hundred, only half of which will receive a full opinion. When the Court decides to hear a case they issue a *writ of certiorari*. The term is from the Latin phrase *certiorari volumus*, which means "we wish to be informed." The term is usually shortened to the terse "cert." An appeal the Court agrees to hear is generally said to have been granted cert; a case they decline to hear is denied cert.

The cases heard by the Supreme Court either involve weighty and significant constitutional issues or concern conflicts between lower courts. If, for example, an appeals court in Louisiana makes a ruling that seems to contradict a ruling made by the Fifth Circuit Court of Appeals (which includes Louisiana, Mississippi, and Texas), the Supreme Court will decide which court is more correctly interpreting the Constitution.

Federal Habeas Corpus

A prisoner whose habeas corpus petition failed at the state level can also file one at the federal level. Like the state courts, the federal appellate courts are very fussy about the use of habeas corpus. Again, a prisoner is generally granted only a single opportunity to use habeas corpus to get his case before the court.

Since the Supreme Court is the highest court of last resort, this is especially significant to inmates on death row. This is the inmate's last chance. Lawyers involved in death penalty appeals have learned to carefully time the filing of writs of habeas corpus. Reviewing an inmate's first writ can take some time. If it's filed shortly before the inmate's execution date, the Court will almost always issue a stay of execution. This effectively stops the execution process and, assuming the habeas petition fails, a new execution date must be set, which also consumes time. A writ filed too soon might be reviewed and decided before the inmate's execution date.

Despite the complaints of politicians who argue that delays in execution make a mockery of justice, the appeals process is an important one. It's especially important in capital cases. If a person has been wrongfully convicted or imprisoned, there is always a chance he or she might eventually be freed. Obviously, however, if a person has been wrongfully executed, he or she remains dead.

There is, of course, no such thing as an error-free process. Factually innocent and wrongfully convicted defendants have been, and will continue to be, executed. The appeals process acts as a buffer, protecting those few wrongfully convicted and factually innocent people. That's what the process is designed to do. It also means that sometimes the guilty benefit from the process. In order to better protect the innocent it's necessary to provide the same protections to the guilty. Again, it's important to remember that we can't always distinguish between the guilty and the innocent.

Death penalty appeals do not make a mockery of justice; they reduce the odds that a wrongfully convicted or factually innocent person will be executed.

LIFE ON DEATH ROW

The United States has over 1.8 million people incarcerated in prison and jail. Approximately one out of every 150 people currently living in the United States is in some form of custody. The number of people incarcerated in the U.S. is six times greater than the number incarcerated in all of Europe. Of those 1.8 million incarcerated Americans, approximately 3,400 are currently on death row, awaiting execution. Who are these people?

According to the Bureau of Justice Statistics, the vast majority of death row inmates are men—approximately 98.5 percent (as of January 1, 1999, there were forty-nine women on death row). More than half (56 percent) are white.* African Americans comprise the second largest segment of the death row population (42 percent, although blacks only account for about 12 percent of the U.S. population), followed by Latinos, American Indians, and Asians.

Their ages vary dramatically; the youngest inmate under sentence of death is eighteen years of age and the oldest is eighty-two. More than half were between the ages of twenty and twenty-nine at the time they were arrested for their capital offense. Approximately 13 percent were nineteen or younger; fewer than 1 percent were age fifty-five or older.

---

*These percentages can only be approximate, of course. The population of death row is fluid; new inmates arrive and old inmates are executed or released.

Not surprisingly, death row inmates tend to be undereducated. A significant proportion (14 percent) had not completed school beyond the eighth grade. About a third (38 percent) managed to attend high school without completing it. An equal number (38 percent) had either graduated from high school or obtained a GED. Only 10 percent had any education beyond high school.

Approximately two-thirds of death row inmates (65 percent) had been previously convicted of a felony; nearly 10 percent had a previous homicide conviction. About 2 percent were actually incarcerated at the time they committed their capital offense.

Civil Death

Inmates on death row have been referred to as "civilly dead." They are as far removed from society as humans can be. Prisons tend to be located in isolated rural areas, and death row is usually isolated within the prison unit. Death row is, in effect, a prison within a prison—a unit physically and psychologically separated from the rest of the prison. Death row inmates are made distant from society, from their families and friends, and from the rest of the prison population and from other death row inmates. Once sentenced to death row, an inmate can expect to live the rest of his life in dull isolation, and when the time comes for him to be executed, he can expect to die in isolation as well.

Isolation from Family and Friends

Prison visitation is often a chore for any inmate's family. Most have to travel great distances to reach the prison. Once there, the family members must clear security checks to ensure they are not smuggling contraband to the inmates. This is an intrusive and time-consuming process, and it often discourages families and friends from visiting. It isn't uncommon for families and friends to visit less often as the inmate's sentence progresses.

This is exacerbated for death row inmates. Visitors have to undergo more rigorous security checks. In some prisons contact visits (in which the handcuffed and shackled inmates are allowed to touch their visitors) are limited to one hour each month. Non-contact visits are permitted somewhat more frequently. All visits with death row inmates are closely monitored and supervised. Packages and gifts from the outside are strictly limited to certain types of items and are always opened and inspected before the inmate receives them.

Isolation from Other Inmates

Death row in most prisons is located in a separate facility, away from the rest of the prison population. This is done primarily for security reasons. It's easier to maintain security in a smaller unit, and removing condemned inmates from the rest of the population reduces the tension that can build when an execution is scheduled. Inmates in the general population may agree that certain condemned prisoners deserve to die, but they often see the execution as another act of "them" versus "us"—the prison staff against the inmates.

The physical isolation from the rest of the prison also results in some small inconveniences to death row inmates. However, in a stimulation-free environment like death row, small inconveniences attain major significance. For example, death row inmates may eat the same food as inmates in the general population, but because they are housed in a separate unit the food must be delivered. Not only is the food generally cold when it arrives, the inmates often fear it may have been adulterated by the guards. Any small amenity, such as receiving library books, takes longer for death row inmates. When the most consequential event of the day is the arrival of a meal, all minor worries and concerns become exaggerated.

Death row inmates are also isolated from each other. Many prisons confine condemned inmates to their cells twenty-three hours a day, with an hour out of the cell for exercise (in a small exercise cage) or a shower. Rarely are two inmates allowed to be out of their cells at the same time. This is done for the safety and protection of both the guards and the inmates themselves.* Regardless of the reasons, the result is the same:

---

*At the prison in Parchman, Mississippi, in January of 1999, Jimmie Mack fatally stabbed fellow death row inmate Donald Leroy Evans. Mack was being led to the shower at the time of the stabbing and Evans was being returned from the shower. Although correctional officers accompanied both men, they were unable to stop the attack. Evans was a self-proclaimed white supremacist; Mack is black.

death row inmates have virtually no physical contact with anybody except the staff who will eventually lead them to the execution chamber.

In general, life on death row is unrelentingly spartan and dull. The inmates, out of touch with the rest of society and powerless in their environment, often become apathetic, listless, and emotionally numb (qualities, by the way, that work to the benefit of the staff during the actual execution process). Many become hypochondriacs. Some become clinically depressed. Some gradually become insane.

Women on Death Row

Women on death row are rare. This isn't surprising; women in general don't commit as much crime as men and certainly not as many capital offenses. Women account for only about 13 percent of murder arrests and less than 2 percent of the death sentences imposed at trial. As was noted earlier, women comprise only about 1.5 percent of the entire death row population. This has been true throughout the history of this nation. There have been fewer than six hundred documented legal executions of women since 1632.

Only three women have been executed in the United States since the lifting of the capital punishment moratorium in 1976 (see pages 241–242). The first was Velma Barfield, a grandmother executed by North Carolina in 1984 for poisoning four people, including her fiance and her mother. Although the Barfield execution attracted some media attention, it was nothing compared to the execution of the second post-moratorium execution of a woman.

Karla Faye Tucker and her boyfriend had used a pickaxe to murder two people. Tucker, a heavy drug user, reported experiencing an orgasm during the murder. What made the execution of Karla Faye Tucker different was that she was young, attractive, and a very vocal born-again Christian. She found support from several normally pro–capital punishment conservatives, including television evangelist Pat Robertson. Tucker became the focus of massive media coverage. The attention didn't help Tucker, however. She was executed by lethal injection as scheduled.

The execution of the third woman since the moratorium, Judy Buenoano, took place in Florida about a month later with virtually no media interest.

Juveniles on Death Row

At the time this was written, there were seventy-four inmates awaiting execution for crimes they committed as juveniles. Since the lifting of the moratorium, twelve condemned inmates have been executed for crimes they committed as juveniles.

Fifteen of the thirty-nine death penalty jurisdictions (thirty-eight states and the federal government) do not permit the death penalty to be imposed on offenders below the age of eighteen at the time the crime was committed. Four states have set the minimum age for eligibility at age seventeen. The remaining twenty states permit capital punishment on juveniles as young as age sixteen at the time the crime was committed. The youngest person to be executed in the U.S. since World War II was fourteen-year-old George Stinny by the state of Georgia. Stinny was so small his mask fell off while he was being electrocuted.

All of the juvenile offenders on death row are male. All were convicted and sentenced to death for murder. Two-thirds of these condemned inmates are minorities. Their victims were mostly adults (83 percent) and mostly white (66 percent).

The United States is one of only a few nations that permit the execution of juveniles. Since 1990, only five other countries have executed people for crimes they committed as juveniles: Pakistan, Nigeria, Saudi Arabia, Yemen, and Iran.

DOCILE BODIES

By his fifth year on death row Colin Brooks felt dead to the world. His emotions were dead; he'd become apathetic about everything except his food. His mind was dead, or at least dying. He received little intellectual stimulation beyond that provided by television, and he found himself growing increasingly dull. At times hours would pass without his having a single conscious thought. At first that frightened him; now he welcomed it. His senses were dead. His smell had been blunted by the stink of prison—mildew and rarely washed bodies. His hearing was dulled by the constant assault of prison noise. Worst of all for a photographer, his world seemed increasingly limited to the colors of institutional grey and green. Brooks even looked dead—five years without direct exposure to the sun had left his skin a dull, pasty white.

Brooks was also increasingly dead to his family. His father had died years ago, when Brooks was still in high school. His mother and sister had come to visit once a month for the first year or so, but the visits had grown so painfully artificial and awkward that everybody was relieved when they gradually became less frequent. Now he hadn't seen his sister in almost a year and his mother in five months.

His world had shrunk, collapsed in on itself. For the most part the boundaries of his life were the boundaries of his cell. Three days a week he was allowed to spend an hour in a small exercise area. Twice a week he was allowed a brief shower. Once a week he was allowed to go to the prison

235

library to work on his appeal. The library was the longest trip he got to make—easily 150 yards from his cell. He rarely did any actual work on his appeal, and hadn't in a year or more. Most of the time when he visited the library he did exactly what he did in his cell. He sat quietly and let the time go by.

The appeal seemed unreal to him, like a mirage he could still see but no longer chased after. He'd exhausted all his appeals to the state courts; he was now working his way through the federal court system. His latest appeal argued that the prosecution had failed to provide him with timely notice of the evidence of the aggravating factors to be presented at the penalty phase—specifically the eleven former models who'd claimed he'd raped them. Because of that he was denied his rights to due process of law, a fair trial, and a reliable penalty determination pursuant to the Constitution.

He found it difficult to care about the appeal. Brooks told himself he was still desperately intent on getting out of prison, but deep inside he recognized he had virtually nothing left in the outside world. Even if he eventually won an appeal, he had no place to go and no way to earn a living. His mother had handled the sale of his house and its contents, including all his photographic equipment. A significant chunk of that money went to Liza Walsh, the lawyer who had failed to keep him out of prison.

Brooks cared only slightly more about the concept of execution. Since his arrival on death row, three inmates had been executed. Two other inmates had been released from death row after DNA testing had proved them innocent of the crime for which they'd been convicted. To Brooks, both groups of inmates were essentially the same. The only thing that mattered was that in both cases they'd left their cells and never returned. Where they really ended up . . . well, it didn't much matter. The cells never stayed empty.

There were twenty-seven inmates on death row. Brooks knew the names of eight of them. He'd never shaken hands with any of them. He'd never spoken to most of them. Most of them he'd only seen when they were being escorted to the showers or exercise yard. He heard them though. He heard them talking with and shouting at each other, he heard them crying or babbling crazily, he heard them using the toilet, he heard them masturbating, he heard their radios and televisions running fourteen hours a day. It was less noisy at night, but even then metal doors clanged as guards went about their business and inmates cried and had nightmares.

There was almost no privacy in the general prison population; there was absolutely no privacy on death row. In five years Brooks had never had a single moment when he could be certain of privacy, never a moment of quiet seclusion.

The inmates were on display twenty-four hours a day. The prison administration even allowed tours to pass through death row on the way to the execution chamber. The hostility of the inmates to the tours was almost palpable and most of the tours passed through quietly, only furtively looking at the inmates. Brooks overheard one member of a tour of criminologists say, "the living conditions on death row seem almost designed to produce docile bodies ready for execution."

Docile bodies. Brooks knew the truth of that and for a moment felt a spark of resentment and anger. But only for a moment. Really, what did it matter?

THE EXECUTION PROCESS

It's not a simple thing for the State to kill one of its own citizens. It's a difficult process legally, procedurally, and physically. We've discussed the legal difficulties; conviction of a capital crime is the beginning of a legal battle between the State and the condemned inmate. The appeals process can last years.

Execution is difficult procedurally in that the State has to design and implement an execution strategy. This involves a careful step-by-step analysis of every aspect of the process—everything from the time and date of the execution to the invitation and arrangement of witnesses, to maintenance of the execution apparatus, to a plan for dealing with potential protesters, to arranging and supervising the inmate's last visit and last meal.

Finally, an execution is difficult physically. This is simply because the human body is resilient. It doesn't die easily. Despite two centuries of practice, the United States still doesn't have a method of execution that is constitutional, acceptable to the general public, and foolproof. The methods we have in place at present are acceptable to large segments of the public and have been declared constitutional, but they are not foolproof. When I say "foolproof" I'm not talking about preventing the possibility of executing an innocent person—that, unfortunately, can't be done. By "foolproof" I mean a method of killing a person that is reasonably quick, relatively painless, and unlikely to go wrong. As will be discussed, a significant number of executions in the United States are botched every year.

A Brief History of Capital Punishment

The first recorded execution in the English colonies in America took place in 1608. George Kendall of Virginia was executed for treason against the king; he was said to have plotted with the Spanish to betray British interests.

Colonial laws included a wide variety of capital offenses. In seventeenth-century Virginia, for example, a person could be executed for murder, sodomy, witchcraft, adultery, idolatry, blasphemy, assault in anger, rape, manstealing, rebellion, bestiality, stealing grapes, killing chickens, or trading with Indians. The penalties were reduced in 1619 for fear they might make new colonists reluctant to settle in Virginia.

After the American Revolution there was a great deal of debate in the new United States about the usefulness and propriety of capital punishment. Thomas Jefferson proposed that only two crimes merited death: murder and treason. In 1793 the attorney general of Pennsylvania published *An Enquiry How Far the Punishment of Death is Necessary in Pennsylvania*. In this report he admitted the death penalty didn't prevent crime. He also noted that the death penalty made it more difficult to convict criminals. In Pennsylvania, as in other of the newly formed states, the death penalty was mandatory for certain crimes. This made some juries reluctant to convict. Nonetheless, the attorney general argued that the death penalty should be retained for the public good. Modern scholars and legislators make these same arguments.

Little changed until the mid-1800s, when public executions sparked a reform movement. Public executions were rowdy events. Huge crowds attended, hawkers sold souvenirs, pickpockets worked the crowds, public intoxication and street fighting were common. In 1835 local authorities had to restrain a crowd of over ten thousand spectators who became violent during a public hanging in Maine. A crowd of that size in a relatively unpopulated state like Maine was remarkable. It would be difficult to draw a crowd of that size to a public event in parts of Maine today!

Many states enacted legislation to reduce the spectacle and the concomitant disorder that accompanied public executions. Some passed laws that required executions be delayed for at least one year after conviction, hoping the public outrage against the criminal would abate in the meantime. There was also a determination that executions should no longer be

240

public events. Instead they should be conducted in private on prison grounds. Death penalty abolitionists of the era opposed this move, arguing that public executions would eventually outrage the public to the degree that the penalty would be eliminated.

In 1846, Michigan became the first state to abolish the death penalty.* Rhode Island followed in 1852, and the following year Wisconsin rescinded its death penalty after a botched hanging in which the condemned inmate dangled at the end of the rope for nearly twenty minutes before dying. Other states passed laws against mandatory death sentences and in favor of discretionary capital punishment.

For the next hundred years legislative support of the death penalty waxed and waned. Some states eliminated it, restored it, and eliminated it again. The topic became a national debate again in the 1950s, sparked in part by the publication of two books by condemned inmate Caryl Chessman (*Cell 2455 Death Row* and *Trial by Ordeal*). A popular movie entitled *I Want to Live!* was based on the life and execution of Barbara Graham.

Opponents of capital punishment, however, found that abolition of the death penalty on a state-by-state basis was ineffective. They switched tactics. Rather than attempt to convince individual state legislatures to repeal their death penalties, they took their fight to the United States Supreme Court. They would try to convince the court that capital punishment as it was practiced at the time was a constitutionally inappropriate penalty.

They succeeded. In 1972 the U.S. Supreme Court handed down the decision in the case of *Furman v. Georgia*. By a five-to-four vote[†] the court struck down all federal and state capital punishment laws. In essence, the court found that all existing capital punishment laws were flawed in design or implementation. They ruled that capital punishment violated the Eighth Amendment protection against cruel and unusual punishment if any of the following applied:

- It was too severe for the crime.
- It was arbitrary.

---

*For all crimes except treason.

[†]Each of the nine Justices wrote a separate opinion, two concurring that capital punishment was unconstitutional in all instances, three focusing on the arbitrary application of the punishment, and four arguing there was no constitutional violation.

• It offends society's sense of justice.

• It was not more effective than a less severe penalty.

A moratorium on executions went into effect.* Over six hundred death row inmates who had been sentenced between 1967 and 1972 had their death sentences changed to life imprisonment.

Advocates of the death penalty set about rewriting individual state laws to comply with the ruling of the Supreme Court. Mandatory death sentences (against which the attorney general of Pennsylvania had argued 180 years earlier) were scrapped in favor of sentences that could be imposed at the discretion of a jury or a judge. The bifurcated trials (with distinct guilt and punishment phases) we are now familiar with were instituted.

In 1976 the Supreme Court (in the case of *Gregg v. Georgia*) ruled that the death penalty was not always cruel and unusual punishment. Executions resumed the following year when convicted murderer Gary Gilmore was executed by firing squad in Utah.

The Execution Process

An execution involves much more than simply strapping the condemned inmate into an electric chair or onto an execution table. It's a process that may take as long as two weeks and involves a variety of prison staff. It's a slow, methodical process in which the staff and inmate are gradually but systematically desensitized to what will eventually take place.

Although the process is slightly different in each state, all follow the same basic pattern. Approximately ten days to two weeks prior to the execution, a death warrant is issued, directing the prison to enforce the death sentence imposed at trial. At some point during the week before the execution date, the condemned inmate is moved from death row to a holding cell closer to the execution chamber. From that point until the execution, the inmate is never left alone; at least one correctional officer is in the room with the inmate at all times. The deathwatch has begun.

---

*During the writing of this book, the Nebraska legislature voted to impose a two-year moratorium on executions while a study into the fairness of the death penalty is undertaken. Courts are still able to impose the death sentence, but no executions will take place.

Deathwatch

The deathwatch serves both a security purpose and a psychological purpose. The security purpose is threefold. First, to ensure the condemned inmate doesn't attempt to escape. Although it's exceedingly difficult to escape from death row, it's not impossible. On Thanksgiving Day 1998, seven inmates managed to escape from Texas's death row in Huntsville. Only one of the inmates actually managed to climb over the two ten-foot-tall fences topped with razor wire and leave the prison grounds; the other six were driven back by gunfire from the guard towers. The sole escapee, however, drowned in a creek a couple of miles from the prison. His body was found a week later.

The second purpose of the deathwatch is to protect the inmate from other death row inmates. Just as it's difficult, but not impossible, to escape from death row, it's also difficult, but not impossible, for one death row inmate to kill another. An inmate who has sworn to kill another inmate might consider it a point of honor to kill the condemned man before the State can execute him. More commonly, however, the condemned inmate needs protection from the jibes and jeers of some other death row inmates. The population of death row isn't known for its compassion.

Third, and most important, the deathwatch is to prevent the condemned inmate from attempting to cheat the executioner by committing suicide. A paradox of capital punishment is that the condemned inmate is prohibited from killing himself. If a condemned inmate attempts it, all efforts are made to revive and treat him so that he remains healthy enough to be executed.

Deathwatch cells are often equipped with a television and VCR. This may seem an odd extravagance but it serves a purpose—it helps keep the condemned inmate pacified and makes the time pass more quickly. Similarly, the inmate is often granted free canteen privileges, allowing him all the soft drinks and snacks he wants. Visiting hours are extended, although many death rows place a strict limit (generally two) on the number of visitors who can be in the deathwatch cell.

Inmate Preparation

Depending on the mode of execution, there are certain preparations to be made for and by the inmate. For example, if the inmate is to be executed in the electric chair his head needs to be shaved, as well as one wrist and one leg near the ankle—the spots where the copper electrodes will be attached. Many states provide special clothing to the inmate; it appears to be standard, respectable clothing but is in fact cutaway clothing designed to be opened at the back in order to facilitate its removal from the dead inmate.

Within the final twenty-four hours the inmate is given a physical examination by a prison doctor. This is obviously a cursory examination; it is difficult to imagine what the doctor could find that would matter to an inmate who is expected to be dead by that same time the following day. The doctor also informs the condemned inmate that he can have a sedative prior to the execution to ease his anxiety.

The condemned inmate must also make some decisions. He must decide what will happen to his few possessions. He has to authorize somebody to claim his body. He has to decide on a last meal and last words.* He has to decide whether or not to take the sedative. These are, admittedly, small concerns, but they often take on enormous importance to the inmate.

The Last Walk

For many condemned inmates, their greatest fear isn't the fear of death, or fear about the manner of their death—it's the fear of the last walk. The very last task of a condemned inmate is to walk to the death chamber. In effect, they are expected to cooperate in their execution. Many inmates fear they will break down or panic, a response they see as unmanly and humiliating. It is important to them that they not leave behind a last image of weakness.

Some condemned inmates do, in fact, collapse emotionally and require assistance on the last walk. A very few others actively resist, forcing the execution team members to restrain them and convey them kicking, screaming, and weeping to the execution chamber. Most inmates however, recognize that willingly or not they *will* be going to the execution chamber. That very knowledge contributes to the numbing effect that has

*In Ohio condemned inmates are not allowed to make a final statement to witnesses just before execution. Instead, the last words are trascribed, copied, and forwarded to the warden, who releases them after the execution. The ACLU has brought suit, arguing condemned prisoners have a constitutional right to give a final statement just before death.

been so carefully nurtured from the time the inmate was transferred to the deathwatch chamber. When the time comes, most inmates appear to cooperate passively in a sort of detached haze.

Execution Methods

At present there are five different methods used to execute condemned inmates in the United States: firing squad, hanging, electrocution, lethal gas, and lethal injection. Several states offer more than one method of execution. This is usually as a result of the advent of lethal injection. In some states the inmate is given a choice between the state's traditional mode of execution and the new method of lethal injection. Many inmates refuse to choose. Refusal to make a choice results in death by lethal injection.

In other states with two methods of execution the method used depends on the date the inmate was sentenced to die. Inmates convicted and sentenced prior to authorization of lethal injection are executed by the state's traditional method; those convicted after are given lethal injection.

Each death penalty state has its own execution protocol. The descriptions presented below are representative protocols; they may not be identical in all states using that particular method of execution.

Firing Squad

Three states* permit execution by firing squad. The firing squad consists of six volunteers—a squad leader and five squad members—all of whom are certified police officers from various state law enforcement agencies.† Each of the volunteers is supplied a 30-30 caliber rifle by his agency. No special ammunition is used.

The inmate is dressed in a dark blue outfit. Prior to being moved to the execution chamber a white cloth circle is attached over the inmate's heart

---

*Idaho, Utah, and Oklahoma. In Oklahoma a firing squad is authorized if execution by lethal gas becomes unconstitutional.

†Prison staff aren't used as squad members to prevent situations like that of the 1951 execution of Elisio Mares. Mares had been popular with the staff. Each of the marksmen, not wanting to be responsible for Mares's death and unaware of the intent of the other team members, aimed away from his heart. None of the shots fired was immediately fatal and Mares slowly bled to death.

by a Velcro strip. In the execution chamber the inmate is restrained in a specially designed chair. Restraints applied to the chest, arms, and legs are intended to immobilize the inmate. A separate head restraint is designed to keep the inmate's head in an upright position after death. Beneath the chair is a large pan to catch the inmate's blood and other bodily fluids. Behind the execution chair is a wall of sandbags draped with dark sheets intended to absorb the gunshots and prevent ricochets. Approximately twenty feet in front of the inmate is a wall containing six firing ports.

After the condemned inmate is restrained, the warden asks if he has a final statement to make. Following the statement, a hood is placed over the inmate's head and the warden leaves the execution chamber. The firing squad then assumes the firing position, aiming through the firing ports at the target affixed to the inmate's chest. The squad fires simultaneously on command. One rifle is randomly selected to be loaded with a blank round. This is to salve any qualms a squad member might have about the execution. This seems a pointless nicety since the firing squad is comprised of volunteers and since a blank round fired from a rifle generally feels different than a live round.

After the shots have been fired a physician and medical personnel enter the execution chamber to confirm the inmate's death. The average elapsed time from the moment the inmate is restrained to the chair until death is confirmed is approximately eight to ten minutes. Death is caused by massive trauma to the heart and central nervous system or, in botched executions, by hemorrhage.

Hanging

Death by hanging is authorized in three states.* Some states maintain a gallows, others have a balcony with trapdoors. Prior to the execution, the trapdoors are tested to ensure they are in working order. Based on the inmate's height, weight, musculature, and any possible physical deformities a determination is made regarding the appropriate drop height. Drop height refers to the length of rope required to ensure a quick death.

---

*Washington, Delaware, and New Hampshire. New Hampshire authorizes death by hanging if lethal injection is banned. In Delaware inmates sentenced to death prior to June 1986 are hanged; those sentenced later are executed by lethal injection.

A hemp rope approximately thirty feet in length, between three-quarters of an inch and one and a quarter inches in diameter, is soaked, then stretched while drying. This greatly reduces the stiffness of the rope and eliminates the potential for the rope to spring or coil. The hangman's knot is treated with wax, soap, or oil so that it slides smoothly.

The inmate is escorted in restraints to the execution chamber and required to stand on the trapdoor. After being given the opportunity to make a last statement, a long hood is draped over the inmate's head (it also covers much of his chest and back), and he is further restrained. If the inmate is unable or unwilling to stand he is leaned against a "collapse" board. The noose is then slipped over the inmate's head with the knot placed behind the left ear on the lower jaw.*

At a command given by the warden or prison superintendent, a member of the execution team presses a button mechanically releasing the trapdoor. The inmate drops through the trapdoor. The execution team then moves to the lower level of the gallows or balcony to assist in removing the inmate's body. After an appropriate amount of time the warden signals a physician to make the pronouncement of death.

The estimated length of time from the moment the condemned offender is restrained until death is determined is approximately five to ten minutes. In a properly conducted hanging, death is caused instantly by snapping the inmate's third and fourth cervical vertebrae. Too short a drop results in a slow death by strangulation. Too long a drop can result in decapitation.†

Lethal Gas

At present six states execute condemned inmates using lethal gas.‡ The execution team consists of the warden, deputy warden, three executioners, a three person medical team, the chaplain, an escort team of four prison staff, and the security coordinator. Except for the warden and deputy warden all members of the execution team are volunteers.

*The knot is placed on the left side to ensure it snaps the neck. A knot on the right side tends to throw the head forward, and the inmate will slowly strangle to death.
†In 1930 Eva Dugan, the first woman executed in Arizona, had her head ripped from her body when the hangman misjudged the drop.
‡Arizona, California, Maryland, Missouri, and Wyoming. North Carolina offers condemned inmates the choice of lethal injection or lethal gas.

Prior to the execution the team will conduct several rehearsals of the event, including at least three involving the chemicals used to activate and release the lethal gas. This is done to test both the execution process and the integrity of the gas chamber. The chamber must, of course, be airtight to prevent the lethal gas from escaping and endangering the staff and witnesses. Most gas chambers are octagonal and constructed of steel with glass panels set in airtight seals. A chair is mounted within the chamber (California has a gas chamber that seats two). Beneath the chair is a metal container in which cyanide pellets are placed before the execution. There is also a canister containing sulfuric acid, which, when introduced to the container of cyanide pellets, will create the lethal gas. The chamber also includes a heart monitor, which permits the medical staff to determine the condemned inmate's heart function from the safety of the control room. Off to one side is a small control room containing the device that causes the sulfuric acid to mix with the cyanide.

The inmate is escorted into the gas chamber and strapped to the chair using chest, waist, arm, and ankle restraints. The heart monitor is attached to the inmate's chest. The inmate is permitted to make a final statement. In some states a mask is then placed over the head of the condemned inmate.

After the escort team leaves the execution chamber and seals the door, the three executioners each turn a key in the control room. An electric switch causes the cyanide container to open, allowing the pellets to fall into the sulfuric acid solution, producing a lethal gas. Inhalation of the gas is intended to first render the inmate unconscious, followed rapidly by death.

Death occurs when the gas blocks the body's ability to process blood hemoglobin (which transports oxygen from the lungs to body tissue). The prisoner becomes unconscious and chokes to death. The estimated elapsed time from when the inmate is restrained in the gas chamber until death is pronounced is generally six to eighteen minutes, and can be as long as thirty-eight minutes.

After the inmate is pronounced dead, the gas chamber is pumped full of ammonia to neutralize the lethal gas. Exhaust fans are used to vent the inert fumes, a process that takes approximately half an hour. Once the execution chamber has been cleared of lethal gas, the execution team dons protective clothing and oxygen masks and enters the chamber to contend with the inmate's body. The body itself has become poisonous and must be scrubbed with ammonia or chlorine bleach. The inmate's clothes, also contaminated with the lethal gas, must be bagged and burned. After the inmate's body has been removed, the entire gas chamber must be carefully scrubbed with ammonia to remove the last vestiges of lethal gas.

Electrocution

Electrocution is the chosen method of execution in eleven states.* The size and composition of the execution team varies from state to state. South Carolina relies on a ten-member execution team comprised of the warden, the associate warden, a major, six captains and lieutenants, and a doctor. In Georgia the team consists of six special escort officers and three executioners operating under the supervision of the deputy warden of security. Kentucky's execution team consists of a dozen security staff under the direction of a senior captain.

The electric chair, constructed of wood, is tested prior to the execution. Most states conduct periodic tests throughout the year to ensure the chair remains in proper working condition. In addition, the execution team practices the actual execution protocol to ensure that each member is familiar with his assignment.

Prior to being moved to the execution chamber, the condemned inmate's ankle, and head are shaved to ensure the conductors will be securely attached. The inmate is escorted to the execution chamber and strapped into the electric chair. Each officer has an assigned strap (right leg, for example, or chest). After the inmate is secured to the chair the death warrant is read and the inmate is given the opportunity to make a final statement.

An electrode is then affixed to the inmate's shaven leg. A headpiece containing a natural sponge soaked in brine is fitted to the inmate's head. Any excess moisture is wiped from the condemned inmate's face with a towel. A mask or hood is then placed over the inmate's head.

At a signal, generally given by the warden, the executioner engages an automatic electrocution cycle. An electrical current is passed through the inmate's body from the top of the head to the leg. In Florida the automatic

---

*Arkansas, Florida, Georgia, Kentucky, Nebraska, Ohio, Oklahoma, South Carolina, Tennessee, and Virginia.

cycle begins with 2,300 volts for eight seconds, followed by 1,000 volts for twenty-two seconds, followed by 2,300 volts for another eight seconds. In Georgia the cycle consists of 2,000 volts for four seconds, 1,000 volts for seven seconds and 208 volts for one minute and forty-nine seconds. Nebraska favors 2,450 volts for eight seconds, then 480 volts for twenty-two seconds, followed by a brief pause, then an automatic repeat of the same cycle.

When the cycle is complete, the current is turned off. Approximately two minutes later a physician examines the inmate's body for vital signs. If the inmate isn't yet dead, the execution cycle is repeated. Depending on the state, the elapsed time for a successful first-run execution is from ten to twenty-five minutes from the time the inmate is restrained until he is pronounced dead. Death results from disruption of the autonomic nervous system and heart seizure.

Lethal Injection

Lethal injection is the most popular method of execution. Thirty-three states rely on lethal injection, as do the U.S. military and the federal government.* As noted earlier, the protocol for each state varies. Most states using lethal injection have two separate execution teams, one to escort the condemned inmate and a medical team to administer the lethal drugs.

The inmate is escorted to the execution chamber (Texas has a four-room execution suite—a room for the injection team, the execution chamber, and two separate witness rooms). He is then placed on a gurney and secured at the wrists, biceps, chest, stomach, and legs with straps. In Missouri the inmate's head is covered with a hood; in all other states the inmate isn't masked or hooded. The inmate's head is not secured by a strap, so that he may turn his head to face the execution witnesses. The inmate is given the opportunity to make a final statement.

Prior to the arrival of the witnesses the medical team starts two intravenous lines on the inmate, one in each arm. The second IV line is used as

*Arkansas, California, Colorado, Connecticut, Delaware, Idaho, Illinois, Indiana, Kansas, Kentucky, Louisiana, Maryland, Mississippi, Missouri, Montana, Nevada, New Hampshire, New Jersey, New Mexico, New York, North Carolina, Ohio, Oklahoma, Oregon, Pennsylvania, South Carolina, South Dakota, Tennessee, Texas, Utah, Virginia, Washington, and Wyoming

a contingency line in the event the first line malfunctions or is blocked. A normal saline solution flow is begun.

After the condemned inmate makes his last statement he is given a sequence of three drugs. In some states this is done by machine, in other states the drugs are manually injected into the IV line. First, a lethal dose of a barbiturate, sodium thiopental or sodium pentothal, is administered to render the inmate unconscious. The line is then flushed with saline. Next a muscle relaxant, pancuronium bromide, is administered to paralyze the inmate's diaphragm and lungs. Again the line is flushed with saline. Finally a dose of potassium chloride is injected to stop the inmate's heart.

The administration of drugs takes less than two minutes. The average length of time elapsed from the moment the inmate is restrained until the time of death is approximately seventeen minutes. Death is caused by cardiac arrest.

Botched Executions

No current execution method is foolproof. Botched executions are alarmingly common. Firing squads and executions by hanging have been the most reliable methods in the post-*Furman* era, possibly because they have been used less often than the other methods.

Executions by lethal gas frequently go awry. Witnesses to the 1983 execution of Jimmy Lee Gray report that the inmate suffered convulsions and banged his head against the chair for at least eight minutes. Prison authorities escorted the repulsed witnesses away from the scene before Gray died.

Errors in executions by electrocution are even more dramatic. During the 1990 electrocution of Jesse Tafero, six-inch flames shot out from behind the mask covering the inmate's face and smoke rose from his head. The current was shut off. When a second jolt was applied, flames and smoke again were visible. In 1991 mechanical difficulties and voltage errors resulted in steam pressure building up in condemned inmate Alberta Clozza's head. His eyes popped and blood ran from the sockets onto his chest. More recently, in the 1997 execution of Pedro Medina, the first jolt of electricity caused foot-long blue and orange flames to shoot

251

from the mask covering his face. The execution chamber became clouded with smoke, and the smell of burnt flesh filled the witness room.*

A manufacturer of execution equipment described botched electrocution results in this way: "If you overload an individual's body with current . . . you'll cook the meat on his body. It's like meat on an overcooked chicken. If you grab the arm, the flesh will fall right off in your hands. That doesn't mean he felt anything. It simply means that it's cosmetically not the thing to do."

Botched executions using lethal injection are less spectacular, but more common. The primary difficulty appears to be in finding a vein through which the lethal drugs may be injected. A large proportion of death row inmates have been IV drug users, a population with notoriously bad veins. In 1986 condemned inmate and drug user Randy Woolls had to assist the medical team when they were unable to find a good vein for the execution. It took nearly an hour for the medical team to find a vein in the 1992 execution of Rickey Ray Rector. Three additional medical technicians were summoned to assist the original two team members. Witnesses were unable to view the scene but reported hearing Rector's loud moans throughout the process. Inmate Stephen McCoy, at his 1989 execution, had an unintended adverse reaction to the drugs. His chest began to heave, and he began to gasp and choke. One witness fainted. The 1995 execution of Emmitt Foster took half an hour. Several minutes into the process members of the execution team could not understand why Foster was still alive. After twenty minutes the coroner, who was at the scene to pronounce Foster's death, informed the execution team that the straps securing Foster's arms were so tight that the flow of chemicals into his veins was restricted.

---

*Following Medina's execution, Florida corrections officials decided to replace the old electric chair, known as "Old Sparky." They did not, however, replace the electrical equipment. The first inmate to die in the new chair, Alan "Tiny" Davis, died bloodily. Blood flowed from beneath the face mask, soaked his white shirt, and oozed through the buckle holes on the leather chest strap holding him to the chair.

IS THAT IT?

They were all volunteers. They had no official title, but everybody referred to them as the "death team." A dozen correctional officers, each selected by an interview team comprised of administrative staff, including a warden and a mental health professional. Although all twelve were correctional officers, none of them worked at the prison that housed death row. It was a good policy. It would not be wise, prison officials reasoned, to have the officers who routinely guarded the inmates be the same ones who executed them.

Six of them were assigned to the deathwatch, staying with Colin Brooks during each minute of the final 120 hours of his life. The other six would be involved in the actual execution.

The execution of Colin Brooks would be Correctional Officer Mickey Gibson's fifth. This time he'd been promoted to operate the execution machine—the device that actually delivered the lethal dose of drugs. His first execution he'd served on the deathwatch squad; the other three he'd been on the execution squad. He'd been assigned to the condemned inmate's right arm, although during practice the squad members had trained to fill each of the positions. His task had been to ensure the inmate's right arm was securely strapped down. Securely, but not too securely—he didn't want to reduce the circulation of the arm. The right arm was the spare arm; if the intravenous line in the inmate's left arm failed to work correctly it would be necessary to shift arms. He also had to pass the chest strap over the inmate's body so it could be secured by the squad member assigned to the left arm.

Gibson's new task was less complex but carried more responsibility. He would no longer be in the execution chamber; he would be next door in the injection chamber. All he had to do was turn on the injection machine and, at the appropriate moment, push the button that started the injections. He then had to call out the different injection steps. If the injection machine failed for some reason, Gibson would be required to manually depress the syringes. Gibson didn't think of himself as the executioner, though. He was simply assigned to the injection machine.

It was John Huff's first execution, and he was nervous. He'd been assigned to the deathwatch squad. From the moment the condemned inmate was moved to the deathwatch cell, at least one member of the deathwatch squad would be there in the cell with him. They worked in shifts—four hours on, eight hours off. After four hours of deathwatch a correctional officer needed a break.

Huff's task would end when the condemned inmate was taken to the execution chamber. They would wait until word arrived that the inmate had been executed, then the members of the deathwatch squad would gather up the condemned inmate's few belongings and deliver them to one of the prison administrators.

Huff and another more experienced execution team member were waiting in the deathwatch cell the evening the death row guards brought Brooks in. Huff introduced himself. In training he'd been told to be courteous and professional. The members of the deathwatch squad weren't expected to be friends with the condemned inmate, but it was important that the process went smoothly. If that meant being courteous to a convicted murderer, then the correctional officer would just have to suck it up and be courteous. Being part of the execution team wasn't about the CO's feelings; it was about getting the job done with as little fuss and as much dignity as possible.

Huff's first shift went quickly enough. All Brooks had wanted to do was watch videos. Huff sat through a stupid Adam Sandler comedy and a pretty good Kevin Costner golf movie. Except for an awkward moment when Brooks had a particularly foul-smelling bowel movement, Huff felt his first shift had been a success.

Huff put in four more shifts, most of which were spent watching movies and eating snacks with Brooks. Brooks hadn't seemed particularly interested in the movies, but they served to reduce any awkward silence. Huff wondered how the guards were able to stand a deathwatch in the days before television in prison.

Huff was off duty when Brooks was taken to the execution chamber. It left him feeling a little . . . unresolved. Oddly, Huff found himself wishing he'd said goodbye to Brooks when he left his last shift.

The parents of Carla Willis arrived at the prison ninety minutes before midnight. They were met at the administration building by a member of the treatment staff who explained to them, step by step, what was going to happen. Both of the Willises were nervous and anxious, but were determined to see the event through.

After getting their orientation briefing the Willises were escorted to the room holding the other witnesses—Detective James Dietz, a few other law enforcement officers, two reporters, and Brooks's appellate attorney. Coffee was available and most of the witnesses poured a cup, though not all drank it. There was little conversation. At 11:45 P.M. the witnesses were taken to the witness chamber. It was a small room with a dozen chairs facing a large window concealed by a curtain. There they waited.

Mickey Gibson stood in the door to the injection chamber as the execution squad brought Colin Brooks into the execution chamber. Brooks had the same look as all the other condemned inmates he'd seen—sort of confused, sort of frightened, mostly stunned.

Brooks laid on the execution gurney when asked. He was quickly and efficiently strapped to the gurney. Gibson nodded to the medical technicians waiting in the injection chamber. They entered the execution chamber and started intravenous lines in each of Brooks's arms. The medical techs were relieved to see Brooks's arms. He had good veins; it took less than three minutes to get both IV lines going. They then connected the IV lines leading from the injection machine and returned to the injection chamber.

It was five minutes to midnight.

At midnight the curtain in the witness chamber was opened. The witnesses could see Colin Brooks strapped to the gurney. His eyes were closed.

255

At 12:01 the warden coughed quietly and read the death warrant aloud. When he finished he stepped closer to Brooks. "Is there anything you'd like to say?" he asked.

Brooks opened his eyes. He had a million things he wanted to say. He'd planned and rehearsed a final statement. But he couldn't remember it. All he could think to say was "This isn't right. This just isn't right."

The warden hesitated a moment, in case Brooks had more to say. Then he stepped into the injection room. He nodded to the execution team.

"Green light," Gibson said quietly, and turned on the injection machine. He let it warm up for a minute. It was working fine.

"Foxfire one," Gibson said. He pressed the button and the injection of sodium thiopental began.

Brooks, eyes closed, was unaware that he was drifting into terminal sleep. There was no clear border between being awake and not being awake.

Another minute. "Foxfire two." Gibson didn't have to say it; it was an automatic process. At this point the machine was in control. The lethal injection of pancuronium bromide was sent on its way.

Brooks's lungs became paralyzed. His breathing stopped. His body and brain were suddenly deprived of oxygen. His body struggled to survive, causing his heart rate to increase. Although his heart continued to beat, at the cellular level death had already begun. Indeed, at the cellular level Brooks was experiencing exactly what Carla Willis experienced. He was dying from lack of oxygen.

Another minute. "Foxfire three." The potassium chloride. Three times the normal lethal limit. Brooks's heart seized and stopped. In the injection room the prison physician watched as Brooks's EKG went perfectly flat.

"Flatline," the physician said.

Gibson nodded. He gave the password to the member of the execution team in the witness chamber. The curtain was drawn closed, leaving the witnesses with nothing to look at but each other.

The witnesses were a little surprised. There had been no drama, no sense that something meaningful or profound had taken place. No sense that they'd witnessed justice taking place. All they had seen was a man strapped to a gurney, a man who had quietly closed his eyes. That was all.

"Is that it?" Mrs. Willis asked. "Is that all there is?"